he
European
Union

The
European
Union

Structure and Process
Third Edition

Clive Archer

CONTINUUM
London and New York

Continuum
The Tower Building, 11 York Road, London SE1 7NX
370 Lexington Avenue, New York, NY 10017-6550

First edition published 1992
Second edition published 1996, reprinted 1999
Third edition first published 2000

British Library Cataloguing-in-Publication Data
A catalogue record of this book is available from the British Library.

ISBN 0-8264-5109-8 (hardback)
        0-8264-4781-3 (paperback)

Library of Congress Cataloging-in-Publication Data
Archer, Clive.
   The European Union: structure and process / Clive Archer. — 3rd ed.
      p. cm.
   Includes bibliographical references and index.
   ISBN 0-8264-5109-8 (hb) — 0-8264-4781-3 (pb)
      1. European Economic Community. 2. European Union. I. Title.

   HC241.2. S743 2000
   341.24'22—dc21   00-055477

Typeset by YHT Ltd, London
Printed and bound in Great Britain by Biddles Ltd, *www.biddles.co.uk*

Contents

List of tables

List of abbreviations

AAMS	Association of African and Malagasy States
ACE	EU programme with CEECs on economics
ACP	African, Caribbean and Pacific states
AEMM	ASEAN-EU Ministerial Meeting
AFTA	ASEAN Free Trade Area
ALTENER	EC programme for renewable energy
APEC	Asia-Pacific Economic Co-operation
ARF	ASEAN Regional Forum
ASEAN	Association of South East Asian Nations
ASEM	Asia-Europe Meeting
Benelux	Belgium, the Netherlands and Luxembourg (customs union)
CAP	Common Agricultural Policy
CCP	Common Commercial Policy
CCRE	Council of Municipalities and Regions of Europe
CEEC	Committee for European Economic Co-operation
CEECs	Central and East European Countries
CEMR	Council of European Municipalities and Regions
CEN	European Standardization Committee
Cenelec	European Standardization Committee for Electrical Products
CEP	European public sector confederation
CESDP	Common European Security and Defence Policy
CET	Common External Tariff
CFE	Conventional Forces in Europe (Agreement)
CFP	Common Fisheries Policy
CFSP	Common Foreign and Security Policy
CIREA	Centre for Information, Reflection and Exchange on Asylum Matters
CIREFI	Centre for Information, Reflection and Exchange on Crossing of Borders and Immigration
CIS	Commonwealth of Independent States (ex-USSR)
CITES	Convention on the Trade in Endangered Species
CJTF	Combined Joint Task Forces
CMEA/Comecon	Council for Mutual Economic Assistance
Comett	Community in Education and Training for Technology
COPA	Committee of Professional Agricultural Organizations

CoR	Committee of the Regions
Coreper	Committee of Permanent Representatives
COREU	Telegram system between EU ministries
Cosine	EU programme with CEECs on infrastructure
CSCE	Conference on Security and Co-operation in Europe (became OSCE)
CSF	Community Support Framework
Daphne	European action programme to combat violence against women and children
DGs	Directorate Generals
EAEC/Euratom	European Atomic Energy Community
EAGGF/FEOGA	European Agricultural Guidance and Guarantee Fund
EAPs	Environmental Action Programmes
EAPC	Euro-Atlantic Partnership Council
EBRD	European Bank for Reconstruction and Development
EC	European Communities
ECB	European Central Bank
ECHO	European Community Humanitarian Office
ECJ	European Court of Justice
ECMM	EC Monitoring Mission
ECOFIN	Economic and Finance Council
Ecosoc	Economic and Social Committee
ECSC	European Coal and Steel Community
ECU	European Currency Unit (replaced by the euro)
EDC	European Defence Community
EDF	European Development Fund
EDU	Europol Drugs Unit
EEA	European Economic Area
EEC	European Economic Community
EFTA	European Free Trade Association
EIB	European Investment Bank
ELDR	European Liberal, Democrat and Reform Party
EMCF	European Monetary Co-operation Fund
EMI	European Monetary Institute
EMS	European Monetary System
EMU	Economic and Monetary Union
EP	European Parliament
EPC	European Political Community
EPC	European Political Co-operation
EPP/ED	European People's Party/European Democrats
Erasmus	European Community Action Scheme for the Mobility of University Students
ERDF	European Regional Development Fund
ERM	Exchange Rate Mechanism
ESA	EFTA Surveillance Authority
ESC	Economic and Social Committee

ESCB	European System of Central Banks
ESDI	European Security and Defence Identity
ESF	European Social Fund
Esprit	European Strategic Programme of Research and Development in Information Technology
ETUC	European Trade Union Confederation
EU	European Union
EUA	European Unit of Account (replaced by the ECU)
Euratom	European Atomic Energy Community
euro	'Euroland' currency from 1 January 1999 (replaced the ECU) (€)
EWCs	European Works Councils
FAQs	Frequently Asked Questions
FAWEU	Forces Answerable to WEU
FDI	Foreign Direct Investment
FIFG	Financial Instrument of Fisheries Guidance
FRG	Federal Republic of Germany
GATS	General Agreement in Trade in Services
GATT	General Agreement on Tariffs and Trade
GCC	Gulf Co-operation Council
GDP	Gross Domestic Product
GDR	German Democratic Republic (former East Germany)
GNP	Gross National Product
GSP	Generalized System of Preferences
IDOs	Integrated Development Operations
Helios	European action programme for the disabled
IFOR	Implementation Force (in former Yugoslavia)
IGCs	Inter-governmental Conferences
IMPs	Integrated Mediterranean Programmes
INF	intermediate-range nuclear forces
Interreg	EC programme for border regions
IRA	International Ruhr Authority
ISPA	Instrument for Structural Policies for Pre-Accesssion
IULA	International Union of Local Authorities
JET	Joint European Torus
JHA	Justice and Home Affairs
LDCs	Least Developed Countries
Lingua	European Union Action Programme to promote foreign language competence
MAGP	Multiannual Guidance Programme
MCAs	Monetary Compensatory Amounts
MEP	Member of the European Parliament
MEPP	Middle East Peace Process
Mercosur	Southern Cone Common Market
MFN	Most Favoured Nation
MGQs	Maximum Guaranteed Quantities

NACC	North Atlantic Co-operation Council
NAT	North Atlantic Treaty
NATO	North Atlantic Treaty Organization
NCE	Non-Compulsory Expenditure
NICs	Newly Industrializing Countries
NOW	New Opportunities for Women
OCCAR	Joint Armaments Co-operation Structure
OCT	Overseas Countries and Territories
OECD	Organization for Economic Co-operation and Development
OEEC	Organization for European Economic Co-operation
OPs	Operational Programmes
OPEC	Organization of Petroleum Exporting Countries
OSCE	Organization for Security and Co-operation in Europe
PCA	Partnership and Co-operation Agreement
PES	Party of European Socialists
PfP	Partnership for Peace scheme
Phare	Poland-Hungary Assistance for Economic Reconstruction or Poland-Hungary Aid for Reconstruction of the Economy
POs	Producers' Organizations
PPEWU	Policy Planning and Early Warning Unit
QMV	Qualified Majority Voting
RACE	Research and Development in Advanced Communications Technology for Europe
Rechar	EC initiative programme for the conversion of coal mining areas
Renaval	EC initiative programme for the conversion of shipbuilding areas
Resider	EC initiative programme for the conversion of steel areas
Sapard	Support for Pre-Accession Measures for Agriculture and Rural Development
SAVE	EC programme for energy efficiency
SEA	Single European Act
SEM	Single European Market
SFOR	Stabilization Force (in former Yugoslavia)
Sigma	EU programme with CEECs on government and management
SIS	Schengen Information System
SLIM	Simple Legislation for the Internal Market
SMEs	Small and Medium-Sized Enterprises
SOCRATES	European programme for education
Stabex	Export revenue stabilization scheme
Star	EC programme for high technology and communications
Sysmin	Mineral export revenue stabilization scheme
Tacis	Technical Assistance to the Commonwealth of Independent States
TACs	Total Allowable Catches

TECS	The European Computer System
Tempus	Trans-European Mobility Programme for University Students
TENs	Trans-European Networks
TEU	Treaty on European Union
UK	United Kingdom
UN	United Nations
UNCTAD	United Nations Conference on Trade and Development
UNICE	EU employers' organization
UNRRA	United Nations Relief and Rehabilitation Agency
USA	United States of America
USSR	Union of Soviet Socialist Republics (Soviet Union)
Valoren	EC programme for local energy sources
VAT	Value-Added Tax
VER	Voluntary Export Restraints
WEU	Western European Union
WTO	Warsaw Treaty Organization
WTO	World Trade Organization

Preface

The entry into force of the Treaty of Amsterdam in May 1999 and the move towards the further enlargement of the European Union, with a preparatory Inter-governmental Conference aimed at reforming the EU's institutions, mark further steps in the process of integration in Europe. Both the attempts to deepen integration within the EU and to widen its membership have led to problems, a number of which remain unsolved. Furthermore, there are disputes about the very nature of the EU and its aims and objectives. Nevertheless, the European Union continues to be a beacon for those European states that are not yet members, and has become an important actor on the world scene. This book is about the European Union, its history, institutions, policies and relations with other areas of the world. It also considers the theories and ideas about European integration and the nature of the EU.

The book is set out to be accessible to the student. It starts, in the Introduction, with a brief political history of Europe from the rise of the sovereign state to the post-Second World War period. Since 1945 integration has been an important phenomenon in Europe, and this is placed in its wider context. Chapter 1 examines the theories and concepts of European integration and relates these to the life and times of the European Communities and European Union. The EU's institutions and budget are covered in Chapter 2, which also sets out the legislative processes of the EU and discusses its democratic element. Chapter 3 looks at the completion of the Single European Market or internal market over the period since the establishment of the European Economic Community, and the move to economic and monetary union, with the creation in January 1999 of the euro currency, is related in Chapter 4. The following three chapters are about important policy aspects of the EC/EU: Chapter 5 is on the social dimension, covering a range of policies; Chapter 6 gives a central place to the Common Agricultural Policy, a key element of the EC, but also deals with environmental policy; and Chapter 7 gives an account of the EC/EU's regional and structural policies. Chapter 8 traces the EC/EU's relations with its citizens, and co-operation in judicial and police matters. The Common Foreign and Security Policy, including the burgeoning defence co-operation, is the theme of Chapter 9. The EC/EU's relations with the other countries of Europe is the subject of Chapter 10; Chapter 11 covers the wider map of EU relationships with the rest of the world. Each chapter has a bibliography at the end with both references and further reading. Where appropriate, web sites have been noted and these were current as of the end of July 2000. Their URLs or nametags should be preceded by http://

A note on names may help at this early stage. The European Union (EU) covers, after the 1997 Treaty of Amsterdam, the institutions and activities of the European Communities, of the Common Foreign and Security Policy (CFSP) and of police and judicial co-operation in criminal matters (Justice and Home Affairs in the 1992 Maastricht Treaty). The European Communities (EC) were made up of the European Economic Community (EEC), the European Atomic Energy Community (Euratom) – both created by treaties signed in Rome in 1957 – and the European Coal and Steel Community (ECSC), set up by the 1951 Treaty of Paris. To the extent that this book deals with each of these separately, then the terms EEC, Euratom and ECSC will be used. However, for the period after the 1965 Merger Treaty – when the institutions of the three were drawn together – the term European Communities (EC) will be employed. A further complication is that the Maastricht Treaty transformed the EEC into simply the European Community. EC/EU budgets were reckoned in ECUs (European Currency Units, formerly the European Unit of Account) until 1 January 1999 when the new currency, the euro, took over. By July 2000, the euro was worth £0.60 or $0.88. Readers should note that this rate could fluctuate – either upwards or downwards.

The author would like to thank Fiona Butler, who co-authored the first two editions of this text. Though the earlier material has been largely rewritten, the structure – and some of the ideas – of the earlier collective effort broadly remains. Also thanks are due to the following for their assistance: Chris Jones, Neill Nugent, Janet Mather and those who made constructive comments about the first two editions. Of course, any mistakes are my own. Finally, I would like to thank my wife, Elizabeth, for her supreme tolerance while I was writing this volume.

Clive Archer
September 2000

This book is dedicated to my mother
and to the memory of my father

Introduction: a changing Europe

At the beginning of the twenty-first century, Europe is coming to terms with the end of one historic period – that of the Cold War – without the system that may replace it yet being apparent. Europe has to live with the consequences not just of the Cold War but also of four historic settlements: Westphalia, the Vienna Congress of 1815, Versailles and the post-Second World War deals arranged at Yalta and Potsdam. The Westphalian settlement of 1648 saw the genesis of the sovereign state system in Europe. This is now being challenged by the creation of the European Union and by the Organization for Security and Co-operation in Europe (OSCE), which has made human rights and minority issues subjects of international activity as never before. The balance of power system entrenched in Europe with the Vienna Congress has been undermined by the end of the Soviet Union in 1991 and by a stress on co-operative security in the OSCE. A couple of states created by the Versailles settlement of 1919 – Yugoslavia and Czecho-slovakia – split up, while others, notably Estonia, Latvia and Lithuania, re-emerged, and a unified Germany dominated central Europe. The divided Europe of spheres of influence, brought about by the Yalta and Potsdam agreements of the victors of the Second World War, faded away after the Berlin Wall was torn down in November 1989. A look back to the history of modern Europe helps in understanding the debates about the nature and possible development of the European Union.

The rise of the sovereign state

It is necessary to understand the sovereign state in order to comprehend the European Union. The genesis of the sovereign state as a European creation can be traced back to the fourteenth century (Strayer, 1970: 57) with the essential element of 'constitutional self-containment' (Manning, 1962: 166) having been established in a number of states by the Peace of Westphalia in 1648. If sovereignty 'consists of being constitutionally apart, of not being contained, however loosely, within a wider constitutional scheme' (James, 1986: 24), then many city-states and principalities failed this test in the late Middle Ages. After all, they were regarded as being under the jurisdiction – the legal authority – of either the Holy Roman Emperor or the Pope.[1]

In the Peace of Westphalia the ruling houses of Europe agreed on that which was already a fact: that sovereign states in Europe could not be contained within the Habsburg-run Holy Roman Empire or within the writ of the Pontiff in Rome. It 'paved the way for a system of states to replace a hierarchical system under the leadership of the Pope and the Habsburg family complex that linked the Holy Roman and Spanish Empires' (Holsti, 1991: 26). This was as much a recognition of the consequences of the Reformation, which had splintered Christendom in Europe, as a triumph for such monarchs as the kings of Sweden and of France. The acceptance of the higher authority of an emperor or a pope within a set of rules, institutions and sanctions was replaced in the Peace of Westphalia by 'the first successful attempt in European history to establish a continental diplomatic order that was based on the sovereign state' (Holsti, 1991: 34). This allowed sovereign rulers not only to make agreements but also to decide how these should be interpreted and whether they should be kept.

From the seventeenth century until the Napoleonic Wars of the early nineteenth century, Europe was divided into a patchwork quilt of states. Some were sovereign, some subject, and they had war as a common form of interaction with diplomacy as a means of ending one conflict or preparing for the next. Grand Designs were advanced by the likes of Dante, Dubois and Sully to re-unite Christendom. Later writers, such as Penn, Rousseau and Kant, were more concerned with bringing peace to what had become an anarchic system, that is, one without an overall authority (Hinsley, 1963: Part I).

Concert and nation

The Napoleonic Wars led to the short-lived, near-unification of the European continent under one political system. During the Revolutionary and Napoleonic Wars, warfare became popularized in the sense that French governments undertook it on behalf of 'the peoples'. The Congress of Vienna (1814–15) re-established many of the states abolished by Napoleon and sought to create a balance of power in order to maintain stability in Europe. The Great Powers accepted that there should be occasional gatherings of their representatives to manage change in the system. This Concert System hid a number of disagreements between the major powers in Europe, not least as to the occasion for a joint intervention and the form it might take (Holsti, 1991: 132).

The Concert was supplemented by agreements such as the 1856 Congress of Paris, which added to the laws of war and the law of the sea and brought the Ottoman Empire into the comity of European states (Hinsley, 1963: 231–7). By the latter half of the nineteenth century, nationalism had become a significant force in Europe. The nation-states of Italy and Germany had been created from smaller entities and the hopes of other national groupings – the Poles, Slavs, Bulgars and Romanians – started to threaten the very existence of the large, multinational European empires.

Attempts to manage and organize the European system took a severe blow with the First World War. The destruction of 1914–18 led to the downfall of the continental empires – Imperial Germany, Austro-Hungary, Czarist Russia and the Ottoman Empire – and the creation of a number of nation-based states such as Estonia, Latvia, Lithuania, Poland and Czecho-slovakia. As the war was won with American assistance, President Woodrow Wilson of the United States helped to fashion the Versailles settlement both in general outline and in detail. Versailles was founded on the assumption of continued American involvement in Europe but Wilson was unable to persuade the US Congress to ratify the treaty. The new system had to be upheld in Europe without US assistance or membership of the League of Nations. In addition, the new states created in Europe were not really economically viable and were unable to withstand the growing trade protectionism of the inter-war period. Many states included ethnic minorities, the international guardianship of which proved less than satisfactory. The mixture of disputed frontiers, discontented national groups, political instability and economic turbulence proved too testing for a Europe that had few instruments to manage change or disruption, except the diplomatic efforts of the French and British, cloaked in the garb of the League of Nations, and their peacetime armed forces.

Proposals for the peaceful collaboration of former enemies were advanced during the 1920s (Stirk and Weigall, 1999: 2–5) and, in an attempt to break through the mistrust of the inter-war European relations, the French Prime Minister, Aristide Briand, in 1930 circulated to other European leaders a proposal for a confederal Europe. Though the Briand Memorandum was sidelined into a study group (Urwin, 1991: 7), an alternative way forward for Europe had been signposted.

Europe divided

The Second World War – like the First – started as a European civil war and spread to other continents. Its outcome was again decided by outside powers: the United States and the Soviet Union. The Soviet Union (USSR) had been distanced from the mainstream of European politics after European, and other, powers had tried to strangle the Soviet state at birth from 1918 to 1921. After failing in this, most states in Europe isolated the Soviet Union, a process mirrored by the policies of Stalin, the Soviet leader, in cutting off his population from what was considered to be the corrupting influence of capitalism. Even during the Second World War, when the United Kingdom and the United States were fighting on the same side as the

Soviet Union, contact was minimal and controlled. The United States was an ocean away from Europe and, after the First World War, had slipped back into isolationism. However, by the end of the war in Europe in May 1945, both the USSR and the USA had large numbers of troops on the continent of Europe and had been central to the defeat of the Axis powers of Germany and Italy.

This outside presence was to mould European – and world – politics in the post-Second World War era. The phrase 'the Cold War', an expression that described the relationship between the United States and the Soviet Union, typified much of that time. It was not a 'hot war', since neither side pitched its armed forces directly against those of the other side, but each used other means – espionage, economic warfare, terrorism and surrogates – in the struggle against its adversary. Both built up nuclear arsenals aimed at the other side. The conflict was one of power, involving control and influence; it was also ideological with the free-enterprise, elected-democracy beliefs of the USA and its Western supporters pitched against the central-market, communist-controlled system of the Soviet bloc countries. However, the East–West relationship was not always conflictual: even at the height of the Cold War there were elements of co-operation. There were also periods of lesser tension, such as the couple of years after Stalin's death in 1953 or the period of détente in the late 1960s to the late 1970s.

Europe in 1945 was an exhausted and devastated continent. The inter-war great powers had lost something of their greatness. Germany had been overrun and divided by its conquerors. Italy's African empire had ended. France was burdened by its defeat in 1940 by Germany and its subsequent occupation. The United Kingdom, which had stood alone against Nazi tyranny and domination of Europe, was economically bankrupt.

In 1945 American troops were in France, Germany, the Low Countries, Italy, parts of Austria and Czechoslovakia, and US money was being used to provide the basics for the peoples of occupied and liberated Europe alike. The Soviet Red Army backed up the USSR's presence in Central and Eastern Europe. The Soviets had liberated Poland, Romania, Bulgaria, Hungary and parts of Germany, Austria and Czechoslovakia, but the Soviet Union scarcely had the resources to feed its own people, let alone those in the occupied regions. What it was able, and willing, to offer the people of these newly liberated lands was an alternative political and economic system: that of Soviet socialism.

Thus European political leaders were faced with two outside powers dominating their continent in 1945. However, at that stage both could be considered to be there 'by invitation' of the Europeans, who had been unable to throw off the tyranny of Nazi occupation by themselves. The main hope of Europe's politicians was to build a prosperous, peaceful and free Europe. In 1945 prosperity was a long way off; it was more important to provide the basic goods and services, and then to attempt to rebuild the economies of Europe. Peace in 1945 meant 'no war' and in particular the prevention of a recurrence of the post-First World War situation, where Germany had risen again to challenge the Versailles settlement. Freedom was an end to the Nazi yoke and the establishment of governments representing those forces that had fought against tyranny during the war.

However, as the fog of war lifted and long-term goals were considered, then the consensus on the meaning of prosperity, peace and freedom started to crack. The differences were defined by the division of the continent at the end of the war by the two superpowers of the United States and the Soviet Union, and became institutionalized in the Cold War. As Buzan *et al.* have typified the situation:

> With overlay from 1945 to 1989 [by the superpowers], the European security complex virtually ceased to exist as an entity defined by its own interactions. It became instead the nut in the nutcracker of global rivalry dominated by the two superpowers. (1991: 31)

This division did not form immediately with the onset of peace in May 1945, though even then there were signs of disagreement between the USA and USSR (Feis, 1970: Part Three). The four victorious powers – France, the Soviet Union, the United Kingdom and the United States – jointly ran Germany and Austria, and the United Nations established an Economic Commission for Europe, drawing membership from all of the continent. Most of the governments in Europe – outside the United Kingdom, the Soviet Union and the two Iberian states of Spain and Portugal – were coalitions including communists, socialists, liberals, agrarians and Christian democrats.

By early 1946 a war of words had started between the Soviet Union and its erstwhile Western allies. Stalin, in his February election speech, looked forward to the triumph of Marxism over capitalism. Churchill – the United Kingdom's wartime leader but by then Leader of the Opposition – warned in his Fulton, Missouri, speech:

> From Stettin in the Baltic to Trieste in the Adriatic, an iron curtain has descended across the Continent. . . . [T]he populations . . . in what I must call the Soviet Sphere . . . are subject in one form or another, not only to Soviet influence but to a very high and, in many cases, increasing measure of control from Moscow. . . . (Halle 1967: 103–4)

Although the United States had nuclear weapons (though only a few), its troops had been rapidly withdrawn from Europe, whereas the Red Army still seemed to remain in Eastern Europe in large numbers.

Churchill's Iron Curtain represented a political, military and economic division of Europe. During 1946 and 1947 the Communist parties in

Eastern Europe, France and Italy were expanding their influence and support. In March 1947 the French and British governments signed the Treaty of Dunkirk, which allowed for defence co-operation between the two, ostensibly against German revival but with the main eye on the Soviet Union. A few days later, the United States' President announced the Truman Doctrine – that the USA would support all free peoples resisting subjugation, with the implied enemy being Soviet communism. In June 1947 US Secretary of State George Marshall proposed massive American aid to help with the rebuilding of Europe. This offer was only taken up by the Western European states, with Moscow forbidding the participation of countries of Eastern and Central Europe that it dominated. The economies of these excluded states would now be very different had they been allowed to participate in what became known as the Marshall Plan and Marshall Aid. The Soviet reaction was defensive: the Cominform – an organization to co-ordinate action by communist parties throughout the world – was formed in October 1947, and by the end of the year non-communist parties were being dissolved all over Eastern Europe on Moscow's instructions.

The turning point

Events in 1948 clarified what had happened almost by stealth: the creation of a communist-run Eastern Europe tied to Moscow opposed by a capitalist-dominated Western Europe eager to enrol the United States in its cause. In response to a communist takeover in Czechoslovakia, the United Kingdom and France agreed to expand their defence agreement to include the three Benelux states – Belgium, the Netherlands and Luxembourg – on 29 February 1948. It was feared that Norway and Denmark were next on Stalin's list. It seemed that there was little peace for Europe while freedom had been extinguished in one part of the continent and was being threatened in the other.

However, instruments were being forged to offer at least the Western Europeans the prospect of re-establishing their prosperity, guaranteeing some form of peace and proclaiming their freedom.

By 1948 the Western European states had agreed on the distribution of assistance provided (mainly from the USA) by the European Reconstruction Plan and formed a permanent instrument of economic co-ordination, the Organization for European Economic Co-operation (OEEC, later the OECD, the Organization for Economic Co-operation and Development).

In March 1948 France, the United Kingdom and the Benelux states signed the Brussels Treaty creating the Western Union, which, as well as promising common action in the political and economic field, provided a 50-year mutual defence guarantee for its members. Its real importance, however, lay more in the expression by the five countries to defend themselves and the positive effect this had in encouraging the United States (and Canada) to join talks about a wider self-defence treaty. Though this agreement was less all-embracing in content than the Brussels Treaty, it did include states such as Iceland, Denmark and Norway in Northern Europe and Italy and Portugal in the south, as well as the two North American states. The resulting North Atlantic Treaty (NAT) was signed in April 1949 and came into force in August of that year.

On the political side, a number of groups had been forming associations to promote closer political and economic unity in Europe, examples being the United Europe Movement in the United Kingdom and the Europa-Bund in Germany. These organizations brought together a wide range of opinions and personalities at the Hague Congress of May 1948, which established the influential European Movement, a non-governmental organization (Urwin, 1991: 27). In particular, the French and Benelux governments quickly took up the Movement's ideas on European unity. At a meeting of the Brussels Treaty powers, they proposed a parliamentary Council of Europe. The British were reluctant to have such a body discuss important matters, which they thought should be dealt with by ministerial consultation. The statute of the Council of Europe signed in May 1949, was a compromise with the United Kingdom's wishes dominating: a Committee of Ministers was established together with a Parliamentary Assembly, which was to have only a consultative status. The Council's aim, as stated in its Statutes, was the achievement of closer unity of those European states that accepted the values of 'individual freedom, political liberty and the rule of law, principles which form the basis of all genuine democracy' (Preamble). This aim was to be achieved by 'discussions of questions of common concern' and agreements and common action in economics, social, cultural, scientific, legal and administrative matters' (Article 1.b).

The OEEC, the Brussels Treaty – and the subsequent North Atlantic Treaty – and the Council of Europe represented both the institutionalization of the division of Europe and – especially in the case of Marshall Aid and the NAT – an underpinning of Western Europe's future by the United States. This response was important in reassuring the governments of Western Europe that they could draw on outside support if facing attacks from either within their country or outside.

These institutional responses by no means solved all the main outstanding problems in Western Europe; neither did they represent an attempt to transcend the politics of Europe as the supporters of European federalism had hoped. The OEEC, the Brussels Treaty organization and the NAT were all traditional intergovernmental agreements, and even the Council of Europe, with its innovative Parliamentary Assembly, had no real powers, at that stage, to act without governmental consent. The institutions established in 1948 and 1949 were aimed at underpinning the existing sovereign states in Western Europe.

The Community method

The main problem not addressed during this period was that of an emerging Germany and its relations with the rest of Western Europe, especially France. By September 1949 the three Western allies – France, the United Kingdom and the United States – had merged the administrations of their occupation zones in West Germany. They agreed on a Basic Law for a federal German state which came into being in September 1949, with a democratic government headed by Konrad Adenauer.

France, in particular, had doubts about this renaissance. After 1945 the French government had expressed concern that the untrammelled economic revival of Germany could lead to that country gaining political and military dominance, as had happened after the First World War. The French, in particular, wanted a careful control of the industrial areas of Germany – mainly in the Rhineland – that had provided the powerhouse of German rearmament in the 1930s. The British and Americans were more willing to bring the Germans back into the comity of nations and recognized that the economic revival of Europe had to include West Germany.

The International Ruhr Authority was created in January 1949 to ensure that 'the resources of the Ruhr shall not in the future be used for the purpose of aggression' (Preamble of draft agreement). This authority was a management board for those resources, on which were represented the United Kingdom, France, Germany, the three Benelux states and the USA. However, the French considered that the British and Americans were allowing too much coal and steel production in the Ruhr, which was part of Germany, while the Germans thought it unfair that only their heavy industries were under international control. The new democratic Federal German government could not be expected constantly to pay for the sins of its Nazi predecessors. Other solutions to this problem were on offer. Karl Arnold, a prominent German politician, suggested that the Authority be extended to include French Lorraine, the Saar (a former German territory then in economic union with France), Belgium and Luxembourg. The powerful US Commissioner in Germany, John McCloy, and a number of other spokesmen, ranging from socialist politicians to businessmen, took up this idea (Diebold, 1959: 35–46).

The coal and steel industries of continental Western Europe straddled the frontiers of France, Germany, Belgium and Luxembourg and were interdependent. Coal and steel then represented the heartbeat of an industrial society and the life-blood of any rearmament plans. There was also the fear that, as after the First World War, the post-war boom would be followed by a recession, forcing such industries into protective cartel agreements that would be difficult for national governments to control.

So by 1950 the coal and steel industries of Western Europe offered fertile ground for a political initiative that could help solve their problems, which could address Franco-German relations and which might even touch on the wider issues of the peace, prosperity and freedom of Europe. Jean Monnet, who had headed the French post-war planning effort and who was a staunch supporter of a federal Europe, planted the seed of the new approach. He persuaded the French Foreign Minister, Robert Schuman, to advance an ambitious plan in May 1950, that had repercussions for the organization of post-war Europe.

The basis of the Schuman Plan was simple. Taking up Karl Arnold's point, it proposed 'that Franco-German production of coal and steel as a whole be placed under a common High Authority, within the framework of an organization open to the participation of the other countries of Europe' (Robert Schuman, 9 May 1950, cited in Stirk and Weigall, 1999: 76). This Authority would oversee the reduction of coal and steel trade barriers between the participating states, thereby rationalizing them not just on a basis decided by narrow national interests or by a cartel of the companies. This French proposal was strengthened because it referred to more than just the German industries.

Second, the proposal bound the fate of Germany and France together. By placing their coal and steel under common control, it was felt that neither state would be able to build the sinews of war for use against the other. This would make 'any war between France and Germany . . . not merely unthinkable, but materially impossible' (Robert Schuman, 9 May 1950, cited in Stirk and Weigall, 1999: 76).

Third, Monnet had imported some federalist ideas into the proposal, though – for the time being – these were to be exercised in a limited sphere. The High Authority was to be a functional body covering only coal and steel, but it was also 'a first step in the federation of Europe' (Stirk and Weigall, 1999: 76) and a 'first decisive act in the construction of Europe' (Willis, 1968: 80). Thus, the Schuman Plan represented not just a solution to an immediate set of problems but also the beginning of a wider enterprise that had a United States of Europe as its end product.

The response to the Schuman Plan from the Federal Republic of Germany, Italy and the Benelux states was positive, and by April 1951 these five countries plus France – the Six – had signed the Treaty of Paris establishing the European Coal and Steel Community (ECSC). This Treaty came into force on 25 July 1952.

The Preamble of the Treaty of Paris set as an aim for the member states 'to substitute for age-old rivalries the merging of their essential interests'. They recognized 'that Europe can be built only through practical achievements'.

The Coal and Steel Community was to be founded upon 'a common market, common objectives and common institutions'. The attainment of its objectives was to be ensured by a High Authority, a body created to consider 'the general interest of the Community' and independent of the demands of member states (Article 9). The signatories undertook to respect the 'supranational character' of the High Authority (Article 9), which suggested that this institution should be above the workings of the nation-state.

Another unresolved issue in 1950 was the contribution to be made by the states of Western Europe to their own defence. By signing the North Atlantic Treaty the United States had agreed to regard an attack on a European signatory as being equivalent to an attack on itself, and the USA had made available armaments for the hard-pressed Western European states. However, no additional American troops were stationed in Europe. Hope that the US monopoly of nuclear weapons might deter a Soviet attack was dented in 1949 when the Soviet Union exploded its own nuclear device.

One way to prevent the Soviet occupation of Western Europe, which was presumed in most Western military plans, was to build up Western armies in Europe so that they might repulse the might of the Soviet forces. In the absence of the Americans and with the British and French both stretched by their global colonial commitments, the natural choice seemed to be that of West Germany. The US Joint Chiefs of Staff encapsulated the problem as early as April 1947: 'Without German aid the remaining countries of western Europe could scarcely be expected to withstand the armies of our ideological opponents until the United States could mobilize and place in the field sufficient armed forces to achieve their defeat' (US Department of State, 1947: 741).

However, the idea of placing the Germans in uniform so shortly after the end of the Second World War was not one that attracted European approval, nor indeed was it popular in Germany. Chancellor Adenauer of the Federal Republic had addressed both concerns – the need to defend Western Europe and the fear of a revived militarized Germany – when in 1949 he announced that 'The question of the re-establishment of our army can only be brought up within the framework of the Western Union [Brussels Treaty]. We are ready to participate in the formation of a European army' (cited in Greiner, 1985: 169). It was this notion that was taken up by one of Schuman's colleagues in the French government, René Pleven. He adapted the Community idea – as outlined in the Schuman Plan – and proposed a European Defence Community (EDC) to bring the European armed forces of 'the Six' under a common control which would be regulated by a European Political Community (EPC).

While the Schuman Plan was quickly adopted, that of Pleven ran into difficulties. The outbreak of the Korean War in June 1950 was seen by many in the West as a precursor to a Soviet attack on Western Europe. As a result US forces in Europe were bolstered, leading to greater pressure on the Europeans to increase their contribution. This fired the debate on German rearmament, with the British wanting it within a North Atlantic context and the French preferring a Western European solution. In the end, the EDC fell by the wayside, and the compromise was an expansion of the 1948 Brussels Treaty to create the Western European Union (WEU), of which West Germany and Italy would be members. West Germany also joined the North Atlantic Treaty Organization (NATO) and its rearmament was undertaken within the framework of NATO and the WEU. The Soviet Union established the Warsaw Treaty Organization (WTO) in May 1955 with the communist governments of Eastern Europe as a riposte to German membership of NATO. The WTO institutionalized the close control of the defence policies of these states, exercised by the Soviet Union since 1945.

Relaunch and schism

By 1955 progress had been made towards the settlement of the two major political problems that Western Europe had faced in the early 1950s. France and Germany had started to pool control of their coal and steel industries and had embarked on a qualitatively new relationship. The creation of the WEU had allowed the rearmament of West Germany to go ahead within a wider Western European and NATO context and it also had re-established the commitment of British forces to the defence of the European continent. Other advances had been made. A multilateral payment system for trade had been established between the OEEC countries. At the outbreak of the Korean War, the North Atlantic Treaty had begun to build an organization – NATO – that included a joint military structure. The Nordic states had formed the Nordic Council in 1952 (with Finland joining in 1955) with the aim of enhancing co-operation between those states and societies. In December 1954 the United Kingdom had signed a treaty of association with the ECSC that established a working relationship between the two sides.

However, certain problems endured. The USA, in particular, felt that the Europeans were not contributing enough to their own defence and the gap was filled by an increased dependence on nuclear weapons in Europe in order to deter the expected Soviet attack.

The ECSC started to run into trouble within a couple of years of its creation. By 1954 it was being adversely affected by recession and the French and West Germans were increasingly resorting to a bilateral approach to solve their problems (Haas, 1968: 265). In addition, suggestions for the creation of separate agricultural, transport and health communities – based on the ECSC model – had not been taken up, and by

August 1954 the EDC had also failed. It seemed that the British government – which had scorned the Community idea – would be proved right.

In November 1954 Jean Monnet, the first President of the ECSC High Authority, resigned from his post in order to supervise the 'relance' – the relaunching of the Community idea. He supported a memorandum by the Benelux governments that expanded the Community idea to include a common market in all goods traded between the ECSC members, and which was submitted to the ECSC governments at a meeting in Messina in June 1955. This gathering of 'the Six' prepared the ground for two further Community institutions – one to cover trade and other economic activities and the other to embrace the emerging nuclear energy industry.

From July to December 1955 the details of these Communities were worked out in the Spaak Committee, named after the Belgian Foreign Minister who chaired it. The Six wanted to abolish trade restrictions among them and to standardize their tariff level with the rest of the world. Goods, capital, services and labour would eventually be free to move between the six members as easily as within each state. As well as this customs union element, there would be a harmonization of financial, economic and social policies, as well as aid to the poorer areas such as Southern Italy. The institutions matched those of the ECSC, though they were to be less 'supranational' with the governmental representatives having a greater say.

In April 1956 the Spaak Report was presented to the ECSC governments. It recommended the creation of a European Atomic Energy Community (Euratom) and a European Economic Community (EEC). The latter would be based on a common market made up of a customs union and common economic policies and would be supervised by common institutions fashioning and enforcing common regulations for the entire Community area. A close relationship with other Western European states was recommended by the Spaak Report. In May 1956 the Foreign Ministers of the Six adopted the Spaak Report, with the addition of a section on overseas territories and colonies. It was intended that two treaties to be signed in Rome in March 1957 would establish the EEC and Euratom.

The British attitude to the ideas of the Spaak Report was, in the words of the then Chancellor of the Exchequer, R.A. Butler, that they felt 'it was not going to work' (Charlton, 1983: 195). When it appeared that the Six were going to adopt the Report, the United Kingdom advanced its own ideas. They proposed that an OEEC study group should examine possible forms of association between the nascent customs union and other OEEC states. From mid–1956 until early 1959, after the Six had introduced their first tariff cuts, the British and other OEEC states tried to persuade the Six to subsume their customs union within a OEEC-wide free trade area. However, the Six, led by the French, did not wish to allow the rest of the Western

Europeans to benefit from access to their markets through a free trade area without taking the full responsibilities – and costs – of a customs union. In particular, the United Kingdom wanted to accept only a free trade area that would allow it to maintain its own preferential tariff system with Commonwealth countries. The Six also insisted that agricultural trade should be included in any deal and that social policy also should be considered, both notions that the British rejected. The United Kingdom wanted the institutions that managed the free trade area to be loose and intergovernmental; the Six wanted a tighter arrangement with more powerful institutions that could enforce what had been agreed.

Once the EEC had been formed and had started to implement its own policies and the OEEC negotiations had failed, some of the non-Six OEEC states (principally the United Kingdom, Sweden and Switzerland) decided to form their own trade arrangement. Representatives from the United Kingdom, Denmark, Norway, Sweden, Austria, Switzerland and Portugal met in the summer of 1959 and agreed on a smaller free trade area among themselves. The European Free Trade Association (EFTA) started work in May 1960 with the above seven states as members. It had intergovernmental institutions, excluded most agricultural trade from its remit and aimed at creating free and fair trade – rather than a customs union – among its members. By the start of the 1960s Western Europe was 'at Sixes and Sevens'.

Further division

European integration received two major setbacks in the 1960s. First, the division between the EFTA Seven and the EEC Six continued, and was to endure in one form or another until 1993. It was aggravated by the attitude of President de Gaulle of France (who had come to power in 1958) to British attempts to join the European Communities (as the ECSC, the EEC and Euratom became collectively known). By summer 1961, the British government decided that the EEC was going to survive and that the United Kingdom should be on the inside. Pressure by the US administration on the United Kingdom to join and the expected economic benefits of membership were key in this decision. An application for membership was submitted but negotiations were broken off in January 1963 when de Gaulle exercised a French veto, claiming that the British were not yet ready for membership. In May 1967 the Labour government in Britain re-submitted a request for membership negotiations but de Gaulle again stopped this in November 1967.

Division was also growing within the European Communities (EC). De Gaulle's attitude to the EC was different both from his predecessors' and from most of the other leaders of the Six. He accepted the reality of the EC and the need for close Franco-German relations, but he rejected the idea that the EC should have supranational institutions. When the EEC Commission attempted to use the development of the Common Agricultural Policy (CAP) – from which the French farmers benefited – to increase their own powers, French ministers boycotted the EC Council of Ministers (the 'empty chair' policy) in order to get their way on agriculture without having to pay the price in terms of supranational institutions. Though this particular crisis was resolved with the Luxembourg Compromise of January 1966, it nevertheless circumscribed the development of the Communities' institutions at a time when the economic success of the EC was beginning to slow after the rapid growth of the 1950s.

At the Hague Summit of December 1969 the new French President, Georges Pompidou, accepted both the necessity for widening the membership of the EC and for deepening co-operation, including the prospect of political co-ordination of foreign policies and of economic and monetary union. Membership negotiations with the United Kingdom, Denmark, Ireland and Norway were opened by the EC in 1970 and a Treaty of Accession for the four – the Treaty of Brussels – was signed in January 1972. Norwegians rejected membership in a referendum in September 1972, but the three other states joined the EC on 1 January 1973. A major step had been taken to mend the Franco-British rift within Western Europe and to develop the EC beyond the status of a customs union with a Common Agricultural Policy.

The widening of EC membership and the deepening of its policies did not come at an auspicious time for Europe. The October 1973 Middle Eastern War led to a massive increase in oil prices brought about by the Arab members of the Organization of Petroleum Exporting Countries (OPEC). This dampened the growth of the European economies, the success of which had been fired by cheap oil prices in the 1950s and 1960s. The response of the EC member states to the oil price increases and the resulting economic depression in the 1973 to 1974 period was to resort to national instruments both to obtain more oil and to cope with unemployment.

The internal development of the EC was also impeded by the election of a Labour government in the United Kingdom in 1974, which insisted on 'renegotiating' the terms of British membership of the Communities. The British people accepted the results of a referendum in the summer of 1975, but Labour's lack of enthusiasm for the EC encouraged the re-emergence of a Franco-German axis within the Communities. Margaret Thatcher's accession to power in May 1979 led to a more aggressive approach towards the EC with demands to 'give us our money back' – a reference to the unequal burden of the cost of the CAP that the United Kingdom had to bear – being made at the highest level.

The momentum that the EC had gained in the early 1960s was soon squandered in a number of internal disagreements in the 1960s and 1970s. These included divisions between de Gaulle and the other members, then between the British and most of their partners, and were exacerbated by the adverse conditions such as the oil price increase of 1973–74 and the international recession of 1979–81.

A second relaunching

The start of the 1980s saw Europe as divided as ever: between East and West, the United Kingdom and the continental EC states and between federalists and intergovernmentalists.

In a global context, the Soviet invasion of Afghanistan in December 1979, the election of Ronald Reagan in November 1980 and the declaration of martial law by the Communist regime in Poland in December 1981 all signalled the return of a period of chilly relations between the two super-powers, called the 'New Cold War'. Until 1987, Western Europe was in dispute as to whether US intermediate-range nuclear forces (INF) should be placed in Europe to strengthen the military links between the United States and Western Europe. The response of the decrepit Soviet leadership was to place equivalent forces into Eastern Europe (then under Soviet domination) and to raise the stakes in the international arms control negotiations. It seemed that one half of the Western Europeans feared the United States deserting them to face a highly armed Soviet Union by themselves, while the other half feared too close an embrace by the US president.

Even within Western Europe, the European Communities seemed rudder-less. Though Greece had joined in 1981 and Spain and Portugal were lining up for membership, there was little impetus towards political development. One of the most strident opponents of such moves was the British Prime Minister, Mrs Thatcher, and the EC institutions spent much of the early 1980s responding to British demands for a reconsideration of the budgetary question.

A turning point for Europe came in 1985 with a new Soviet leader, Mikhail Gorbachev. He reversed the hard-line Soviet foreign and defence policy and initiated reforms at home. His 'new thinking' in external affairs led him to jettison the previous confrontational approach of the Soviet leadership and to place emphasis on achieving 'common security' with the West by a series of arms control and disarmament agreements.

During the New Cold War an institution had been kept alive in Europe that later proved to be of some value – the Conference on Security and Co-operation in Europe (CSCE – later the OSCE, the Organization for Security and Co-operation in Europe). Its genesis lay in the period of détente – in 1972 – when all the European states (including the Soviet Union) plus the

United States and Canada (which both had troops in Europe) had met in Helsinki to discuss a more long-term institutionalization of détente. The result was the Final Act of the CSCE, signed in Helsinki in August 1975 by 33 European states, the United States and Canada. This Act set down the principles governing security in Europe, allowed for prior notification of military manoeuvres, outlined a programme of co-operation in economic, scientific and other fields, and introduced human rights as a specific element in European inter-state relations. During the period of the New Cold War in the late 1970s and early 1980s, the Helsinki Final Act was used by both sides against their adversaries, though the CSCE-offshoot Stockholm Conference in 1983 allowed a continued discussion of disarmament and security in Europe. With an impetus from the new Soviet leadership, the Stockholm meeting in September 1986 agreed a tighter arrangement for checking military activities in Europe. The 1987 INF treaty was an agreement to remove all intermediate-range nuclear forces from Europe and to destroy them. By November 1990 the NATO and Warsaw Treaty Organization members had signed the far-reaching Conventional Forces in Europe (CFE) Agreement, which limited the size of armed forces across the European continent and introduced an intrusive verification system to ensure that the demobilization went ahead.

The Milan Summit of EC leaders also marked a watershed as a reform of the Treaty of Rome (which had established the EEC) was agreed. The changes were included in the 1986 Single European Act, which strengthened the institutions of the EC, gave them greater competence and increased their involvement with foreign and security matters. These changes were part of the relaunching of the Community idea in the mid–1980s with the intention of creating by the end of 1992 a large home market of the then 12 member states – the Single European Market ('1992'). This was to reflect the internationalization of capital and business in the EC, which had been taking place for some time, and which would eventually provide industry and commerce with a market larger than that of the United States. These moves gave a new confidence to the EC at a time when the Soviet Union and its Eastern European allies were having problems with their economic and political reforms.

A new Europe

In 1989 the strain of imposing reform on an inflexible Communist system in Eastern Europe became too much, and the face of Europe changed fundamentally and with extensive consequences. At the same time it seemed that the EC was about to embark on a period of entrenchment, though the 1990s proved to be one of transformation and crisis.

A wave of protest swept over Eastern Europe in 1989, and this culminated in the dismantling of the Berlin Wall, which had been built by the East German Communist regime between East and West Berlin in 1961. Earlier in 1989 President Gorbachev had made it clear to the leaders of the Warsaw Treaty Organization – which had originally been established to entrench Soviet military power throughout Eastern Europe – that the Soviet Union would not send their tanks to rescue Communist leaders from their people. One after another Communist government in Eastern Europe folded, with avowedly pro-Western administrations taking their place. With the exception of fighting in Romania, the process was almost without bloodshed as discredited regimes buckled under the pressure of public opinion. It seemed that anything was possible.

These upheavals changed the security situation in Europe, and by 1991 the Warsaw Treaty Organization was defunct, the Soviet armies in Eastern Europe were returning home and massive cuts in armaments in Europe were presaged by the CFE Agreement. At a CSCE meeting in Paris in November 1990, the Cold War was effectively ended and plans were laid for the CSCE to become more active in monitoring human rights and elections and in preventing the outbreak of conflict. The success of a Western-led coalition of forces in the 1991 Gulf War suggested that a new world order might be attainable, in which the EC and NATO would have important roles.

Change had its casualties. The first was the German Democratic Republic (East Germany), which was incorporated into the Federal Republic of Germany – and into the EC – in October 1991. Later that year both Yugoslavia and the Soviet Union broke up, with the latter jettisoning over 70 years of communism and fragmenting into its 15 constituent republics. At NATO's Rome Summit in November 1991 the ex-communist states of Eastern and Central Europe and the decaying Soviet Union were welcomed into a new forum: the North Atlantic Co-operation Council (NACC, now EAPC, the Euro-Atlantic Partnership Council). A new agenda was set for the CSCE that included the possibility of intervention in a state without the consent of its government (NATO Review, 1991: 21). By 1994 the former members of the Warsaw Treaty Organization were being drawn ever closer to NATO by that organization's Partnership for Peace (PfP) scheme. The PfP's Framework Document emphasized transparency in national defence planning and budgeting and the democratic control of armed forces; individual partnership programmes were tailored to suit the needs of co-operation between the partnership country and NATO (von Moltke, 1994: 3–7; Rose, 1994: 13–17). By September 1995 NATO was considering enlargement of its membership with many of the partnership countries clamouring to join. First, NATO had to regularize its relations with Russia and this was done in May 1997 with the signing by both sides of the Founding Act on Mutual Relations, which established a permanent Joint

Council of Russian and NATO members. In April 1999 the Czech Republic, Hungary and Poland became members of NATO with the prospect of membership being held out to other Eastern and Central European states.

In its search for a post-Cold War role, NATO increasingly stressed its potential as an operational body for peacekeeping and humanitarian activities, sanctioned either by the CSCE/OSCE or by the UN Security Council. By far the most difficult situation that these organizations have had to face has been the succession of conflicts in former Yugoslavia, starting with that in Croatia, spreading to include Bosnia-Herzogovina and culminating in the Kosovo conflict. In response to a UN call, NATO provided air-strikes against Bosnian-Serb forces in early 1994 and again in August and November 1994 (*NATO Review*, 1994–95: 11). Neither the UN nor the OSCE sanctioned the wider bombing of Serbia, which was intended to wrest control of the province of Kosovo from that country in early 1999, so this action incurred opposition from Russia.

The former communist-led countries were eager to join other organizations in Europe. As they developed parliamentary systems and moved towards the market economy, so they became eligible for membership of the Council of Europe (Tarschys, 1994–95: 8–12). The European Bank for Reconstruction and Development (EBRD) was formed by the OECD countries with a directorate of the most economically important of those countries known as the Group of Seven (G7). The purpose of the EBRD was to funnel aid and assistance – especially from commercial sources – into Eastern and Central Europe. It had neither the vision nor the resources of the Marshall Plan and made an uncertain start.

The Central and Eastern European states also joined regional organizations such as the central European Initiative, the Visegrad co-operation scheme of the Czech Republic, Hungary, Poland and Slovakia, and the Council of Baltic Sea States. However, such organizations alone have not been able to 'guarantee long-term security, stability and prosperity' (Roucek, 1992: 28) and their member states have instead looked to both NATO and the European Union for such benefits. Much of their concern has been about Russia. The attempted coup against President Yeltsin in 1993 helped to undermine the stability of that country, as did its internal war in Chechnya. Its dire economic and social situation, represented by the collapse of the value of the Russian ruble during 1998 and 1999, adversely affected its neighbours and trade partners. Its alienation from the West during NATO's Kosovo operation in early 1999, and over the renewal of war in Chechnya, brought back a whiff of the Cold War. The most certain element of Russia's future is uncertainty, and the states of Eastern and Central Europe have turned to Western institutions such as NATO and the European Union as, at least, an insurance against this great unknown.

Amid the turmoil of the early 1990s, the EC members were trying to plan their future. Preparations were made for two Inter-governmental Conferences (IGCs), one on political union and the other on economic and monetary union, culminating in a heads of state and government meeting in Maastricht in December 1991. The resulting Treaty of European Union (see Chapter 2) was an agreement to create a European Union, consisting of the three European Communities (with the EEC renamed the European Community) including economic and monetary union (see Chapter 4), the institutions of foreign and security co-operation (previously European Political Co-operation, see Chapter 9) and intergovernmental co-operation of justice and home affairs (see Chapter 8). This tripod arrangement meant that there was often no clear division between areas covered by Community competence and those subject to intergovernmental activity. A question of sanctions on third countries, for example, covered both trade (a Community competence) and diplomatic relations (intergovernmental). Nevertheless, the Maastricht treaty represented an advance in European integration, not least because it set out a road map for a single currency for the members.

The new European Union seemed to offer a beacon of attraction to other European states. The EFTA countries first signed a European Economic Area agreement with it and then four EFTA states applied for full membership of the European Union (see Chapter 10). In June 1993 the Copenhagen European Council set out the criteria for membership by the states, mainly from Eastern and Central Europe, that were knocking on the door of the nascent European Union (the Maastricht Treaty came into force on 1 November 1993). Meanwhile Europe Agreements were signed with a number of potential applicants, offering them aid and limited access to the EU's markets (see Chapter 10, and Avery and Cameron, 1998).

However, the core of European integration was by no means vibrant. The ratification of the Maastricht Treaty proved to be long and arduous with the Danish electorate rejecting it in 1992 and then accepting a slightly revised version in 1993. This 'euroscepticism' seemed to spread to the United Kingdom, France and even Germany. EU members squabbled among themselves and with the USA about the signing of a General Agreement on Tariffs and Trade (GATT) deal and about the creation of a World Trade Organization (WTO) (see Chapter 11). The Swiss did not ratify the agreement with the EFTA states and its implementation was postponed. Plans to enlarge membership to the EFTA states met with the opposition of the Norwegian electorate, obliging that country to stay out while Austria, Finland and Sweden joined on 1 January 1995. Agreements with the Eastern and Central European states turned out to be less advantageous than anticipated, and the EU's attempt to broker a peace in the wars of former

Yugoslavia was frustrated by internal differences between EU members and the organization's lack of access to military force.

Nevertheless, by the end of the 1990s, the possible future shape of Europe was emerging. An Inter-governmental Conference opened in March 1996, bringing modest revisions up of the Maastricht Treaty, increased activity in the EU's defence and security engagement and greater powers for the European Parliament in the Treaty of Amsterdam (in force on 1 May 1999). Also, as from 1 January 1999, 11 of the 15 members of the EU had embarked on the road to economic and monetary union by permanently fixing their currencies to the value of the euro, the new EU currency (see Chapter 4). By the end of 1999, the European Council had agreed on a strategy of enlargement for all applicants, and had opened accession negotiations (see Chapter 10, and Avery and Cameron, 1998). Agenda 2000 had been agreed to finance the EU into the twenty-first century and to underwrite the strategy for enlargement. By the start of 2000 the EU was engaged in the process of rebuilding the South-West Balkans, the scene of the wars in former Yugoslavia.

Many issues remained to be faced by the EU: the inter-relationship of its institutions; trade relations with the US; the form of its engagement with Russia and with the area to the south of the Mediterranean; the nature of its defence identity; the future of economic and monetary union; the speed and extent of its enlargement; and the legitimacy of the Union in the eyes of its own citizens. Successive chapters will deal with these issues, which are so important for the successful continuation of the European Union.

Note

1   The notion of sovereignty in European history and in the present world is much discussed. Newman (1996: 5–8) identifies seven varieties of the concept. For a critical appreciation see Hoffman (1998).

References and further reading

Avery, G. and Cameron, F. (1998) *The Enlargement of the European Union*, Contemporary European Studies 1, Sheffield Academic Press, Sheffield.

Buzan, B., Kelstrup, M., Lemaitre, P., Tromer, E. and Wæver, O. (1991) *The European Security Order Recast*. Pinter Publishers, London.

Charlton, M. (1983) *The Price of Victory*. British Broadcasting Corporation, London.

Diebold, W. (1959) *The Schuman Plan*. Praeger, New York.

Feis, H. (1970) *From Trust to Terror*. Anthony Blond, London.

Greiner, C. (1985) 'Rearmament of West Germany 1947–1950', in O. Riste (ed.), *Western Security: The Formative Years*. Universitetsforlaget, Oslo, pp. 150–77.

Haas, E.B. (1968) *The Uniting of Europe: Political, Social and Economic Forces, 1950–1957.* Stanford University Press, Stanford.

Halle, L. (1967) *The Cold War as History,* Chatto and Windus, London.

Hinsley, F.H. (1963) *Power and the Pursuit of Peace,* Cambridge University Press, Cambridge.

Hoffman, J. (1998) *Sovereignty.* Open University Press, Buckingham.

Holsti, K.J. (1991) *Peace and War: Armed Conflicts and International Order 1648–1989.* Cambridge University Press, Cambridge.

James, A. (1986) *Sovereign Statehood: The Basis of International Society,* Allen & Unwin, London.

Manning, C.A.W. (1962) *The Nature of International Society.* Bell, London.

NATO Review (1991) 'The Rome Summit', 39 (6): 19–33.

NATO Review (1994–95) 'NATO aircraft attack Udbina airfield', 42 (6): 11.

Newman, M. (1996) *Democracy, Sovereignty and the European Union.* Hurst, London.

Riste, O. (ed.) (1985) *Western Security. The Formative Years.* Universitetsforlaget, Oslo.

Rose, C. (1994) 'Democratic control of the armed forces', *NATO Review,* 42 (5): 13–17.

Roucek, L. (1992) *After the Cold War: The New International Relations in Eastern Europe.* Royal Institute of International Affairs, London.

Stirk, P.M.R. and Weigall, D. (1999) *The Origins and Development of European Integration: A Reader and Commentary.* Pinter, London and New York.

Strayer, J. (1970) *On the Medieval Origins of the Modern State.* Princeton University Press, Princeton, NJ.

Tarschys, D. (1994–95) 'The Council of Europe: towards a vast area of democratic security', *NATO Review,* 42 (6): 8–12.

Urwin, D.W. (1991) *The Community of Europe: A History of European Integration Since 1945.* Longman, London and New York.

US Department of State (1947) *Foreign Relations of the United States, 1947, Volume 1.* US Government Printing Office, Washington, DC.

von Moltke, G. (1994) 'Building a partnership for peace', *NATO Review,* 42 (3): 3–7.

Willis, F.R. (1968) *France, Germany, and New Europe, 1945–1967.* Stanford University Press, Stanford.

1 The theory, concepts and practice of the European Union

Introduction

The European Union is often seen as an entity in itself that acts – effectively or otherwise – on the world stage. It can also be broken down into a number of elements – states, institutions and non-governmental elements. Unlike the European Communities (EC), which form part of it, the European Union has no international legal existence, though it certainly can present a unified political presence in international relations.

This chapter will look at the nature of the EU and of its predecessor and component, the EC. It will examine the theoretical and conceptual approaches used to understand and explain the post–1945 political development of Western Europe.

Kelstrup (1992: 17) noted how 'the way problems related to European integration 'fall between' two major sub-disciplines within political science, international relations theory and comparative politics', thus pointing up the ambiguous nature of both the EU and its study. The EU cannot be satisfactorily placed at the international level (as some form of international organization), or at the domestic level with its politics merely a continuation of those of national governments.

Nevertheless, much of the theory and conceptualizing about the EU and the EC has approached its subject from two different *levels*: from above, where the international system and the study of international relations are overriding, or from the unit level, with domestic and comparative politics being dominant. Likewise, some writers have tended to stress the importance of the role of government in the workings of the EC/EU as the *pivot* of the EC/EU's politics. Others have given preference to the Community nexus and the influence of interest groups – representatives of political parties, industry, agriculture, the workforce, and so on – often working through the Community-based institutions such as the Commission and the European Parliament. The matrix in Table 1.1 is based on the view from above (the systems level – the international relations approach) versus the view from below (the unit level – favouring the study of government and comparative politics) along one dimension. Along the other dimension are approaches that stress the pivotal role of governments in the working of the EC/EU as against those approaches that put more emphasis on the importance of Community institutions. In the four boxes are examples of approaches to the understanding of the European Union. These approaches, and other related ones, will be explored below.

Table 1.1 *Explaining the European Union*

Pivot	Level of approach	
	International	Domestic
Government	Neo-realist	Intergovernmentalist
Community	Neo-liberal	Neofunctionalist

The emphasis placed on the pivotal role of governments or on that of Community-based institutions has an element of 'more or less' attached to it. If a writer thinks that the role of governments is important in the integration process that saw the creation of the European Union, then he or she tends to downgrade the relative importance of the Community institutions and the interest groups based at the Community level. However, examining the EC/EU from above – the systems level – certainly does not preclude looking at it from below as well – from the unit level. This chapter develops these themes by looking at the major ways in which writers on the EC/EU have explained both the nature of the beast and how it has evolved into its current form.

The system level

The first level of approach used to explain and understand the phenomenon of European integration is that which stresses a structural or systems-level approach, that is, one that looks at the EU from the vantage point of international relations. Some of these views are similar to intergovernmentalist theories (see next section), but identify and emphasize fundamental characteristics of state behaviour resulting from constraints and incentives afforded by the structure of the international system.

Realist and *neo-realist* analyses are similar in assuming the importance of states in a world that has no central authority to enforce promises or provide protection. This anarchic international system results in a 'security dilemma' that leads states to maximize their pursuit of the national interest of security and survival by increasing their economic and military power. Since realists emphasized the centrality of power politics, strong foreign policy and war as possible instruments of policy, they viewed any inter-state co-operation and/or alliances instrumentally, seeing such action as tempo-rary and expedient in balancing against threats. The construction of the EC was, therefore, an important foreign policy success for the United States – to balance Western Europe against the Soviet threat – and was expedient for the Western Europeans themselves in order to manage threats posed by Soviet communism and a historically insecure bellicose Germany (van Ham, 1993).

Neo-realism claims to advance the explanatory power of realist thought by defining more rigorously the properties of the international system in shaping the behaviour of its units (see Grieco, 1993: 132). An anarchic and bipolar system was, according to the neo-realists, more stable and less prone to war than previous multipolar systems, especially since the costs of using force were prohibitive, given nuclear weaponry and levels of intra-bloc economic and military interdependence. Neo-realists attempted to quantify more precisely the importance of structural incentives and costs of potential co-operation between states. The existence of 'relative gains' considera-tions, deriving from states' positional insecurities, means that 'in addition to concerns about cheating, states in cooperative arrangements also worry that their partners might gain more from cooperation than they do ... achieve-ment of joint gains that advantage a friend in the present might produce a more dangerous potential foe in the future' (Grieco, 1993: 118).

Due to ever-present concerns for present and future security, some neo-realists have suggested that stable intra-alliance relations ultimately depend upon the protection provided by a hegemonic power. This means the existence of a state capable of using its power and influence to maintain the framework of co-operation and the rules of behaviour.

In the post–1945 bipolar system, which lasted until 1989, the super-powers – the USA and the Soviet Union – provided hegemonic stability. The so-called 'long peace' in Europe has been seen as being dependent on system-level features of bipolarity, approximate equality in military power between the two superpowers and the deterrence effect of nuclear weapons. Unit-level factors of declining hyper-nationalism and the establishment of stable liberal democracy in Western Europe were seen as secondary factors (Mearsheimer, 1993: 147).

Stress upon the system-level determinants of behaviour led many neo-realists to feel sceptical about the prospects for regional and global security – 'without a common Soviet threat and without the American nightwatch-man, Western European states will begin viewing each other with greater fear and suspicion ... they will worry about the imbalances in gains as well as the loss of autonomy that results from co-operation' (Mearsheimer, 1993: 183). However, one critic suggested that if 'the long peace and end to the Cold War have co-varied with and been facilitated by both the growth of transnational co-operation and the security provided by the post-war alliances and nuclear umbrella ... the integrative progress in Europe requires us to broaden the realpolitik view of ethical possibilities' (Kegley, 1991: 112–13).

Kegley's preference for 'principled realism' did not necessarily provide the major incentive for neo-liberal institutionalist challenges to neo-realism. *Neo-liberal* analysis has accepted the importance of 'anarchy' – or the lack of a central power in the world system – but preferred to emphasize interdependence as the overriding condition of world politics. Norms and rules of international society, international regimes and institutions, and the creation of incentives and penalties would manage state interests and facilitate co-operative outcomes. This emphasis is of more relevance to post-Cold War politics (Keohane, 1989).

Neo-liberal institutionalism's primary claim is that states' preferences are themselves shaped by membership of international institutions (Keohane *et al.*, 1993: 401). Sustained patterns of co-operation and institution-building do matter, since 'balance exchange' or reciprocal distribution of gains from co-operation can prevent states from emphasizing the relative gains they make from any deal (Baldwin, 1993: 5–6). Such theorists highlight the centrality of analysis of domestic politics for understanding how choices and preferences are constructed and for how 'common interests' can be identified for successful co-operation. Conditions that will favour sustained co-operation include mutual interest and the achievement of joint (absolute) gains, long-term relationships engendering trust among actors, and expectations of reciprocal behaviour (Keohane *et al.*, 1993).

Neo-liberal institutionalist analyses agree that the European integration process can meet many of these criteria: the failure of independent (national) decision-making; the roles of bargaining and side-payments in preventing each state from always trying to gain advantage over the other; and structuring incentives for pan-European stability (Baldwin, 1993). However, a major disagreement remains between the neo-realists and neo-liberals on the existence of 'common interest' in military and defence aspects of security (Lynn-Jones and Miller, 1993). The neo-realists emphasize the role of the superpowers in enhancing European integration, while the neo-liberal position places emphasis on the move to a European 'society' being underpinned by the integration process and with importance being attached to the role of institutions and norms.

In these explanations, little reference has been made to the internationalizing effects of post-war economic developments and their influences on the European integration process. Ross (1992) revives the importance of the agents of capital in the move towards the Single European Market (see Chapter 3), while an earlier book by Galtung (1973) pointed to the penetration of the European periphery by its economic and political centre – Brussels – as one of the motive forces behind the integration process.

Kelstrup (1992: 48) notes how the mid–1980s move towards a single market was facilitated by the European fear of loss of competitiveness compared with the USA and Japan. This points to a specific effect of the international economic system on the thought processes of the EC decision-makers, and the need for research on how the changes in the international economy have altered the options available for the European elites and their electorates. In particular, it will be instructive to see how changes brought about by the rise of the Newly Industrializing Countries (NICs, such as South Korea and Malaysia), the supposed globalization of capital and commerce agreed within the World Trade Organization (WTO) and the technological changes in the world market will affect the progress of European integration (Axtmann, 1998: 5–20). This will require theorists increasingly to switch away from the more malleable research programmes of the unit level in order to examine the macro-level factors that shape the choices available for Europe and its citizens.

The unit level

Federalist, consociationalist, intergovernmentalist and neofunctionalist approaches have tended to stress the unit-level – that of the nation-state – in explaining European integration and the development of the EU. Activities at the international level have not been ignored but have received secondary consideration.

Federalist concepts and strategies contributed considerably to defining the goals of post–1945 integration. The twentieth century witnessed the growth of political movements in Europe devoted to the creation of federal political union (Bosco, 1991; Lipgens, 1980). There are a number of understandings of the term 'federal' and many of these refer to existing federations such as those of the United States or the Federal Republic of Germany. Broadly, federal states have central institutions that exercise policy powers but also have regionally based institutions that also have considerable authority, with the division of these powers normally being set down in a constitution and overseen by a judicial body. Comparing the EU to existing federal states may show how far it has to go to become a federation.

Nevertheless, as ideas contributing to the goal and meaning of 'union', federalist contributions are important in providing prescriptions for institutional reform, especially in terms of retaining 'unity in diversity'. Throughout the history of post–1945 integration (see Introduction), federalist convictions have been associated with a number of leading individuals, including Adenauer, Delors, Monnet, Spaak and Schuman. One sympathetic author noted that 'the real argument is about the deepening and extension of an existing federal structure, an argument that is not only about strengthening the powers at the centre, but also about the guarantee of the powers of the members' (Forsyth, 1994: 57). However, there is no agreement that these individuals were primarily motivated by federalist ambitions. One study suggests that 'we have not seen the belief that a united Europe is in itself a desirable ideal as having any strong explanatory force outside its capacity to help in consensus-building in the post-war nation-state' (Milward *et al.*, 1993: 185).

Margaret Thatcher (1993: 551–90), the British Prime Minister from 1979 to 1990, often saw a federalist goal behind the works of the Delors Commission. However, to use this approach as a way of understanding the integration process makes the mistake of equating the features of an integrating political system with those of domestic federal political systems, leading to the assumption of a federal outcome for the EU. Other writers have emphasized that the EC/EU's political system borrows from several traditions in its member states, co-operative federal traditions being only one (Kirchner, 1992; Scharpf, 1988), and therefore the value is in making a 'federal analogy' (Pinder, 1999: 16).

The legal and political process of transferring and pooling sovereignty have led some such as Sæter (1991) and Warleigh (1998) to see the EU as being more *confederal*, meaning that the constituent states are still the sources of power and authority. Aspects of the confederal system include the use of the veto within the Council of Ministers on vital issues as opposed to the use of Qualified Majority Voting (QMV); national financial contributions balanced by the EU's system of own resources in budgeting; and the lack of competence of EC law in criminal cases and in many civil ones weighed against the direct applicability of EC law to citizens without the mediation of governments. Indeed, the German Constitutional Court ruled that the Maastricht Treaty was not contrary to German Basic Law, or constitution, as the EU constituted a confederation rather than a federation.

Since the ratification of the Maastricht Treaty (the Treaty on European Union – TEU), there has been greater power-sharing among the Community institutions, especially between the Council and the European Parliament (see Chapter 2), economic and monetary union with a European central bank, and greater political integration in foreign and security policy, even in the defence field. What Pinder (1991) earlier called 'neo-federalism' seems to have overtaken more state-based federal models and this represents decentralizing and 'constitutionalizing' tendencies more than straight centralization in 'Brussels' as seen by Margaret Thatcher.

Drawn from the comparative politics research of the 1960s and 1970s, *consociational* theory has had a limited application to the study of European integration. Arend Lijphart originally suggested that consociational democracy was characterized by a 'grand coalition' of political leaders, the existence and use of a 'concurrent majority' or veto rule, proportionality in participation and representation, and the maintenance of substantial autonomy for constituent groups (Lijphart, 1977: 25). He wished to understand how democracy could survive and work effectively in extremely divided or fragmented societies. Consociational democracy described stable but fragmented polities, and how institutions and procedures were constructed to ensure the survival of democratic political systems and accommodation of particularistic interests. Consociationalism can 'describe the decision-making environment as it stands at the present time ... [and] institutional features that organise the behaviour of the actors, and structure the conflict' (Hix, 1994: 20).

Paul Taylor (1991: 111) suggested that 'the central problem of consociation is the maintenance of stability in a situation of actual or potential mutual tension'. Consociation helps illustrate the nature of tensions within EC/EU politics where

> ... members of the cartel of elites are likely to be faced with a dilemma: they will have an interest in increasing the size of the pie, and the share obtained by their own segment, whilst ... protecting the distinctiveness of their segments in comparison with others, since they serve as each member's individual constituency and power base (Taylor, 1991: 114).

This approach helps to explain the propensity for clashes of interests among members of the elite, and between elite and mass members of the same segment or interest group. Consociationalism can be a useful complement to the explanatory power – or otherwise – of conventional international relations theories since it locates conflict, bargaining and outcomes in national political cultures and systems rather than in the nature of the international system. It may also refine intergovernmentalist and institutionalist approaches by looking at the politicization of issues and the quality of agreements and rules managed by elites, and by gauging the cost of 'exit' or exclusion, that is, in remaining outside an agreement.

Chryssochoou (1994) has portrayed the EU as a confederal consociation with the states merging 'in some form of union to further common ends without losing either national identity or resigning individual sovereignty' (*ibid.*: 55), thus resembling the marks of a confederation, mentioned above. He calls this a case of 'inverse federalism' where 'political authority tends to be diffused as much as possible to the executive branches of the constituent units, rather than to the common central institutions' (1997: 530).

A well-established approach is provided by *intergovernmentalist* theory. Intergovernmentalism assumes that states are the primary actors in the integration process – it is the states (or, rather, their representatives) that determine the structures and outcomes of co-operation. As Hoffmann (1968: 199–200) remarked of the early Community, the logic of diversity ... sets limits to the degree to which the 'spill-over' process can limit the freedom of action of the governments; it restricts the domain in which the logic of functional integration operates to the area of welfare ... in areas of key importance to the national interest, nations prefer the certainty, or the self-controlled uncertainty, of national self-reliance.

He argued that in diverse domestic environments, the effect of bipolarity (the domination of the world scene by two major power blocs, that of the West and that of the Soviet Union) in reducing autonomy and changes in the cost of using force resulted in a governmental desire to retain ultimate control of the speed and direction of the integration process. Hoffmann suggested that strategic calculations led governments to resist the incorporation of "high politics" (that involving security and diplomatic relations) into a process of integration concerned mainly with 'low politics' (that involving mainly welfare, educational or commercial questions). He thought that 'the nation-state survives, preserved by the formidable autonomy of politics, as manifested in the resilience of political systems, the interaction between separate states and a single international system, the role of leaders who believe both in the primacy of "high politics" over the kind of managerial politics susceptible to functionalism, and the primacy of the nation' (Hoffmann, 1968: 219). The latter element was certainly strengthened in the United Kingdom under the leadership of Margaret Thatcher during the 1980s, but this could not hide the changes in the other factors that weakened the nation-state, not least the move to the single market and to monetary union.

Later theorists turned their attention to bargaining strategies and how issue-linkage may, or may not, be pursued by governments when forming 'bargains' about integrative remedies (Huelshoff, 1994; Weber and Wiesmeth, 1991). Taylor's study of the EC during the 1970s emphasized centralized power in Community institutions, vulnerability to external shock, and the impact of enlargement in creating a more heterogeneous and differentiated membership. He argued that incentives to maintain state attachment to the EC included the benefits of predictability in policymaking, overcoming the 'relative gains' considerations and the 'psychological inheritance' of security concerns in the 1950s (Taylor, 1983).

Works on 'elite-preference convergence' (Garrett, 1992; Sandholtz and Zysman, 1989) and liberal intergovernmentalism (Moravcsik, 1991, 1993, 1998) introduce refinements. Moravcsik pointed out that government strategies were based upon preferences and power. Power was dependent on a number of factors, which would determine whether bargaining and issue-linkage strategies were successful for governments. These included the level of intensity of national preferences in a specific issue-area, the relative costs and benefits of potential agreements, whether alternative courses of action were available, fears of exclusion and the government's willingness to seek compromise, linkage or side payments.

Co-operation and integration can be useful or beneficial where these strengthen national government's control over domestic affairs and agendas. Moravcsik claimed that liberal intergovernmentalism 'provides explanations for some nagging anomalies inherited from neofunctionalism' (1993: 518; see below for an explanation of neofunctionalism) since it could more readily explain variations in domestic constraints, the existence of externalities in promoting agreement, and used 'two-level games' analysis (linked bargaining at the domestic and international levels) to explain domestic government strategies. So the EC 'can be analysed as a successful intergovernmental regime designed to manage economic interdependence through negotiated policy co-ordination' (Moravcsik, 1993: 474). Some historical studies have agreed with this, finding that extension of intergovernmental co-operation is the likeliest method of expanding the scope of the integration process. Thus the EU was shown 'to be an international framework constructed by the nation-state for the completion of its own domestic policy objectives ... reflecting changes in domestic politics rather than the incremental progression postulated by other integration theories' (Milward *et al.*, 1993: 20–1).

Neofunctionalism tried to address both the dynamics and tactics of the actors involved, and the likely end-goal of integration, the creation of a federal body. Neofunctionalists, mainly American scholars writing from the 1950s to the 1970s, saw integration based on a process of gradual and incremental transfers of national sovereignty in specific functional policy areas to a new political centre which would be above the member states, or supranational. The process was also described as 'spillover' insofar as benefits and advantages reaped from successfully integrating one set of welfare tasks would both demand further action in related areas in order to continue successfully and would increase popular and elite support for the process. For the integration of the coal and steel sectors of industry to be successful, further common agreement would be needed about the social welfare provisions for the workers in the coal-mines and steel factories, and so on. Integration would thus spill over into further sectors (Haas, 1961: 368).

Haas originally saw 'spillover' as being part of the 'expansive logic' inherent in neofunctionalist integration. The concept was subsequently modified to allow greater political and institutional roles in the process (Lindberg and Scheingold, 1970). From the mid–1950s until the mid–1970s neofunctionalism was the dominant explanation for the dynamics and potential of the Community experiment. Both Lindberg and Scheingold (1970) and Joseph Nye made refinements that tried to quash the idea that there was 'a single path from quasi-functional tasks to political union by means of spillover' (Nye, 1970: 797). Neofunctionalism emphasized the primary role of group interests, particularly those of the economic and political elites, and the role of technocratic management in shaping and brokering agreement on integrative outcomes. Haas claimed that increased and improved welfare tasks carried out by central (Community) institutions would enable the growth in scope of the integration process. This was because gaols and institutional mechanisms would spill over into new functional areas. It would also result in the creation of a new political entity resulting from the switch of political loyalties from the national to the European level (Haas, 1968). As the development of the neofunctionalist explanation became directly linked to the fortunes of the EC, the mismatch between empirical realities and theoretical predictions led neofunctionalists to re-assess their project by the mid–1970s (Haas, 1975).

Set in the wider context of pluralist theories of politics, neofunctionalism was important in challenging assumptions about the primacy of nation-states. According to the neofunctionalists the articulation of group interest and the participation of groups in the resolution of political conflict were integral to supranational decision-making methods that upgraded the common interest. The EC's decision-making reflected the formal participation of a variety of sectoral, as well as governmental, interests, and the successful resolution of welfare tasks depended on this co-opting, or 'engrenage', of group interests. Neofunctionalists challenged the claim that sovereignty was indivisible, since a differentiation between sensitive and less important areas for integration seemed possible. In Kelstrup's words, 'regional integration show[s] that sovereignty can be functionally specific, and that states might give up sovereignty to international bodies in certain, functionally specific areas' (1992: 18). Neofunctionalist theory also suggested that the division between the 'domestic' and the 'international' spheres of politics was artificial. A gradual process of integration between territorially and politically separate activities could 'domesticate' conventional inter-state relations and could place traditionally 'home affairs' in the international environment. Neofunctionalism was based on earlier functional assumptions that the spread of technology and communications would help link 'authority to a specific activity', breaking away 'from the traditional link between authority and a definite territory' (Mitrany, 1966: 125).

By the late 1960s it was generally accepted that the prospects for automatic 'spillover', the relative lack of popular support for and identification with the process of integration, difficulties in managing political conflicts and rewards, and lack of substantive progress in developing the EC's institutions had undermined earlier expectations of steady and linear progress towards a federal body. Neofunctionalist explanations and predictive power were hampered by the assumption of the popular transfer of loyalties, its reliance on elitist and technocratic management and underestimating the role of external factors. Also important was the rise of 'dramatic political actors' pursuing divergent political interests, as personified by President de Gaulle of France in the 1960s (Haas, 1975; Hoffmann, 1968; Lindberg and Scheingold, 1970).

Neofunctionalist theory had a partial revival in the 1980s. The distinctiveness of the EC's supranational decision-making method, upgrading the common interest through compromise and bargains, was restored during this decade with institutional reform, greater use of the QMV and less recourse to the veto. Much of this was a direct result of the decision to pursue the completion of the single market (see Chapter 3). 'Spillover' was re-interpreted to emphasize the role of governmental bargains in moving forward the integration process, rather than the earlier neofunctionalist conception of coalitions of sectoral interest responding to new incentives and policy impacts (Keohane and Hoffmann, 1990).

Majone (1994) has in common with the neofunctionalists an emphasis on the 'upgrading of common interests' at the EC/EU level and on interest group activity. However, the story of the creation of the Single European Market (SEM – see Chapter 3) in the latter part of the 1980s and early 1990s is seen in terms of public choice. The move to the SEM was preferred to economic and monetary union or to reform of the Common Agricultural Policy because it satisfied the criteria of technical and economic feasibility, administrative simplicity, value acceptability and political receptivity (Majone, 1994: 11). Also the elites and public opinion were 'softened up' by the utilization of knowledge in the policy community before the Council move towards completion of the single market was taken in 1985 (*ibid.*: 12).

Wessels defined the emergence of transnational decision-making within the EC as a way of trying to control forces that have moved beyond the ambit of the member states. In his 'fusion hypothesis', he saw the EC states as no longer able to satisfy rising expectations of the citizens. They therefore have to 'fuse' their decision-making capabilities in order to provide welfare benefits on an EC-wide basis (Wessels, 1992). Thus a political system shaped by multiple loyalties would be shaped (Wessels, 1997: 291). A different approach by Ross (1992: 63) came to a similar conclusion, that the Europeanization of the 1980s emerged after national strategies had failed, with European capital and its national components being the moving force. Also Sandholtz and Zysman (1989) viewed the move to the single market in 1992 as being guided by Community institutions, industrial elites and governments, with the last being receptive because of changes in the world economy and the domestic political context. Schmitter and Streeck (1994), looking at the same series of events – the move to a single market in 1992 – described a more disorganized structure with a trend towards 'supranational pluralism' and corporate interests shifting their gaze from the national to the Community level.

Another approach that opposed many of the assumptions of the intergovernmentalists when examining the EU was that of *multi-level governance* (Marks *et. al.*, 1996). Though this model did not reject the view that the states remain 'the *most* important pieces of the European puzzle', it asserted that 'the state no longer monopolizes European level policy-making or the aggregation of domestic interests', that decision-making among states involved 'a significant loss of control for individual state executives' and that 'political arenas are interconnected rather than nested'. This meant that, instead of 15 separate political processes making policy in a particular policy area and then the representatives of those states coming together to make a decision, there was a complex of relationships across the member states. 'The separation between domestic and international politics, which lies at the heart of the state-centric model, is rejected . . .' (*ibid.* 346–7). Thus the concepts of governance included in this model provide a conceptual bridge between the domestic and international levels (Hurrell and Menon, 1996). This view saw the supranational elements of the original EEC – keenly identified by the neofunctionalists – as being overshadowed by the 'imposition of intergovernmental institutions in the 1960s and 1970s'. A system of multi-level governance arose in the 1980s 'in which national governmental control became diluted by the activities of supranational and subnational actors' (Marks *et al.*, 1996: 373). However, as shown by events throughout the 1990s, this was 'unlikely to be a stable equilibrium' (*ibid.* 372).

Conclusions

Almost from the beginning of the European Communities in the early 1950s until the present day, there have been two major perceptions of their nature. One has seen the Communities, and now the European Union, as broadly being the creation of the governments of the member states to serve their purposes. There may be complicated institutions that are outside the direct control of governments and sometimes states may find themselves outvoted. But that is the system that they have decided will serve them well. An opposing view is that the European Communities, while depending very much on the co-operation of governments, have been evolving a system that is at least parallel to that of the member states. It increasingly serves some form of collective interest of the Union, which is no longer just the lowest common denominator between the member states.

During the 1980s two individuals personified these two models. The first was Mrs Thatcher's Europe. The Conservative British Prime Minister, as her French predecessor President de Gaulle in the 1960s, considered that the EC should be the servant of its member states and, for her, that meant freeing up trade in the move to a Single European Market. The second view was that held by Jacques Delors, President of the European Commission during much of the 1980s. He wanted more active Community institutions with the European Union of the 1990s emerging as a world actor in its own right. If that meant taking powers from the member states, then so be it: Europe could only act effectively if it had one supranational voice rather than a cacophony of national pleadings.

The succeeding chapters will note where and when these two images of the EC/EU have clashed. They will also show that, especially with the Treaty of Amsterdam, the Union has moved on. So has the academic understanding of its nature. The 1990s saw the emergence of studies that examined the complexities of the European Union that occupied the ground between Delors and Thatcher. Some, such as liberal intergovernmentalism, placed greater emphasis on the role of governments in the system, while others, such as multi-level governance, stressed more the role of Community institutions. Petersen and Bomberg examined the policies themselves, seeing a complex interdependent system in which various organizations – public, private, state, Community – control and mobilize resources as on a giant chessboard (1993: 28). Scharpf (1999) stressed the variety of factors that define the 'game' being played in any one Union policy area.

Furthermore, the study of the EU tended to be divided in the 1960s and 1970s between those who viewed it from above – the international relations perspective – and, on the whole, found it wanting as an international actor, and those who viewed it from below – the government and comparative politics perspectives – who were concerned with its institutions, policy-making and policies. As the European Union has emerged as an actor on the European and the world scene, so there has been a greater cross-over between the two approaches. As Smith (1996: 8–9) noted:

> . . . it is evident that there is an intimate linkage between the internal development of the EU and its institutions and the broader European order, which is not solely attributable to the interests, power and policies of major European states. Whilst some analyses have noted these connections, it is doubtful whether it can be accounted for simply within an interstate or intergovernmental framework.

The above account of the theoretical and conceptual approaches to the study of the EC/EU also shows that as these institutions have changed over time, so have academic views. As the EC and EU took on wider policy remits, then some of the explanations became partial. What could be used to explain the nature of economic and monetary union was not necessarily useful to illuminate the Common Foreign and Security Policy.

What will be the theoretical and conceptual concerns about the future European Union? A number of the issues discussed above – including that of the comparative weight of governmental and Community inputs – will continue to be relevant.

One area that will be of increased importance for academic consideration will be that of increased sectorization in policy-making as a result of enhanced Europeanization (Egeberg and Trondal, 1999). This will encourage a consideration of the complexity of policy-making and implementation across the national and Union board, rather than just a separate consideration of Union policy which is the theme of this book.

Second, the enlargement of the EU will bring more into play questions of identity (Hansen and Williams, 1999). If 'political communities are based not just on rational calculation but on sentiment, solidarity and a degree of political cohesion' (Laffan, 1996: 95), then what sort of political community will emerge with a European Union of 20 members or 25? What effect will changes in identity have on the institutional working of the EU? Will the 2000s bring increased nationalist challenges to the EU as elites lead their bewildered electorates into membership?

Following on from this is the work on the various speeds at which integration may take place but also the functional areas covered (such as agriculture or defence) and the geographical space involved. The relationship between these (Stubb, 1996) will be of increasing concern as enlargement continues.

Finally, the position of the EU in the framework of wider forces will be a matter of research. To what extent will the EU be weakened by a stronger World Trade Organization? Or, as bargaining within the WTO becomes more vital, will the EU show its mettle as an actor on the world stage? Will economic, technological and environmental factors make a geographically limited institution such as the EU redundant? How will the EU manage crises in Europe, the Mediterranean, the Middle East and Africa? Will it take on the mantle of a superpower or will it remain a civilian power?

There is plenty for the future student of the European Union to consider.

References and further reading

Axtmann, R. (1998) 'Globalization, Europe and the state: introductory reflections', in R. Axtmann (ed.), *Globalization and Europe: Theoretical and Empirical Investigations*. Pinter, London, pp. 1–22.

Baldwin, D. (1993) 'Neoliberalism, neorealism, and world politics', in D. Baldwin (ed.), *Neorealism and Neoliberalism: The Contemporary Debate*. Columbia University Press, New York, pp. 3–25.

Bosco, A. (ed.) (1991) *The Federal Idea: The History of Federalism since 1945*, Vol. 2. Lothian Foundation Press, London.

Burgess, M. (1989) *Federalism and the European Union: Political Ideas, Influences and Strategies in the EC 1972–1987*. Routledge, London.

Chryssochoou, D.N. (1994) 'Democracy and symbiosis in the European Union: towards a confederal consociation?', *West European Politics*, 17 (4): 1–14.

Chryssochoou, D.N. (1997) 'New challenges to the study of European integration: implications for theory-building', *Journal of Common Market Studies*, 35 (4): 521–42.

Egeberg, M. and Trondal, J. (1999) 'Differentiated integration in Europe: the case of Norway', *Journal of Common Market Studies*, 37 (1): 133–42.

Forster, A. (1998) 'Britain and the negotiation of the Maastricht Treaty: a critique of liberal intergovernmentalism', *Journal of Common Market Studies*, 36 (3): 347–68.

Forsyth, M. (1994) 'Federalism and Confederalism' in C. Brown (ed.), *Political Restructuring in Europe: Ethical Perspectives*, Routledge, London.

Galtung, J. (1973) *The European Community: A Superpower in the Making*. Universitetsforlaget, Oslo.

Garrett, G. (1992) 'International co-operation and institutional choice: the EC's internal market', *International Organization*, 46 (2): 533–60.

Grieco, J. (1993) 'Anarchy and the limits of co-operation: a realist critique of the newest liberal institutionalism', in D. Baldwin (ed.), *Neorealism and Neoliberalism: The Contemporary Debate*. Columbia University Press, New York, pp. 116–40.

Haas, E. (1968) *The Uniting of Europe: Political, Social and Economic Forces, 1950–1957*. Stanford University Press, Stanford, CA.

Haas, E. (1961) 'International integration: the European and the universal process', *International Organization*, 25 (2): 336–92.

Haas, E. (1975) *The Obsolescence of Regional Integration Theory*. Institute of International Studies, Berkeley, CA.

Hansen, L. and Williams, M.C. (1999) 'The myths of Europe: legitimacy, community and the "crisis" of the EU', *Journal of Common Market Studies*, 37 (2): 233–49.

Hix, S. (1994) 'The study of the EC: the challenge to comparative politics', *West European Politics*, 17 (1): 1–30.

Hoffmann, S. (1968) 'Obstinate or obsolete? The fate of the nation-state and the case of Western Europe', in J. Nye (ed.), *International Regionalism: Readings*. Little Brown, Boston.

Huelshoff, S. (1994) 'Domestic politics and dynamic issue linkage: a reformulation of integration theory', *International Studies Quarterly*, 38: 255–79.

Hurrell, A. and Menon, A. (1996) 'Politics like any other? Comparative politics, international relations and the study of the EU', *West European Politics*, 19 (2): 386–402.

Kegley, C. (1991) 'The new containment myth: realism and the anomaly of European integration', *Ethics and International Affairs*, 5: 99–114.

Kelstrup, M. (ed.) (1992) *European Integration and Denmark's Participation*. Copenhagen Political Studies Press, Copenhagen.

Keohane, R.O. (1989) *International Institutions and State Power: Essays in International Relations Theory*. Westview, London.

Keohane, R.O. and Hoffmann, S. (1990) 'Conclusions: Community politics and institutional change', in W. Wallace (ed.), *The Dynamics of European Integration*. Pinter/RIIA, London.

Keohane, R.O., Nye, J.S. and Hoffmann, S. (1993) 'Strategies of adaptation: international politics and institutions in Europe after the Cold War', in R.O. Keohane, J.S. Nye and S. Hoffmann (eds), *After the Cold War: International Institutions and State Strategies in Europe 1989–1991*. Harvard University Press, Cambridge, MA.

Kirchner, E.J. (1992) *Decision-Making in the European Community: The Council Presidency and European Integration*. Manchester University Press, Manchester.

Laffan, B. (1996) 'The politics of identity and political order in Europe', *Journal of Common Market Studies*, **34** (1): 81–102.

Lijphart, A. (1977) *Democracy in Plural Societies: A Comparative Exploration*. Yale University Press, New Haven and London.

Lindberg, L.N. and Scheingold, S.A. (1970) *Europe's Would-Be Polity*. Prentice-Hall, Englewood Cliffs, NJ.

Lipgens, W. (ed.) (1980) *Sources for the History of European Integration 1945–1955*. Leyden, Sijthoff.

Lynn-Jones, S. and Miller, S. (1993) 'Introduction', in S. Lynn-Jones and S. Miller (eds), *The Cold War and After: Prospects for Peace*. MIT Press, Cambridge, MA.

Majone, G. (1994) 'Ideas, interests and institutions: explaining the revival of policy analysis in the 1980s', paper presented at the XVIth World Congress of the IPSA, 21–25 August 1994, Berlin.

Marks, G., Hooghe, L. and Blank, K. (1996) 'European integration from the 1980s: state-centric v. multi-level governance', *Journal of Common Market Studies*, **34** (3): 341–78.

Mearsheimer, J.J. (1993) 'Back to the future: instability in Europe after the Cold War', in S. Lynn-Jones and S. Miller (eds), *The Cold War and After: Prospects for Peace*. MIT Press, Cambridge, MA.

Milward, A., Lynch, F.M.B., Ranieri, R., Romero, F. and Sorensen, V. (1993). *The Frontier of National Sovereignty: History and Theory 1945–1992*. Routledge, London.

Mitrany, D. (1966) *A Working Peace System*. Quadrangle Books, Chicago.

Moravcsik, A. (1991) 'Negotiating the Single European Act', in R.O. Keohane and S. Hoffmann (eds), *The New EC: Decisionmaking and Institutional Change*. Westview, London.

Moravcsik, A. (1993) 'Preferences and power in the EC: a liberal intergovernmentalist approach', *Journal of Common Market Studies*, **31** (4): 473–524.

Moravcsik, A. (1998) *The Choice for Europe: Social Purpose and State Power from Messina to Maastricht*. Cornell University Press, Ithaca, NY.

Moravcsik, A. and Nicolaidis, K. (1999) 'Explaining the Treaty of Amsterdam: interests, influence, institutions' *Journal of Common Market Studies*, **37** (1): 59–85.

Nye, J. (1970) 'Comparing common markets: a revised neo-functionalist model', *International Organization*, **24** (4): 796–835.

Petersen, J. and Bomberg, E. (1993) 'Decision making in the European Union: a policy networks approach', paper to Political Studies Association annual conference, Leicester.

Pinder, J. (1991) *EC: The Building of a Union.* Oxford University Press, Oxford.

Pinder, J. (1999) *Steps Towards a Federal Parliament* European Essays 2. Federal Trust, London.

Puchala, D.J. (1999) 'Institutionalism, intergovernmentalism and European integration' *Journal of Common Market Studies*, 37 (2): 317–31.

Ross, G. (1992) 'Confronting the New Europe', *New Left Review*, 191, January/February: 49–66.

Sæter, M. (1991) 'Föderalismus und Konföderalismus als Strukturelemente europäischer Zusammenarbeit Zur Vergangheit und Zukunft von EG und KSZE', in W. Link, E. Schütt-Wetschky and G. Schwan (eds), *Jahrbuch Für Politik/Yearbook of Politics*, Nomos, Berlin, pp.103–26.

Sandholtz, W. (1996) 'Membership matters: limits of the functional approach to European institutions', *Journal of Common Market Studies*, 34 (3): 403–29.

Sandholtz, W. and Zysman, J. (1989) '1992: recasting the European bargain', *World Politics*, 42 (1): 95–128.

Scharpf, F. (1988) 'The joint decision-trap: lessons from German federalism and European integration', *Public Administration*, 66: 239–78.

Scharpf, F. (1999) *Governing in Europe: Effective and Democratic?.* Oxford University Press, Oxford.

Schmitter, P.C. and Streeck, W. (1994) 'Organized Interests and the Europe of 1992', in B.F. Nelson and A.C.G. Stubb (eds), *The European Union: Readings on the Theory and Practice of European Integration.* Lynne Rienner, London and Boulder, CO, pp.169–87.

Smith, M. (1996) 'The European Union and a changing Europe: establishing the boundaries of order', *Journal of Common Market Studies*, 43 (1): 5–28.

Stubb, A.C.-G. (1996) 'A categorization of differentiated integration', *Journal of Common Market Studies*, 34 (2): 283–95.

Taylor, P. (1983) *The Limits of European Integration.* Croom Helm, London.

Taylor, P. (1991) 'The EC and the state: assumptions, theories and propositions', *Review of International Studies*, 17 (2): 109–25.

Thatcher, M. (1993) *The Downing Street Years.* HarperCollins, London.

van Ham, P. (1993) 'The EC after hegemony: the future of European integration in a multipolar world', *International Relations*, 11 (5): 451–67.

Warleigh, A. (1998) 'Better the devil you know? Synthetic and confederal understandings of European integration', *West European Politics*, 21 (3): 1–18.

Weber, S. and Wiesmeth, H. (1991) 'Issue linkages in the EC', *Journal of Common Market Studies*, 29 (3): 255–67.

Wessels, W. (1992) 'Staat und westeuropaische Integration; Die Fusionthese', in M. Kreile (ed.), *Die Integration Europas: Politische Vierteljahrresschrift Sonderheit 23*. Westdeutscher Verlag, Opladen.

Wessels, W. (1997) 'An ever closer fusion? A dynamic macropolitical view on integration processes' *Journal of Common Market Studies*, 35 (2): 267–99.

2 The EU's institutions and budget

Introduction

The institutions of the European Union can be traced back mostly to their predecessors in the European Economic Community, Euratom and the European Coal and Steel Community. All these had institutions that were broadly intergovernmental – the European Council, the Council and the Committee of Permanent Representatives – and those that had a supranational character such as the High Authority of the ECSC, the Commission, the Court of Justice and the European Parliament. The former group allowed governments of the member states to make their input to the decision-making process, while the latter, supranational, institutions have often tried to take into account the wider interests of the Communities. This chapter will describe the workings of these various institutions – and others – and will also examine the budget of the EU: where the money comes from and how this is spent. Finally, it will briefly consider the question of democracy and the EU.

Institutional background

The supranational element first came to prominence in the European Coal and Steel Community with the creation of the High Authority, which was intended to set coal and steel policies on a Community-wide basis, and whose members, though appointed by the member states, were independent of their control. The Council allowed the member states to contribute to policy-making; the Court interpreted and applied ECSC law; and an Assembly and a Consultative Committee represented party political and sectional interests respectively. The laws applied by the High Authority were supranational – above those of the member states – and the High Authority was supposed to take into consideration the interests of the Community as a whole rather than just aggregate the demands of the original six member states.

The supranational element was watered down in the EEC and Euratom, which covered a wider range of policies than the ECSC. Over time the institutional balance of the Communities shifted sometimes in favour of the

Community element (the High Authority, the Commission and the Parliament) and sometimes in favour of the national element represented in the Council. The Single European Act (SEA), the Maastricht Treaty (Treaty on European Union – TEU) and the Treaty of Amsterdam have all made important institutional contributions, changing that balance. Both in the Maastricht Treaty and in the Treaty of Amsterdam, a pillar structure was maintained whereby one element – the Community pillar (Pillar I) – dealt with policy covered by the three original Communities' treaties as amended by the SEA, the Maastricht and Amsterdam Treaties, while the other two – the Common Foreign and Security Policy (CFSP – Pillar II) and judicial and related co-operation (Pillar III)[1] – were dealt with along more intergovernmental lines. Clearly the Community-based institutions were more prominent in 'Pillar I' than in 'Pillar II' and 'Pillar III'.

The balance between the supranational and the national elements in the institutions of the European Communities, and now the European Union, is central to the debate about the nature of those entities. A perceived increase in the powers of the supranational element might lead one to compare the EU with a federal authority, while an entrenchment of national involvement could, rather, give the arrangement the appearance of an intergovernmental institution. As seen in Chapter 1, either description would be a simplification. The constant clash of forces within the European Union make it the most sophisticated, complicated and elusive of institutions involved in policy formulation. Two influential writers have noted that 'the European Community can best be viewed as a set of complex overlapping networks, in which a supranational style of decision-making, characterised by compromises upgrading common interest, can under favourable conditions lead to the pooling of sovereignty' (Keohane and Hoffmann, 1990: 277). The advent of the European Union has added to this complexity. The institutional elements of this structure will now be examined.

The Commission

The Commission is the engine of the European Communities element in the European Union. It has a role in EU policy formulation, taking and implementation: it is 'at the very heart of the EU system' (Nugent, 1999: 101). The lifeblood which it supplies is the policies considered by Council and Parliament.

The Commission consists of a fairly modestly sized bureaucracy of about 11,000 civil servants (plus researchers and interpreters) and a College of Commissioners. Of the 15 EU members (EU-15), there are 20 Commissioners, two nominated from each of the 'big five' of France, Germany, Italy, Spain and the United Kingdom, and one each from the other ten member states. Although the national governments nominate the Commissioners, they do not represent that government or, indeed, their own state. They are often chosen on party political grounds as well as for their general competence and experience. Once members of the College of Commissioners, they are expected to act in the interest of the Union as a whole, though there have been cases of Commissioners not being re-appointed by their governments. Mrs Thatcher considered that Lord Cockfield, a minister in her government whom she had nominated to the Commission in 1984, had by 1988 started 'to go native' (Thatcher, 1993: 547) – to become too *'communautaire'* – and she refused to nominate him for a second term. At the start of each five-year term of office of a Commission, the member states nominate a President of the Commission. The first of these was Walter Hallstein from Germany, who took up office in 1958. Jacques Delors from France has been the President who most had 'an acute sense of the urgency of the historical moment' (Ross, 1995: 244) during his crucial terms of office from January 1985 until 1994. Jacques Santer's College of Commissioners had the ignominy of having to resign shortly before its term was completed because of accusations of favouritism, incompetence and secrecy, and Romano Prodi's team has promised to be more open and accountable.

The College of Commissioners has a system of collective responsibility whereby its decisions – if necessary taken by a majority of its members – are those of the College as a whole. Each individual Commissioner heads a subsection of the Commission: these are Directorate Generals (DGs), organized along functional lines, such as agriculture, external affairs and competition. The Prodi Commission, which came into office in September 1999, attempted to trim some of the unwieldy DGs and to have Commissioners more clearly in charge of these offices, thus adding to the element of control that was often seen to be lacking in previous Commissions. Each Commissioner has his or her own private office – a *cabinet* (from the French word) – headed by a *chef de cabinet* who can play a powerful role in organizing the Commissioner's time and contacts. There was at least the expression of intent to curb the power of these influential offices under the Prodi Commission.

The original term for each Commission was four years but the Maastricht Treaty changed both this and the term of office of the President of the Commission to five years, allowing each to run almost in tandem with the new European Parliament's (EP's) five-year term. The Maastricht Treaty allowed for the member states to nominate the President of the Commission who was then appointed after the EP had been consulted (Article 158 TEU, 214 TEC).[2] The EP insisted on subjecting the President and the Commission to a vote of approval. In 1995 the EP only narrowly accepted Jacques Santer (by 260 votes to 238 with 23 abstentions) as President after the British Conservative government had, in 1994, vetoed the nomination of all the other member states, Jean-Luc Dehaene of Belgium (Hix and Lord, 1996).

The Amsterdam Treaty recognizes that 'the nomination shall be approved by the European Parliament' (Article 214 (2) TEC). Again the process of the member states 'consulting' the President-elect about those who they wish to nominate for the Commission (Article 158 (2) TEU) has been transformed by the Treaty of Amsterdam into member states appointing the Commission 'by common accord with the nominee for President'. During 1994-95 the EP subjected the nominated Commissioners to a series of hearings, a process repeated in 1999. The new 1999 EP had a centre-right majority but found itself faced with a College of Commissioners of a centre-left hue, reflecting the governments that had nominated them. Despite some reservations, the EP accepted the new Commission.

The functions of the Commission were set out in Article 155 of the Rome Treaty (211 TEC). The Commission shall:

- ensure that the provisions of the treaty are applied;
- formulate recommendations or deliver opinions on treaty matters and participate in the shaping of legislation by Council and the EP;
- have its own powers of decision and exercise powers conferred on it by the Council in order to implement Council rules.

The Commission's numerous roles can make its work difficult and an appreciation of its nature challenging. First, the Commission ensures that the provisions of the Maastricht Treaty are applied (this is often referred to as the 'watchdog' role). The Commission monitors national agencies and others to see whether they are complying with their treaty obligations and EU legislation. It can use general powers under Article 213 EEC (284 TEC) to 'collect any information and carry out any checks required'. It also has discretion, under Article 169 EEC (226 TEC) to present 'a reasoned opinion' on why a member state may have failed to have fulfilled its treaty obligations. Such an opinion can also be delivered, under Article 170 EEC (227 TEC), when one state brings another before the European Court of Justice for an infringement of a treaty.

Second, the Commission acts as the motor of European integration through its roles of primary initiator of legislation and participant in the decision-making process. At the start of the EEC process in the late 1950s and 1960s, the Council decided on legislation that the Commission proposed. This gave the Commission the power to shape the general direction of the EEC's progress as well as to set the more detailed agenda. Since then, and particularly after the debacle over the CAP in 1965 (see Introduction, p. 14), the Commission's relationship with the Council has developed more into one of give and take. After all, the Council could, under Article 152 EEC (Article 208 TEC), ask the Commission to undertake studies that the Council considers desirable for the attainment of the common objectives' and to submit appropriate proposals. More notable has been the growth of the EP's input into the legislative procedure, with the Parliament using its own Rules of Procedure to allow it to submit its own proposals to the Commission in order to influence draft proposals. It can also formally request the Commission to submit proposals. Nevertheless, during the legislative processes – especially when co-decision is used (see pp. 59–60) – there is much more of a balance now between the EP and the Council, with the Commission often acting as the broker between the two.

Third, the Commission oversees the implementation of Community legislation. According to Article 155 EEC (Article 211 TEC), the Commission was to exercise powers conferred on it by the Council in order to implement rules. The notion was that the Council would delegate responsibilities to the Commission, which, as guardian of the treaties, could more effectively oversee and manage implementation throughout the Union. However, the Commission scarcely had the resources to oversee the implementation of a growing amount of legislation in the expanding European Communities. In most cases national authorities – tax offices, local authorities, customs officers, veterinarians, health and safety officers – implement EU law. This could lead to national differences in implementation. In order to provide national and other authorities with the details of implementation and application, a set of advisory ('Procedure I'), management ('Procedure II') or regulatory ('Procedure III') committees, chaired by the Commission but with national civil servants as members, have been established. Their three main functions are fund-approving, norm-setting (either in general or in technical matters) and approving the rules of implementation. The use of such so-called 'comitology' implementation committees was referred to in an amendment to Article 145, introduced by the Single European Act, and since then they have grown, with their national membership calling into question the Commission's role in this area.

Indeed, the Council has become more involved in the implementation of EU legislation with the growth of these implementation committees. After this was recognized in the SEA amendment to Article 145, the Council made its decision on new procedures in July 1987 whereby some uses of the implementing powers of the Commission can be referred to the Council and blocked indefinitely. Comitology has been described as reducing the transparency of the EU which is necessary for democratic control (Evans, 1998) but there is little doubt that the member states and the Council where these are represented want to retain the ability to influence not only decisions but also their implementation. The Commission has made its own proposals for reform (Kortenberg, 1998) but it may take another IGC to resolve this question (Wessels, 1998).

In relation to its own powers, the Commission, according to Article 205 TEU (274 TEC), 'shall implement the budget . . . on its own responsibility' and, under Article 206 TEU (276 TEC), has to get a discharge from the EP 'in respect of the implementation of the budget'.

The Commission is also responsible for managing most of the external economic relations of the EU and for the EU's relations with international organizations. In dealing with such international agreements, the Commission will put a proposal to the Council, which then gives it a mandate to conduct negotiations with the help of special committees appointed by the Council. Agreements are then concluded by the Council, mainly with the assent of the EP (Article 228 TEU, 300 TEC), though this is not the case for 'combined' agreements (ones that cover economic and other matters) such as those under the World Trade Organization. While it is important that the Commission should represent, in a cohesive fashion, the interests of the EU as a whole in international organizations and negotiations, it is also significant that the member states should still want to retain their own rights of representation in those areas not covered by the Community element of the European Union.

The Council, Coreper and the European Council

The Council of the European Union (hereafter the Council) consists of ministers meeting according to the needs of a particular area of EU competence. Coreper is the French acronym for the Committee of Permanent Representatives, consisting of national officials, which does much preparatory work for the Council. The European Council should not be confused with the Council of Europe, an organization separate from the EU with a wider membership, or with the above-mentioned Council of the European Union. It is the meeting of the heads of state and government of the EU,[3] often assisted by their foreign ministers, together with members of the Commission. Though the level of these three institutions differs, their membership is all based on representatives from the member states and all three organizations are crucial to the taking of decisions within the EU.

The Council has assumed the role of the dominant legislative element in the European Union although, with the Maastricht and Amsterdam Treaties, it has increasingly had to share that role in Community matters with the EP. Nevertheless, it is the 'decision-taking' body for the EU and in the past it was said of the European Communities that 'the Commission proposes; the Council disposes'. The European Parliament has interposed itself in that sometimes uneasy, sometimes cosy, relationship.

The general functions of the Council are, according to Article 145 of the EEC Treaty (as amended by the SEA) (202 TEC),

- to ensure co-ordination of the general economic policies of the member states;
- to take decisions;

- to confer on the Commission powers for the implementation of rules which the Council lays down and also, in specific cases, to exercise implementation itself.

First, it should be made clear that while the term 'Council' suggests a unified body, this is far from the case. Ministers meet in a number of different 'Councils' according to which particular policy area is being discussed. A record of the Finnish Presidency of the Council in the latter half of 1999 shows 21 functional Councils, the most important being General Affairs (at which the Foreign Ministers meet) with six meetings, Agriculture (five meetings) and Economics and Finance ('ECOFIN', also with five sessions). The Environment, the Fisheries, and the Justice and Home Affairs Councils saw their ministers meet three times in the half year, while Civil Protection Council and the Tourism Council planned no meetings (http://ue.eu.int/newsroom/).

Second, while one of the main tasks of the Council, according to the treaties, is economic co-ordination, the role of ECOFIN has been complicated by the meetings of those member states that form the economic and monetary union within the EU (see Chapter 4). The fragmented nature of the Councils and the Commission's sole right of policy initiative mean that much of the co-ordination of policy other than economic is undertaken by the Commission. The Commission's input into the EU's legislative agenda and its longer time horizon than that of most national governments (Smyrl, 1998: 79–99) mean that the Council meetings are more than just a clash of various national preferences.

The way that the Council conducts its business shows the complexity of the national input into EU decision-making. Draft proposals coming from the Commission are not immediately discussed by the relevant Council but first go to a meeting of national officials from the member states, the Committee of Permanent Representatives (Coreper). The task of Coreper is to examine the vast amount of material coming before the Council and to sift it into that which needs the ministers' attention and that which can go through 'on the nod'. Coreper itself is divided into Coreper I, made up of civil servants at the deputy level, and Coreper II, of senior officials at the ambassadorial level, whose concern is mainly economic-monetary matters and foreign affairs. There is also a Special Committee on Agriculture. A number of working groups has been established – an estimated 170 by the mid–1990s – consisting of attachés from members' permanent representation to the EU and national civil servants, who prepare material for Coreper. Where agreement has been reached at working group level, Coreper normally sends proposals to the Council as 'A' points, which need no further discussion. If members of the working group cannot agree, then Coreper either hammers out an agreement (and the matter goes up as an 'A' point) or sends it back to the working group for further discussion, or the matter is put on the Council agenda as a 'B' point, to be negotiated by the Council (Beyers and Dierickx, 1998: 290–1).

Clearly Coreper is important in preparing the ground for Council meetings, though its wider significance is disputed. Wessels (1991: 140) claimed that by the late 1980s about 80 per cent of the Council's work was done at working group level, with Hayes-Renshaw and Wallace (1996: 562) estimating that only about 25 to 35 per cent of agreements were decided by either Coreper or the Council. This may give the impression that the Council acts as a 'rubber-stamp' for most issues coming before it. However, this view is challenged by Skou Andersen and Nordvig Rasmussen (1998: 594–6), who claim that, at least in the case of the Environment Council, although 'it is possible to pass Acts as 'A' points with no substantial discussion among ministers, in practice it only seldom happens'. It would appear that ministers make themselves aware of anything that could have political consequences and that a number of 'B' points return on the 'A' list only after they have been dealt with at Council.

When a matter comes before the Council for discussion, its form of adoption will depend primarily on its treaty basis (see pp. 58–62, 'Legislative process within the EU'). It will have to be presented to a range of other EU institutions before the Council – often in tandem with the European Parliament – makes its final decision. Once the Council has approved a draft proposal, then it is deemed to be in force and is published in the EU's *Official Journal*. For the period up to the Single European Act, implemented in 1987, the EC operated on a basis of decisions by consensus and unanimity in the Council. Though the Treaty of Rome had indicated that Qualified Majority Voting (QMV) could be used for some Council decisions, the tendency after the Luxembourg Compromise of 1966 was to avoid the divisions that this might bring. However, the SEA and both the Maastricht and Amsterdam Treaties have widened the opportunity for QMV decisions in the Council, and it was soon realized that the single market legislation would only be passed if QMV was used.

Qualified Majority Voting means that the Council adopts an issue neither by unanimity nor by a straightforward majority of those ministers present and voting, but by a system of weighted voting in the Council (see Table 2.1).

It can be seen that three larger states by themselves can prevent a positive vote, but that a coalition of the three Benelux states (Belgium, Luxembourg and Netherlands) and of the three Nordic states (Denmark, Finland and Sweden) could not stop the adoption of a measure without the support of, at least, another small state. The Mediterranean states of Greece, Italy, Portugal and Spain have a blocking vote even without France.

In the IGC leading up to the Amsterdam Treaty, there were attempts to reform QMV by, for example, introducing an extra criterion that the states forming any majority should also represent a certain proportion of the EU's

Table 2.1 *Weighting given to states' votes under QMV*

Luxembourg	2
Denmark, Finland, Ireland	3 each
Austria, Sweden	4 each
Belgium, Greece, the Netherlands, Portugal	5 each
Spain	8
France, Germany, Italy, UK	10 each
Total	87

A qualified majority is achieved with 62 votes, though in a few cases eight member states must vote in favour. Thus 26 votes can stop the adoption of a measure; it was agreed in 1994 that if there are 23 to 25 votes against a measure, then it would be withdrawn for further reflection before re-introduction.

population, or that votes should be re-weighted according to population. However, this issue became entangled with that of the size of the Commission and of enlargement, and no agreement was reached, with a decision being postponed to the 2000 Inter-governmental Conference (IGC).

The European Council – consisting of the heads of government or of state of the member countries – has a more recent history than that of the Council. The informal summitry of the 1960s was formalized in 1974 in the meetings of heads of government and foreign ministers. This became known as European Political Co-operation (EPC) and was then distinct from the Community-based process, not subject to ECJ rulings or supervision by the EP. Decisions did not have to await Commission proposals, but senior politicians could broker agreements and set the general framework for the development of the EC. The 1986 SEA legitimized the existence of what was called the European Council, the meeting of Heads of Government (or state in some cases), their Foreign Ministers and two senior members of the Commission. At that stage the European Council was still parallel to the EC institutions and was intergovernmental in nature. The European Parliament tried to exploit Article 30 (4) of the SEA, which said that the Council should be 'closely associated' with EPC and that the Presidency should 'regularly inform the European Parliament of ... foreign policy issues' and take the EP's views into consideration.

The Maastricht Treaty entrenched the European Council, linking it more formally with the Communities' institutions. According to Article D, it was to provide the EU with 'the necessary impetus for its development and shall define the general political guidelines thereof'. Its membership was confirmed and it was to meet at least twice a year under the chairmanship of that state holding the Presidency of the Council (see below). It was to submit a report of its meetings to the EP and an annual written report on the progress of the EU. The Maastricht Treaty also gave the European Council an important role in the establishment of Economic and Monetary Union (Articles 103 and 109 passim, 99 and 111 TEC), and in defining 'principles and general guidelines' for the CFSP (Article J.8.1 TEU, now 18.1). It also provided the guidelines to the Council for matters that were to be the subject of a Joint Action in the CFSP pillar. The Amsterdam Treaty confirmed the CFSP role, adding the right to decide common strategies (now Article 13) for the Union as well as the WEU (see Chapter 9).

The Cologne European Council, chaired by Chancellor Schröder of Germany in June 1999, gives some indication of the work of the European Council. It was the first one after the ratification of the Treaty of Amsterdam. The 102 paragraphs of the subsequent press release dealt with four major areas covered by the Council. The first was the appointment of personnel, in this case Javier Solana to the post of the Secretary-General of the Council and as High Representative of the CFSP. The second was growth, employment and stability. The third was the future development of the EU; it covered the implementation of Agenda 2000, the need for an IGC on institutional matters in 2000 and the general aspects of enlargement. The section on external affairs was dominated by the end to the immediate crisis in Kosovo, the situation in the West Balkans, but also included the new Common Strategy on Russia. The six annexes included a list of the 20 reports submitted to the European Council, including one on the Millennium Bug (http//ue.eu.int/newsroom/press/a/kolnen.htm).

The European Council has long been seen as assuming the 'motor' role in the EC of the 1980s (Lodge, 1993). Another author considered that it has not replaced the Commission 'motor', but had brought 'political force to bear on a necessarily tedious decision making process' (Troy Johnston, 1994: 48).

The Presidency is a key institution as the relevant country co-ordinates the work of the Council and of the European Council. The member states take it in turns to assume the Presidency every six months from 1 January to 30 June and from 1 July to 31 December. The Presidency during 1999 was held, respectively, by Germany and Finland, in 2000 by Portugal and France, and will be held in 2001 by Sweden and Belgium, followed by Spain and Denmark in 2002. The Presidency, as well as hosting at least one meeting of the European Council, provides an exhaustive support mechanism for the Council meetings. It can also help to set the agenda, act as a referee between member states and provide the centre of attention for the other institutions (Kirchner, 1992). Certainly a weak Presidency can affect the political dynamics of the Union (Ludlow, 1994: 9–11).

The Council has a secretariat that also supports the work of the European Council. It 'prepares the Council's work and ensures that it runs smoothly at every level' (http://ue.eu.int/en/info/secretar.htm). The Council appoints the Secretary-General, who heads the secretariat and has a staff of some

2300 officials in his private office, the legal service and ten Directorate Generals. For the five years from September 1994, the Secretary-General was Jürgen Trumpf. However, the Treaty of Amsterdam brought a change in the nature of the secretariat. The new Secretary-General of the Council – Javier Solana, the former Secretary-General of NATO – is also the High Representative in the EU's Common Foreign and Security Policy (CFSP). This role as 'Mr CFSP' means he is the contact person within the EU on foreign affairs issues, as well as having the difficult task of co-ordinating his effort with the Commissioner in overall charge of external affairs and with the Council President (Cameron 1999). Article 151 (2) (Article 207 TEC) creates a deputy Secretary-General's post, responsible for running the secretariat as was the Secretary-General under the old system.

The European Parliament (EP)

The European Parliament's genesis goes back to the European Assembly established by the Paris Treaty of the ECSC. It was then a consultative assembly, and was later shared by the EEC and Euratom. Article 137 of the Treaty of Rome, 1957, stated that the Assembly 'shall consist of the representatives of the peoples of the states brought together in the Community' and shall 'exercise the advisory and supervisory powers which are conferred on it in this Treaty'. The Assembly started to call itself the Parliament in the1960s, a term recognized in the SEA. Since 1957 the EP has sought to increase its authority and legitimacy, but until 1979 it suffered from its members being appointed by national parliaments rather than having them directly elected as in practically all parliaments in liberal pluralistic democracies.

Article 138 of the Treaty of Rome stipulated that a uniform procedure be employed across the Community to elect the members of the European Parliament (MEPs). Though direct elections were introduced in 1979, the procedures were scarcely uniform, with most countries using their own electoral systems. In particular, Great Britain used the 'first-past-the-post' system of voting, which contrasted to the varieties of proportional representation (PR) systems used in the other member states (and in Northern Ireland). The British Labour government that came to power in 1997 introduced a form of PR for the British Euro-elections and, for the first time, the 1999 European elections were held using one form or another of PR in all the member states. Elections are held every five years in June, normally over a period of four days.

The 626[4] members of the EP (since January 1995) – apart from some independents – sit in political groups, of which there are eight in the 1999 Parliament, the largest being the European People's Party (Christian

Democrats)/European Democrats (EPP/ED), the Party of European Socialists (PES) and the Liberal, Democrat, and Reform Party (ELDR). The
1994–99 Parliament had a centre-left majority, reflecting the move to the
left in European politics in the mid–1990s after the right-wing domination
of the 1980s. However, the 1999 election saw a move back to the right (see
Table 2.2) and the new Parliament has a centre-right majority. There were
fewer women in the 1999 EP: 131 compared with 166 in the 1994
Parliament, reflecting the growth of the right-wing, more male-dominated,
parties.

Table 2.2 *Main parties in the European Parliament*

	1994	1999
Party of European Socialists	214	180
EPP/ED	201	233
ELDR	42	51
Greens	27	48
European United Left/Nordic Green Left	34	42

The Parliament has a Presidency consisting of a President (José Maria Gil
Robles of the PES from 1997 to 1999 and Nicole Fontaine of the EPP/ED
after July 1999), 14 Vice-Presidents and a Conference of Presidents consisting of the President of the Parliament and the heads of the political groups.
These help to draw up the EP's agenda and to make sure that it runs as
smoothly as possible.

There are 20 standing committees whose subject areas range from Foreign Affairs, Security and Defence Policy and Budgets to Petitions and
Women's Rights. There are also sub-committees and ad hoc committees.
The EP can establish a Committee of Enquiry as it did on the BSE issue (see
p. 53). The rapporteurs of the committees help to draw up texts and often
act as brokers between the political groups or between the committee and
the Commission and other interested groups (such as interest groups or
lobbies).

The EP's official seat is in Strasbourg, France. Committees meet in
Brussels and much of the Secretariat is in Luxembourg, making sure that
many of the MEPs and the EP's documents are regularly on the move
between the three cities. France has resisted any move away from Strasbourg to Brussels (where most of the work is done) and insisted that their
city was nominated in the Amsterdam Treaty as the meeting-place for the
EP, having constructed a new, but controversial, building for the 1999
parliament. The debates in the EP are simultaneously interpreted and are
translated and published in the EU's 11 official languages (Danish, Dutch,

English, Finnish, French, German, Greek, Italian, Portuguese, Spanish and Swedish).

The EP has steadily increased its powers and influence since 1970. The Parliament's advisory powers meant that the Council consulted it on both legislative and non-legislative matters. However, the EP felt that this process was somewhat desultory and took the Council to the European Court of Justice (ECJ) over the failure to consult. The ECJ's *Isoglucose* ruling of 1980 clarified the legal obligation of the Council to consult the EP before adopting legislation. This *consultation* procedure still applies to the agricultural price review, and, since the Maastricht Treaty, covers more broadly judicial co-operation (Pillar III). The Council could, of course, ignore the EP's advice, though where a Commission proposal has undergone considerable change, the EP now demands 'renewed consultation' (Smith, 1999: 74).

The Maastricht Treaty's introduction of the *co-decision* procedure under Article 189b (Article 251 TEC) considerably strengthened the EP's legislative powers (see p. 59 under 'Legislative process within the EU'). Though the areas covered were limited – they covered approximation of laws for the internal market, education and culture, consumer protection and public health – the Treaty of Amsterdam has extended this list as well as simplified the procedure. In co-decision areas, the EP is an equal partner with the Council and can prevent legislation from being adopted.

The SEA provided for the *assent* of the EP to Association agreements and the accession of new members. It exercised this by withholding its assent to EC-Israel and EC-Morocco Protocols because of alleged human rights abuses in those states (Greilsammer, 1991). The Maastricht Treaty extended the EP's power of assent to include other international agreements, the cohesion fund, free movement and residence issues, and amendments to the Statute of the ESCB.

The SEA also introduced the *co-operation* procedure, in particular for much internal market legislation. This allowed the EP to have a greater say than in the consultation system, but the Council could still override the EP's wishes. The Amsterdam Treaty virtually abandoned its application and it can be seen as a transitional measure in the advance of parliamentary powers in the EU.

Although the EP has been placed more in the thick of the legislative process from such a profusion of powers, it still does not have the additional power of initiating legislation held by most national parliaments. This is still in the hands of the Commission for Community matters, although Article 138b TEU (192 TEC) gave the EP the right to ask the Commission to 'submit any appropriate proposal on matters on which it considers that a Community act is required' to implement the Treaty, a right similar to that held by the Council (208 TEC). This lack of legislative initiation may be one of the reasons why many voters do not regard the EP as a 'proper parliament' and means that any notion of a legislative programme is left in the hands of the unelected Commission.

Nevertheless, the EP has considerably increased its legislative influence since the 1970s. It has progressed from being an assembly that was consulted to being a parliament – with all its limitations – that can affect EC legislation from beginning to end. It can require that the Commission make proposals on certain matters and then can review and amend the legislation proposed. It can reject legislation or force an issue on to the political agenda.

The EP has a number of important supervisory functions. The most important and the oldest of these is the right provided for in the Treaty of Rome (Article 144, 201 TEC) to censure the Commission en bloc, thereby ensuring its resignation. It has threatened this punishment on a number of occasions (Jacobs *et al.*, 1995). In January 1999 a censure motion failed but the EP got its first taste of Commission blood in March 1999 when the prospect of another motion passing led to the resignation of the Santer Commission over accusations of incompetence, lack of control and even corruption. Although the members of the Santer Commission stayed in office as acting Commissioners, Jacques Santer was quickly replaced by Romano Prodi, who was to head the new Commission after the election of the 1999 EP.

Perhaps more important is the Parliament's increased power over appointments to the Commission. By the early 1980s the EP had developed the practice of having a vote of confidence on each incoming Commission, and Jacques Delors' Commission acknowledged the importance of this endorsement to their legitimacy by delaying their oath-taking ceremony with the ECJ until after the EP's vote of confidence. The Maastricht Treaty acknowledged the right of the EP to be consulted over the appointment of the President of the Commission and to submit each new College of the Commission to a vote of approval (Article 158, 214 TEC). In fact the EP's rules of procedure mean that the President-designate has to answer to a plenary session of the EP, which then votes to approve or reject him or her.

It is unlikely that a candidate defeated by the EP would want to take office, even if the member states decided to press on with that candidature. This was the line taken by Jacques Santer in 1994 when he narrowly won the EP's support for his presidency by 260 votes to 238, with 23 abstentions (Hix and Lord, 1996). The Parliament was formally consulted in March 1999 over the appointment of Prodi to succeed the disgraced Santer, although this was only after his nomination had been decided by the member states. Prodi's centre-left political views nevertheless reflected the majority in the 1994–99 Parliament, which confirmed him as head of the retiring Commission in May 1999. However, the new Parliament that confirmed him as head of the new Commission in September 1999 had a centre-right complexion and took a more critical view of his appointment.

MEPs have also taken to inviting individual Commission candidates to answer questionnaires and attend special 'hearings' at which they are questioned about a variety of matters. Some members of the Santer Commission in 1994 were given a tough time by MEPs, either because of their lack of qualifications for their portfolio or, in the case of Ritt Bjerregaard of Denmark, because of her seemingly dismissive attitude towards the EP. The Maastricht Treaty allowed the EP to approve the composition of the College of the Commission. However, although the new 1999 Parliament has a centre-right majority, the governments of the member states – who nominate the members of the Commission – are mostly from the centre-left. The Commissioners chosen in July 1999 were predominantly to the centre-left, and this riled the leaders of the right-wing parties in the new Parliament.

The EP is also consulted over a number of other appointments: to the European Central Bank, the European Monetary Institute and the Court of Auditors. In the last case, votes against the French and Greek nominees in 1989 led to the withdrawal of the former but not the latter, whereas two negative votes in 1993 did not prevent the Council from appointing them (Westlake 1998: 433). The EP has the sole responsibility for appointing the Ombudsman (see p. 56).

Members of the Commission and of the Council appear before the EP to answer for their actions. The Treaty of Rome (Article 140) required the Commission 'to reply orally or in writing to questions put to it by the European Parliament or its members', and the Maastricht Treaty extended this right to the CFSP and JHA areas. Although the same right was not extended over the Council, it became common, especially after British entry to the EC, for the Council President to participate in 'question time' in the EP, a practice formalized in 1983.

The Maastricht Treaty provided the European Parliament with the right to establish a temporary Committee of Inquiry 'to investigate ... alleged contraventions or maladministration of Community law' (Article 138c TEU, 193 TEC). The Parliament did this twice in 1996, once in order to investigate the Community transit system and the other time in order to examine the BSE beef crisis. Before the Maastricht Treaty the EP had established such ad hoc committees, but these had no standing in law (Shackleton, 1998: 115–30).

Important progress has been made in the budgetary powers of the EP. Control of the purse is often seen as a crucial power for any national parliament. The EP has the right to reject the EC's draft budget and, to a significant extent, can decide on the level of Non-Compulsory Expenditure (NCE). The EP then has to adopt the final budget, with the EP President's signature making it legal (see 'The budget', pp. 62–3). On matters of compulsory expenditure (CAP expenditure and expenditure from agreements with third countries), the Council has the final say, whereas the Parliament can alter NCE expenditure. During the early 1980s the EP refused to agree to the final budget on several occasions (the last being in 1985), but since then the emphasis has been on the Council, Commission and EP all agreeing a budget. The EP also has to 'discharge' previous budgets, which means accepting the Commission's use of the money. Increasingly both the Court of Auditors and the EP's committee on budgetary control have become critical of the management of EU funds, in particular of the level of fraud. The matter came to a head in December 1998 with the EP's refusal to allow the discharge of the 1996 budget because of allegations of fraud and irregularities. This led to the EP's attempt to censure the Commission in January 1999, but also to a report that finally led to the March 1999 resignation of the whole of the Santer Commission. The new Prodi Commission has as one of its main aims the tightening of control over expenditure, and the EP will continue to scrutinize progress in this area.

The Amsterdam Treaty improved the powers and position of the European Parliament. It simplified the decision-making process, more or less phasing out the co-operation procedure and enhancing and simplifying the use of co-decision, thus making 'the European Parliament the big winner of Amsterdam' (Duff, 1997: 143). However, despite this, and the Parliament flexing its muscles over the Santer Commission, there was a record low turnout in the June 1999 Euro-elections. As yet the elections for the EP are 'Second-order Elections' (Smith, 1999: 21–4) and as such are regarded as less important than national elections by the electorate. With the proposed new members, the EP will become even more unwieldy and fragmented than with the present 15 EU members, even though the Amsterdam Treaty capped its membership at 700. Until the EP has the right to initiate legislation and, perhaps, to choose the Commission, it will remain 'not a proper parliament' in the minds of many electors. However, over the past decades it has increased its consultative, decision-making and supervisory powers and has started to use these in a way that overshadows some national parliaments.

The European Court of Justice, the Court of Auditors and the Ombudsman

The European Court of Justice is perhaps the most underestimated institution of the EU. It comprises 15 judges – one nominated from each member state – and nine Advocates-General, all appointed by common accord by the 15 governments for renewable six-year terms. They are chosen from jurists 'whose independence is beyond doubt' (Article 167 EEC, 223 TEC) and who are of recognized competence. The Advocates-General assist the Court by delivering to it impartial opinions on the cases coming before the Court. In this way, they prepare the Court for what can be complicated subjects, but they are not prosecutors in any sense. The Court can sit in six chambers of three or five judges as well as in plenary (full) session.

There is also a Court of First Instance, established in October 1988 by the SEA. This also has 15 judges, who are appointed on a similar basis to that of the ECJ. The Court sits in chambers of three or five judges (or in plenary session in important cases); it deals with actions for annulment, failure to act or for damages brought by persons against the Community, competition proceedings, ECSC cases and disputes between the Community and its officials (http://curia.eu.int/en/pres/comp.htm).

The main responsibility of the Court of Justice is to 'ensure that in the interpretation and application' of the Community's treaties that 'the law is observed' (Article 164 EEC, 220 TEC). Its remit thus does not cover the non-Community elements of the European Union, Pillars II and III.

It can hear a wide variety of actions (http://curia.eu.int/en/pres/comp.htm):

- *Proceedings on the failure to fulfil an obligation*, whereby the Court determines whether a member state has carried out its obligations under Community law. The Commission or another member state can bring that state to the Court. If the state is found in breach of its obligation, it must comply without delay.
- *Proceedings for annulment*, whereby one of the Community institutions or a person affected by a legal measure can seek to have that measure annulled. The Court can also review the legality of the acts of Community institutions. If the case succeeds, then the measure in question is made void.
- *Proceedings for failure to act* when the legality of a failure to act by a Community institution is examined.
- *Actions for damages* caused by Community institutions or their servants may be ruled on.
- *Appeals* on points of law against judgments given by the Court of First Instance can be heard.

In most cases it is national courts that have to rule on the implementation of Community law to make sure that there is some consistency in the rulings given, there is a system whereby national courts may seek preliminary rulings from the ECJ on the issue at hand. In such a case, the ECJ will declare what the Community law is, and the national court then has to apply that interpretation to the dispute before it.

Judicial interpretation has been crucial to the process of European integration. The Court has ruled on the nature and supremacy of the EC law, for example in the 'direct effect' of Community law without the need for interpretation by national governments or agencies (van Gend en Loos case 26/62). It has stated that if there is a conflict between national and Community law, then the latter has precedence (Costa v. ENEL case 6/64).

The Court of Auditors was created as a result of amended budgetary procedures in 1975. It carries out an annual review of the EU's financial affairs, especially the management and disbursement of monies. Members are appointed from persons who belong to audit bodies within their own country and they act independently. The Court has collective responsibility and is represented by a President in its relations with other institutions. Its reports, and the criticisms that they have contained, have often caused embarrassment for the institutions of the Communities and for member states. Nevertheless, this institution is seen as being vital in creating a more open and responsible EU.

The Ombudsman is appointed by the EP under Article 138e TEU (195 TEC) and is empowered 'to receive complaints from any citizen of the Union or natural or legal person ... concerning instances of maladministration in the activities of the Community institutions or bodies, with the exception of the Court of Justice and the Court of First Instance acting in their judicial role'. The Ombudsman has to establish whether such a complaint is well-founded and then gives the relevant institution three months to reply. A report is then forwarded to the EP. This system is based on the Nordic practice, since adopted by the United Kingdom, of a person examining cases of administrative mistakes and oversights.

The Economic and Social Committee

Article 193 of the Treaty of Rome established the Economic and Social Committee (ESC, also known as Ecosoc), although the Consultative Committee of the ECSC can be seen as its predecessor. The ESC currently consists of 222 representatives of three groups: employers (Group I), workers (Group II), and various interests (Group III) that voice the concerns of various socio-economic groups such as small businesses, consumer and environmental organizations and co-operatives. Members are nominated by national governments for a renewable four-year term, though they are 'appointed in their personal capacity and may not be bound by any mandatory instructions' (Article 194 EEC, 258 TEC). Germany, France, Italy and the United Kingdom have 24 representatives each; Spain 21; Austria, Belgium, Greece, the Netherlands, Portugal and Sweden 12 each, Denmark, Ireland and Finland nine each; and Luxembourg six.

The task of the ESC is to issue opinions to the Council, Commission and European Parliament. In some cases the Council or Commission have to consult the ESC, for example in aspects of regional and environmental policy. Otherwise such consultation is optional. The ESC can also take its own initiative to issue opinions, which make up about 15 per cent of its approximately 170 advisory documents issued each year (http:/ /www.ces.eu.int/en/org/w_esc.htm). The Treaty of Amsterdam added employment and social matters to the list for obligatory consultation. However, the Treaty also allowed for the creation of an Employment Committee by the Council with advisory status 'to promote co-ordination between member States on employment and labour market policies' (Article 109s, 130 TEC). This Committee will consult the social partners, thus cutting across an important part of the ESC's work.

During the 1990s the ESC developed the notion of it representing civil society, that is, the non-governmental organizations in society. The stress has traditionally been on the 'European model', which embraces agreements between the social partners, and on the so-called Val Duchesse social dialogue between these social partners, the employers and the employees' representatives. This has now been broadened out to include other repre-sentatives, especially those of consumers and women's associations (Rangoni Machiavelli, 1999: 1) and a dialogue has been opened up with equivalent organizations in Central and East Europe.

The Committee of the Regions

The Committee of the Regions (CoR) was set up by the Maastricht Treaty and was implemented in 1994. Like the ESC it is a consultative body, aiming to bring to the EU a 'local and regional point of view' (http:/ /www.cor.eu.int/overview/intro/intro_eng.html). It has 222 members drawn from the 15 member states in the same proportion as the members of the ESC, but from representatives from local and regional government. Such organizations differ widely between the member states, so that a representa-tive of the powerful German Länder (such as Bavaria or North-Rhine Westphalia) may sit near to the Mayor of Barcelona or the chairman of a small Danish municipality or an English district council.

The Committee can provide the Commission, European Parliament or Council with opinions on areas affecting the responsibilities of local and regional government:

- economic and social cohesion, including the structural funds
- trans-European transport, telecommunications and energy infrastruc-tures
- public health
- education and youth
- culture
- employment
- social matters

- Social Fund implementation
- the environment
- vocational training

In its first four years the Committee adopted some 200 opinions (*ibid.*). Both this Committee and the ESC have found themselves sometimes in conflict with the EP as to which organization represents the 'people of Europe'.

Legislative process within the EU

There are four basic forms of EU legislation (Article189 TEU, 249 TEC):

- a 'regulation' has general application, is binding and is applicable to all EU states;
- a 'directive' is binding in terms of the results to be achieved (for example the reduction of automobile exhausts) but leaves the method of achievement to each member state;
- a 'decision' is binding in its entirety to whomever it is addressed, and this may be to commercial enterprises as well as to particular states;
- 'recommendations' and 'opinions' have no binding force but may help to clarify issues and help to guide ECJ judgments.

During 1997 the Commission presented to the Council or the Council and EP 238 regulations, 52 directives, 245 decisions and 14 recommendations. The Council adopted 209 regulations, 34 directives and 164 decisions (Corbett, 1998: 46–7).

There are also a number of ways in which EU legislation may be adopted, with the first three mentioned below being the dominant.

1. Consultation

This is the most traditional method dating from the EEC Treaty. The process is begun by the Commission, which has the sole right to initiate legislation, although it might be instigated by another institution (the EP or the Council) or by particular interest groups (environmentalists, industrial groups). A working draft is normally drawn up in the Commission's Directorate-Generals and it then proceeds to the College of Commissioners. Unless there is a feeling that the proposal stands little chance of adoption, it is then sent to the Council, where the working groups and Coreper briefly examine it in order to get a feel for the response of national governments.

The Council then passes the draft to either the EP or the ESC or both. Once the EP or ESC has given its opinion, the draft returns to the Council and at this stage Coreper examines it in more detail. If agreement can be reached within Coreper, it is placed in section A of the relevant Council's agenda; if there is disagreement, it is placed in section B. When the relevant

Council meets, section A matters go through 'on the nod' while section B matters have been earmarked as being potentially controversial and worthy of further discussion.

Throughout this process the Commission has the right to amend the draft proposal, for example after EP and ESC discussion or during Council sessions.

Once the Council has voted on the draft and it has received the necessary majority, or has been adopted by unanimity, according to its precise legal base, than it is deemed to have passed into law and is subsequently published in the *Official Journal*.

After the Treaty of Amsterdam, the consultation procedure remains for a number of articles including those concerning citizenship measures, reform of the CAP, competition policy and the Common Fisheries Policy, harmonization of indirect taxes, EMU surveillance, budgetary regulations, common immigration policy and the scope of trade negotiations (Duff, 1997: 146–8).

2. Co-decision

The power of co-decision was introduced by Article 189b TEU (Article 251 TEC) but the process was seen as cumbersome and difficult to manage. The Amsterdam Treaty simplified the process considerably and extended its application. In future, more areas of legislation are likely to be placed in this category, which will become the main pathway for legislation certainly within the Communities part of the EU (Pillar I).

As with consultation, the source of a legislative proposal is the Commission, although its inspiration may be found in an interest group or the EP. Unlike consultation, there are up to three readings of the legislation in the EP which, in this case, has equal decision-making power with the Council.

If the EP rejects a proposal, then the Council cannot adopt it. To forestall this, a conciliation committee consisting of Council and EP representatives (and with a Commission member present) will try to prevent such rejection at a third reading of the legislation in the Parliament. The areas of co-decision (with the Council acting by Qualified Majority Voting) include free movement of workers, research and development framework programme, right of establishment, services, internal market harmonization, consumer protection, trans-European networks, social exclusion, transparency and the environment action programme. In the cases of citizens' rights, social security for migrant workers, the rights of the self-employed and cultural measures, the Council has to act unanimously (Duff, 1997: 144–5). In 2004, co-decision will be applied to visa procedures, conditions and uniformity rules; the Council and EP could decide to extend this list.

In 1997 the Council adopted jointly with the EP, using the co-decision procedure, one regulation, 20 directives and seven decisions (Corbett, 1998: 47).

3. Assent

This procedure was introduced by the SEA and extended in the Maastricht Treaty. In this case the EP's agreement is required for the passage of a treaty, agreement or legislation. The EP can either agree to or reject – but not amend – a proposal and, in the case of electoral reform and enlargement, it has to do so by an absolute majority of its members (314 votes in the 1999 Parliament). The Amsterdam Treaty made some small changes to the coverage of the assent procedure but failed to extend it to all international agreements (Duff, 1997: 142).

4. Co-operation

The SEA introduced the co-operation procedure whereby the EP was involved more in the legislative process, especially with regard to the creation of the '1992' internal market. In these cases, if the Parliament's opinion after its first reading of legislation is not sufficiently taken into account by the Council, then the EP can reject a proposal at second reading. The Council can overturn this action only by a unanimous vote. In order to prevent this from happening, the Council has often resorted to compromise with the EP in such areas as the European Regional Development Fund, research, the environment and development (http://www.europarl.eu.int/dg7/survol/en/bro_en3.htm). However, the co-operation procedure has been mostly removed (except in some areas of economic and monetary union) by the Treaty of Amsterdam, which effectively replaced it with co-decision. Nevertheless, this procedure served 'to transform the Council-Commission dialogue into an asymmetrical Council-Commission-Parliament trialogue' (Earnshaw and Judge, 1997: 560).

5. Secondary legislation

The Commission can bring in a limited but increasingly large range of legislation, which provides greater detail to framework legislation already passed by the Council and EP. This 'secondary legislation' is often the result of the comitology activities of expert committees, invariably including national representatives (see p. 43 The Commission).

6. Second and third pillar activities

As a result of the Maastricht Treaty, the activities of the EU under the headings of the Common Foreign and Security Policy (Pillar II) and on

Justice and Home Affairs (Pillar III) were not carried out by any of the Community decision-making methods. The Council did not have to await an initiative from the Commission, nor did it share its decision-making role with the EP. Instead, the Council could principally make decisions by unanimity (although the Treaty of Amsterdam set out the occasions for QMV), with member states, the Commission and the EP bringing CFSP matters to the attention of the Council. This is also the case with Pillar III matters. However, the Treaty of Amsterdam transferred a number of these areas, such as asylum and immigration, from Pillar III to the Community pillar, but not police and judicial co-operation.

7. 'Absent and flexible friends' – decisions by some members

One way around opposition to advance, desired by a large majority of member states, has been to allow for 'opt outs'. The Maastricht Treaty was infested with these – on the social protocol, on economic and monetary union, on justice matters and on defence. In the case of the social chapter, and later on EMU, those members who wished to advance took decisions in the absence of those who did not.

As a result of the Maastricht Treaty some decisions were taken about social policy using Community-based decision-making, but in the absence of the United Kingdom, which had insisted on not being covered by the Social Protocol of the Maastricht Treaty. The decision to go ahead with the third stage of EMU by 11 of the EU states as from 1 January 1999 meant that on certain economic matters 11 states were meeting and taking decisions, while on other related economic issues all 15 members were involved.

The situation was further confused by the Treaty of Amsterdam introducing 'flexibility' clauses whereby closer co-operation between a number of EU states might be allowed, with others opting out. These were particularly noticeable in both Pillar II, where neutral states may not want to go along with certain defence co-operation, and Pillar III, where the United Kingdom and Denmark have reservations about co-operation over justice questions. The treaty also allowed for flexibility in Community (Pillar I) matters not falling 'within the exclusive competence of the Community' (Article 5a TEU, 11 TEC).

It should be noted that the above legislative patchwork quilt, though made a little more patterned in some areas by the Amsterdam Treaty, does not represent a logical, ordered approach to legislation and decision-making. In particular, there is no specific hierarchy of European Union law with certain kinds of legislation (for example legislation that primarily involves international implications, such as treaties, or constitutional legislation) having distinct forms of decision-making.

Limiting the EU's action in line with the principle of subsidiarity was a way of trying to increase its legitimacy. According to Article A of the TEU Preamble, this meant that 'decisions ... are taken as closely as possible to the citizen'. In Article 3b TEU (5 TEC), the Commission shall take action in accordance with subsidiarity, in areas not within its exclusive competence, only if the proposed action 'cannot be sufficiently achieved by the Member States' (see Duff, 1997: 96–106). Though a protocol of the Amsterdam Treaty revived subsidiarity and linked it with proportionality – keeping to what is needed to achieve treaty objectives – its vague nature has limited its utility.

The 2000 IGC aimed to deal with the 'left-overs' of Amsterdam and to prepare the EU's institutions for a possible membership of over 20 states. Ministerial meetings throughout 2000 – with members of the Commission and two MEPs present – prepared for a decision at the Nice European Council in December 2000. Areas covered were the Commission's size (especially whether one Commissioner from each state should suffice); the weighting of votes in the Council (to prevent larger states being outvoted by a group of small states); the possible extension of QMV (73 articles or sub-articles still being subject to unanimity); and reform of other EU institutions, especially the judicial system. The debate and outcome on these issues can be followed at http://europa.eu.int/comm/igc2000/index_en.htm .

The budget

The EU's budget has always been a matter of hard negotiation between the Communities' institutions, especially among the EP, and the member states. As a result of treaties in 1970 and 1975 covering budgetary powers, the EP increased its say in budgetary matters. It could change the compulsory expenditure (basically the CAP, but a majority of the budget); it could increase the non-compulsory element; and it could reject the budget as a whole. The late 1970s and early 1980s saw the EP testing these powers, often leaving the EC without a full budget for a number of months while the Council and EP sorted out their differences.

In June 1988 the Council, Commission and EP signed an inter-institutional budgetary agreement that gave a measure of order and predictability to affairs. The EC was given a financial perspective for the 1988–92 period (extended later to 1993) and the EP enhanced its control over the budget, especially as the non-compulsory element was expanded. The financial perspective set ceilings for both types of EC expenditure and thus for any increase in the EC budget. A seven-year financial perspective was agreed for 1992–99 and another one for 2000–06. The last was based on the Commission's Agenda 2000 document (Commission, 1997), which took into account the proposed enlargement of the EU as well as key reforms in agriculture.

In the context of the wider financial perspective, the Council and the EP agree an annual budget. Each April the Commission puts forward a preliminary draft budget to the Council which, after meetings with the EP about the compulsory element, it adopts in July. The EP has its first reading of the budget in October, when a range of modifications to the compulsory element and amendments to the non-compulsory element are proposed. The EP and Council will meet before the Council has its second reading of the budget in November. The EP then has a second reading in December, with its President's signature making the final budget enforceable.

What is the money spent on? Even by 1999, 41.7 per cent of the budget went towards the CAP. Another 40.2 per cent was spent on structural measures (the Structural Funds and the Cohesion Fund – see Chapter 7), 6.0 per cent on internal policies (such as research and development, energy, telecommunications), and 6.1 per cent on external activities (aid to other states, joint actions under the CFSP, international agreements, Pre-Accession strategy). Administration took 4.6 per cent of the budget and there was a reserve of 1.3 per cent (background information: The 2000 Budget, 21 October 1999 at http://www.europarl.eu.int/).

How is the money obtained? Until the late 1960s, revenue was based on national contributions with each member state's contribution being assessed on the basis of its national wealth. In 1970 the EC was also given its 'own resources', consisting of customs duties on goods imported into the Communities; levies on imported agricultural products, and a proportion of Value Added Tax (VAT – sales tax) receipts, amounting to 1 per cent of total EC VAT receipts. However, the amount that the United Kingdom – a high-importing and high-consuming country – paid into Communities' funding was, under this system, much less than the amount that the UK received, given that agriculture was such a small part of its economy. In 1986 it was decided that the British should have part of their VAT payments back as a rebate. In 1988 the idea of controlling EC expenditure by financial perspectives was introduced and a 'fourth resource' related to members' GNP was agreed. Finance for the EU budget now comes from four sources:

- customs duties;
- agricultural levies on products from third countries which, with the above, provided 17.4 per cent of EU revenue by the late 1990s;
- a share of VAT on goods and services throughout the EU, accounting for 42.3 per cent of revenue;

- a contribution made on the basis of each member state's GNP, providing 38.9 per cent of revenue (with the remaining 1.4 per cent coming from reserves).

The financial perspective for 2000–06 has maintained the EU budget at 1.27 per cent of the EU's Gross Domestic Product (GDP). With the accession of new members a prospect in the near future, a 'disjuncture is clearly emerging between what the EU level does and will be called upon to do, and the means with which it is endowed' (Begg and Grimwade, 1998: 147). There have been a number of suggestions about how the EU might bridge that gap. United Kingdom governments have resisted an end to the British rebate, and the German government – the largest net contributor to the EU budget – has started to raise the question of the imbalance of its expenditure on and income from the EU. On the income side, there have been a number of suggestions for increased own resources (*ibid.*: 146), but none of these have found favour with a solid core of member states. The inability of the EU to solve the mismatch of resources and policies to be financed will be brought home by enlargement or by a downturn in the European economies, which could undermine the basis for EU financing and increase the demands on governments to trim EU expenditure. Either way, the EU will have to solve its budgetary problems before either widening its membership or deepening its level of integration.

Democracy in the EU

As the SEA and the Maastricht Treaty moved a number of policies from the national level to the Communities level, a 'democratic deficit' was identified. This meant that whereas powers had previously been overseen by parliaments at a national level, this was no longer the case at the EU level. This was partly remedied by increasing the powers of the EP and its involvement in the decision-making process (Smith, 1999: 13–14). However, as seen on pp. 49–54, the nature of the EP is quite different from that of a number of parliaments in the member states. It cannot initiate legislation, and neither does it appoint the Commission (although its powers in that respect have increased). The political parties in the EP are nebulous and fractious and it is often difficult to define the Parliament's political complexion. Why should the EP be given a greater say in legislation than the Council, which, after all, consists of ministers responsible to their electorates? The answer to this question depends on one's view not just of what the EU is by nature but, as seen in Chapter 1, what it should be.

The democratic deficit also refers to the *accountability* element of the EU. How should the institutions of the EU be accountable for what the organization does? There are other elements of democracy to be considered. What about the *representational* element? Should the EP be made more representative by the number of electors represented by an MEP being made more equal? Should residents in the EU, and not just citizens of EU states, be able to vote for MEPs? Are the ESC and Committee of Regions more representative of civil society and local and regional democracy than the EP is of the total EU electorate? Another element in the democratic debate is that of *identity*. Do the peoples living in the European Union regard themselves as an entity with not only common institutions but also with shared meanings and norms? If they do – or if they begin to – then maybe they will pay greater attention to the forms – and democratic nature – of the institutions, requiring them to be at least as sound as national ones. Until then, the general public's view of the EU is to see it as an elite institution – 'them' – that imposes rules and regulations of doubtful legitimacy, and to which they feel little loyalty compared with their nation (Lord, 1998: 112).

Notes

1   In the Maastricht Treaty Pillar III was titled 'Justice and Home Affairs', but this was changed to 'Police and Judicial Co-operation in Criminal Matters' in the Amsterdam Treaty, in which a number of matters were transferred from Pillar III to Pillar I.

2   The Treaty of Amsterdam tried to make sense of numbering and lettering in the EU treaty articles by renumbering them and providing a Table of Equivalence. Throughout this text the renumbered European Union element (which previously had letters in the Maastricht Treaty) will be referred to as such: 'Article J.1 TEU, now 11'. The European Community part (bringing together the EEC, ECSC and Euratom treaty elements) is referred to in the Table of Equivalence as the Treaty establishing the European Community (TEC). Thus in this text 'Article 155' of the original Treaty of Rome (EEC) becomes 'Article 211 TEC' while 'Article 4a TEU' becomes 'Article 8 TEC', all according to the Table of Equivalence.

3   Some heads of state of EU countries – especially those of France and Finland – have some executive function and insist on attending European Council meetings, although together with their country's Prime Minister.

4   The 1999 European Parliament was made up from 99 MEPs from Germany, 87 each from France, Italy and the UK, 64 from Spain, 31 from the Netherlands, 25 each from Belgium, Greece and Portugal, 22 from Sweden, 21 from Austria, 16 each from Denmark and Finland, 15 from Ireland, and 6 from Luxembourg.

References and further reading

Begg, I. and Grimwade, N. (1998) *Paying for Europe*, Contemporary European Studies 2. Sheffield Academic Press, Sheffield.

Beyers, J. and Dierickx, G. (1998) 'The working groups of the Council of the European Union', *Journal of Common Market Studies*, 36 (3): 289–317.

Cameron, F. (1999) *The Foreign and Security Policy of the European Union: Past, Present and Future*, Contemporary European Studies 7. Sheffield Academic Press, Sheffield.

Commission of the European Communities (1997) *Agenda 2000: For a Stronger and Wider Union*, COM. (97) 2000 final. Office for Official Publications of the European Communities, Luxembourg.

Corbett, R. (1998) 'Governance and institutions', in G. Edwards and G. Wiessala (eds), *The European Union 1997: Annual Review of Activities*. Blackwell, Oxford, pp. 39–49.

Duff, A. (ed.) (1997) *The Treaty of Amsterdam: Text and Commentary*. Sweet and Maxwell, London.

Earnshaw, D. and Judge, D. (1997) 'The life and times of the European Union's Co-operation procedure,' *Journal of Common Market Studies*, 35 (4): 543–64.

Evans, A. (1998) 'European Union decision-making, third states and comitology', *International and Comparative Law Quarterly*, 47 (2): 257–77.

Greilsammer, I. (1991) 'The non-ratification of the EEC-Israel protocols by the EP', *Middle Eastern Studies*, 27 (2): 303–21.

Hayes-Renshaw, F. and Wallace, H. (1996) *The Council of Ministers*. Macmillan, Basingstoke.

Hix, S. and Lord, C. (1996) 'The making of a President. The European Parliament and the confirmation of Jacques Santer as President of the European Commission', *Government and Opposition*, 31: 62–76.

Jacobs, F., Corbett, R. and Shackleton, M. (1995) *The European Parliament*, 3rd edn. Harper, London.

Keohane, R.O. and Hoffmann, S. (1990) 'Conclusions: Community politics and institutional change', in W. Wallace (ed.), *The Dynamics of European Integration*, Pinter/RIIA, London.

Kirchner, E.J. (1992) *Decisionmaking in the EC: The Council Presidency and European Integration*. Manchester University Press, Manchester.

Kortenberg, H. (1998) 'Comitologie: le retour', *Revue trimestrielle de droit europeen*, 34 (3): 317–27.

Lodge, J. (1993) *The EC and the Challenge of the Future*, 2nd edn. Pinter, London.

Lord, C. (1998) *Democracy in the European Union*, Contemporary European Studies 4. Sheffield Academic Press, Sheffield.

Ludlow, P. (1994) 'The Greek Presidency', *ECSA Newsletter*, 7 (3): 9–11.

Nugent, N. (1999) *The Government and Politics of the European Union*, 4th edn. Macmillan, Basingstoke.

Rangoni Machiavelli, B. (1999) 'The focal point of a citizens' Europe', *Eur-op News, Economic and Social Committee Supplement*, 2.

Ross, G. (1995) *Jacques Delors and European Integration*. Polity Press, Cambridge.

Shackleton, M. (1998) 'The European Parliament's new Committees of Inquiry: tiger or paper tigers?' *Journal of Common Market Studies*, 36 (1): 115–30.

Skou Andersen, M. and Nordvig Rasmussen, L. (1998) 'The making of environmental policy in the European Council', *Journal of Common Market Studies*, 36 (4): 585–97.

Smith, J. (1999) *Europe's Elected Parliament*, Contemporary European Studies 5. Sheffield Academic Press, Sheffield.

Smyrl, M.E. (1998) 'When (and how) do the Commission's preferences matter?', *Journal of Common Market Studies*, 36 (1): 79–99.

Thatcher, M. (1993) *The Downing Street Years*. HarperCollins, London.

Troy Johnston, M. (1994) *The European Council: Gatekeeper of the EC*. Westview Press, Oxford.

Wessels, W. (1991) 'The EC Council: The Community's decisionmaking center', in S. Hoffmann and R.O. Keohane (eds), *The New European Community: Decision-making and Institutional Change*. Westview, Boulder, CO, pp. 133–54.

Wessels, W. (1998). 'Comitology: fusion in action. Politico-administrative trends in the EU system', *Journal of European Public Policy*, 5 (2): 209–34.

Westlake, M. (1998) 'The European Parliament's emerging powers of appointment', *Journal of Common Market Studies*, 36 (3): 431–4.

Web sites

curia.eu.int/	European Court of Justice
eib.eu.int/	European Investment Bank
europa.eu.int/agencies.html	EU agencies and bodies
europa.eu.int/comm/igc2000/index_ en.htm	2000 Intergovernmental Conference
europa.eu.int/comm/commissioners/index_ en.htm	The 20 Commissioners – peoples, portfolios and homepages
europa.eu.int/comm/index_en.htm	European Commission
europa.eu.int/inst_en.htm	Institutions of the EU
ue.eu.int/en/summ.htm	Council of the European Union
ue.eu.int/newsroom/	Council of the European Union newsroom
www.ces.eu.int/	Economic and Social Committee
www.cor.eu.int/	Committee of the Regions
www.eca.eu.int/	Court of Auditors
www.ecb.int/	European Central Bank
www.euro-ombudsman.eu.int/	EU Ombudsman
www.europarl.eu.int/	European Parliament

3 Completing the single market

Introduction

For many years the European Economic Community, established by the Treaty of Rome in 1957, was known in common parlance as 'the Common Market', reflecting both the central core of its activities and popular perception of what the EEC was about. Indeed the EEC was part of the general trend since 1945 to integrate the markets of Western Europe. The process had started in the late 1940s with the economies of the three Benelux states, had progressed with the sectoral approach of the ECSC and had advanced more generally with the negotiations for the Treaty of Rome on the basis of the Spaak Report (see p. 12). By the 1990s, the aim was to create a Single European Market – an internal market – within the European Communities and then the European Union, with the broad intention that goods, services, capital and labour would be able to move as easily between Paris and Rome or Copenhagen and Madrid as they could between Munich and Bremen or Aberdeen and Manchester.

Original plans

The original outline of a common market, including a customs union, can be found in the Treaty of Rome. One view, expressed by Jean Monnet (1978: 440), was that those pressing for European integration used plans for a customs union in order to 'relaunch' the Community idea in autumn 1955, once the scheme for a European Defence Community had failed. Milward (1992: 119) challenges this idea, pointing out that the customs union plans had been well discussed before that date and had merely re-emerged once the question of security had been sorted out on an intergovernmental basis. Neo-mercantalism – trade protectionism – could no longer work soundly at the nation-state level and had to be 'guaranteed by its Europeanization'. It had to have the Federal Republic at its core (*ibid.*: 134).

The Treaty of Rome emphasized the creation of a common market and customs union between the member states. The customs union meant the removal of tariffs and other obstacles to trade between the Six, and the adoption of a common trade policy towards non-members, as expressed through the Common External Tariff (CET) and the Common Agricultural Policy's variable levy on imports (see Chapter 6). While the customs union allowed for the free movement of goods between member states, the common market involved the acceptance of joint rules allowing the free movement of the other factors of production – labour, capital and services.

The customs union was to be established in stages according to the Treaty of Rome, which came into force on 1 January 1958:

- Articles 12 to 17 allowed for the elimination of customs duties between members by stages over a period of four years;
- under Articles 18 to 29 the Six were to establish a common customs tariff by stages with the first one lasting a period of four to five years, and the tariff level was to be calculated as being 'at the level of the arithmetical average of the duties applied in the four customs territories' of the Six (the Benelux states, Italy, the Federal German Republic and France) (Article 19.1 EEC);
- Articles 30 to 37 abolished quantitative restrictions on trade between the member states, required members to convert their quotas open to other member states into 'global quotas without discrimination to all other Member States' (Article 33.1 EEC), and for all six member states to aggregate and increase their global quotas over a period of four years.

Separate arrangements were made for agricultural trade (see Chapter 6).

The customs union and the Common Agricultural Policy were the main building-blocks of the proposed common market. The other elements can also be seen in the Treaty of Rome:

- in principle the free movement of labour, services and capital was established (Part 2, Title III EEC), though the practical details were left to be arranged at a later date;
- likewise a common transport policy was to be established (Part 2, Title IV EEC), though little indication was given of how this might be achieved;
- Part 3, Title 1 of the Treaty set out rules of competition that would ensure fair trade within the customs union: these included the removal of potentially distorting measures such as state aids or subsidies to domestic industries (Articles 92–4 EEC), an end to dumping (Article 91), and cartels and monopolies were to be investigated and prohibited (Articles 85–90);
- member states were to agree on a common commercial policy (Articles 110–16 EEC) that would co-ordinate their trade policy to third countries, leading to a common policy for external trade;
- closer co-ordination was promised in social provision, though the detail was left to be worked out later (Articles 117–22 EEC);

- a European Social Fund (ESF) was to be established to help improve employment opportunities and to raise living standards (Articles 123–8 EEC);
- A European Investment Bank (EIB) was set up in order to encourage the development of the common market and to help the less-developed regions (Articles 129–30 EEC).

Clearly this represented a full range of activities for the new EEC and, as indicated, most of the common market element – apart from the CAP and the customs union – was left to be developed at a later stage. Both the ESF and the EIB were established in the early years of the EEC and acted as springboards for later Community action in the social and regional spheres. The common commercial policy saw the EEC establish itself as a participant in trade negotiations, especially in the General Agreement on Tariffs and Trade (GATT) Dillon and Kennedy Rounds, which ended in agreements in, respectively, 1962 and 1967. Bilateral trade agreements were also signed with such countries as Iran (1963) and Israel (1965).

Although tariff barriers were removed 18 months ahead of time in July 1968, non-tariff barriers proved more stubborn. National protection and preference continued and the free movement of services, labour and capital remained an aspiration. Court cases played their role in overcoming some barriers to the free movement of persons, fiscal harmonization of indirect taxes and excise duties, in such cases as Defrenne v. SABENA, Reyners v. the Belgian state, and Van Gend en Loos (Stirk and Weigall, 1999: 174).

The Commission attempted to harmonize industrial standards throughout the EC through a system whereby, from 1983, new national technical regulations and industrial standards would be scrutinized by the Commission working with the European Standardization Committee.

During the early 1980s, there were changes that encouraged the EC to re-examine the common market elements of the Treaty of Rome and to consider a move towards what became known as the Single European Market (SEM). Right of centre governments, especially in the United Kingdom and Germany, placed an emphasis on the freeing of the market and allowing greater competition. They looked to extend these national policies to the EC. It was also a time when both Japan and the USA were competing more openly in the world market. The EC seemed to have been left behind after the period of 'eurosclerosis' of the 1970s when their economies seemed to be unable to stand up to the younger and fitter American and Asian competitors. A new revived Commission in the 1980s took up the challenge from industry and national governments that the early promises of the Treaty of Rome should be fulfilled. They also saw this as a way of renewing the activities and power of the EC, particularly of the

Commission and the Parliament. The move to a more complete common market brought another issue to the fore – that of a single currency.

The 1985 White Paper and the SEM

The Delors Commission which first came into office in 1985 unveiled a White Paper at the Milan Council in June of that year. This White Paper proposed a legislative programme that would remove many of the barriers to the free working of the common market throughout the EC (Featherstone, 1990). It sought to identify the problem areas within the EC that were forming barriers to this market and to deal with them both through specific EC legislation and also through a new approach known as mutual recognition and equivalence.

To provide evidence of the necessity of their new programme, the Commission supported a major study of the 'costs of non-Europe', in other words, what would be the estimated cost if the single market – as it became known – was not completed. The widely circulated Cecchini Report brought together a range of information which claimed to show that maintaining the barriers to the freedom of movement within the EC of goods, services, labour and capital (the 'four freedoms') would cost more than ECU200bn. It claimed that liberalization of these restrictions would bring a 4.5 per cent benefit to the EC's Gross Domestic Product (Cecchini, 1988; Commission of the European Communities, 1988).

Even before the publication of the Cecchini Report, industry and commerce were warming to the Commission's notion of creating a Single European Market (SEM) by 31 December 1992. Indeed, some writers have emphasized the importance of a coalition between the Commission and transnational business elites in the move to the SEM (Sandholtz and Zysman, 1989: 95–128). Others, such as Moravcsik (1991: 651–88), have placed greater emphasis on governmental acceptance of the plans. Even the British Prime Minister, the eurosceptic Margaret Thatcher, saw the SEM in positive terms. It was 'intended to give real substance to the Treaty of Rome and to revive its liberal, free trade, deregulatory purpose' (Thatcher, 1993: 547).

The 1985 White Paper, drafted by the British Commissioner Lord Cockfield, who had previously been a minister in Mrs Thatcher's government, advanced almost 300 measures that could be taken to eliminate the barriers to the 'four freedoms'. The aim was to remove the *physical*, *technical* and *fiscal* barriers to the single market (Pelkmans and Robson, 1987).

The *physical* barriers were represented by customs controls at the frontiers between EC states and the main costs here were those of delays in journey times leading to extra transport costs as well as the extra administrative burden – the 'red tape'. Cecchini argued that the cost of such barriers was about ECU8bn 'or getting on for 2 per cent' of the total value of intra-EC trade, while 'the turnover companies forgo as a result is at least ECU4.5bn' (1988: 8–9). In 1988 the Single Administrative Document replaced the plethora of import and export documents that existed before within the EC, and its use was later extended to the EFTA countries before it was phased out altogether on 1 January 1993. The Benelux states, Germany and France created the Schengen Agreement in 1985 in order to allow them to abolish border controls between their countries and thereby to facilitate not just the free movement of goods but also that of people. This led to closer co-operation between governments and their agencies on matters such as the movement of illegal aliens, drugs, arms and criminals and Schengen was later extended to include most of the EC states (see Chapter 8).

The reduction of physical barriers brought up the question of the regulation of transport throughout the EC, leading to a deregulation of the road haulage industry and air transport with a series of directives from 1987 to 1992.

Technical barriers to the SEM were removed by the harmonization of technical standards, the liberalization of public procurement and service provision, the resolution of differences in qualifications that hindered the free movement of labour, and by the removal of conflicts in business laws and practices.

Technical standards on an EC-wide basis had previously applied to EC laws covering a wide range of requirements for goods and services, ranging from teddy bears to car exhaust emissions, from additives and preservatives in food to listing the nutritional information on processed food. From 1985 the Commission adopted a more flexible approach. First, they promoted EC standards in the fields of health, safety, protection of workers and the environment through the European Standardization Committee (CEN) and the European Standardization Committee for Electrical Products (Cenelec) (Pelkmans, 1987: 249–69). Second, the 1986 Single European Act introduced changes to the EEC treaty (Articles 100A and 100B EEC) that allowed the approximation of laws to be adopted by the Council by a qualified majority. The Commission was given the task of rounding up before the end of 1992 the national laws that needed harmonizing on the grounds of health and safety. Third, the European Court of Justice's ruling in the Casis de Dijon case in 1979 had broadly meant that standards accepted in one EC country should also be acceptable in other EC states. This mutual recognition saved much bureaucratic effort in trying to find a common denominator in the technical standards of all EC member states.

The mutual recognition of most higher educational qualifications for professions meant the removal of one substantial barrier to the free movement of some labour. The Community in Education and Training for

Technology (Comett) programme led to further academic-practitioner co-operation in information technology.

One highly protected trade sector was that of the tenders and contracts offered by local and central government. Cecchini (1988: 16) estimated that the total purchasing power of the public sector in 1986 was about 15 per cent of the EC's GDP. He thought that liberalization of this sector would lead to the cheapest bid being accepted (and not necessarily from a domestic supplier), to reduced prices as a result of opening up competition, and to the long-term rationalization of this sector (Cecchini, 1988: 17–18). EC directives in this area meant that closed markets such as those in tele-communications, water and energy supplies and transport – which had been liberalized to some extent in the United Kingdom – would be opened up for EC-wide competition, with contracts advertised through the Official Journal of the EC.

The Second Banking Directive of 1989 allowed free operation and establishment throughout the EC for banking and other financial services. Insurance companies, mortgage lenders and other credit institutions were also placed on a EC-wide basis. A number of directives covered the insurance business, harmonizing certain procedures and establishing common rules on, for example, the trans-border sale of life insurance. Cecchini had estimated that the liberalization of the banking sector would result in direct savings of some ECU22bn with an equivalent amount saved should interest rates also be reduced in consequence (Cecchini, 1988: 37–42, 84, 95). These reforms also helped to free the movement of capital within the EC and acted as a catalyst both for moves towards an economic and monetary union and for a tightening of government budgetary controls (Grahl and Teague, 1990; Pinder, 1991: 134).

Attempts to harmonize company law and practice through the draft Fifth Directive on company structure were opposed especially by the British Conservative government because of the Directive's inclusion of worker involvement in the running of companies. Instead the Commission emphasized plans for a European Company Statute – which also ran into opposition and again had to be shelved – and the Thirteenth Directive on takeover bids.

The *fiscal* barriers to the SEM were also tackled. National differences in indirect taxation levels – such as the Value Added Tax (VAT) on sales – and excise duties, the 'sin taxes' mainly on tobacco and alcohol, could severely prejudice those businesses in relatively high-tax areas and encourage smuggling from one tax-zone to another. Proposals to approximate VAT rates – which differed by about 10 per cent for the standard rates throughout EC countries – ran into trouble when governments realized that they might lose useful sources of income and may have to impose or increase the tax on certain goods – such as children's shoes and clothing – which would produce a backlash from voters. An agreement in October 1992 allowed for a standard rate in each member state of 15 per cent or above and with a lower rate to be applied to a list of agreed goods. Luxury rates were abolished. In October 1992 the member states also agreed on the harmonization of excise rates. The abolition of restrictions on cross-border purchases had already been agreed with customs officers being given indications – such as 90 litres of wine – as to what might be accepted as the maximum level that could be transported across an EC frontier for the consumer's own use. However, it was only by mid-1999 that the logical consequence of a single market – the abolition of 'duty free' shopping within the EU – finally took place after a long campaign to retain this 'perk' by airlines, ferries and, of course, the duty-free shops.

Taken as a whole, the legislation passed to achieve the SEM by the end of 1992 represented a frontal assault on the barriers to the 'four freedoms'. By that date, trade restrictions throughout the EC had been decimated; the movement of labour had been eased especially for the professions; capital was able to flow between EC countries without the raft of restrictions experienced previously; and it was easier to offer services such as banking, insurance and advertising on an EC-wide basis. However, the move towards a single market clearly had other consequences. First, it was an engine for political change within the EC, leading directly to the Single European Act and the increase in the use of majority voting in the Council and in the powers of the European Parliament. Second, it increased the pressure for change in other policy areas. The extension of the freedom of movement of labour meant that the member states had to reconsider their co-operation in the area of criminality, immigration and protection of frontiers generally (see Chapter 8). Perhaps most important, the idea of a single internal market implied that it would be as easy to sell a product made in Rome, in Copenhagen or in Edinburgh as it would have been before within Italy. However, this was clearly not the case as long as member states had their own currencies. Selling goods and services across even an EC frontier would incur the extra cost of currency transactions. Thus the pressure increased for Economic and Monetary Union (see Chapter 4).

Completing the internal market

What had been trumpeted to be an auspicious occasion – the inauguration of the SEM from 1 January 1993 – passed by quietly. The optimism of the late 1980s had turned into the uncertainties of 1991 and 1992 with the West European economies dipping into recession and the EC itself falling into the quagmire of Yugoslavia and the extended embarrassment of the ratification of the Maastricht Treaty on European Union. The collapse of the Soviet

Union on Christmas Day 1991 only added to a sense of international confusion.

Nevertheless, '1992' represented quite an achievement. The Council adopted something like 280 directives, sometimes by majority voting and after much disagreement. Most of the White Paper's aims had been turned into Communities' legislation by the end of 1992, although the level of transposition into national legislation remained low – at 85 per cent – at the start. Most of the 'four freedoms' were extended to six of the then seven EFTA members through the European Economic Area as from 1 January 1993 (the electorate of the seventh member, Switzerland, having rejected the agreement in a referendum).

Nevertheless, a number of White Paper proposals remained outstanding, such as the details of a VAT regime, the idea of a European Company Statute and work on intellectual property. Furthermore, much of the legislation was subject to national interpretation, varied transposition rates, a number of derogations and transitional measures. To achieve a truly single market, the EC had to go beyond '1992', and this was just what it did. Apart from the plans for an Economic and Monetary Union, there were other elements of continuation. The Sutherland Report (Commission of the European Communities, 1992) on the operation of the single market after 1992 and the Commission's Strategic Plan for the Internal Market (1993) both identified areas for further progress in achieving the White Paper's aims. The former recommended changes to combat a lack of openness and problems in monitoring legislation. The latter responded by proposing better administrative co-operation, surveillance and information; it also identified measures to accompany the single market such as stronger enforcement of competition, further proposals on transport and intellectual property and the development of Small and Medium-Sized Enterprises (SMEs). There was also a call for the environmental policy and the SEM to act in tandem.

The push towards '1992' was, as mentioned on p. 70, spurred on by the fear of the EC losing its international competitive position. The creation of the SEM – however imperfect – had implications internationally. One example was the transposition of national quotas, kept under the safeguard measures allowed by Article 115 EEC, into a standard EC quota. Under the 1991 EC-Japan agreement, member states phased out their individual voluntary export restraints (VERs) and quantitative restrictions on the import of Japanese cars by 1993 and replaced these with an EC-based VER that would last until 1999.

The GATT Uruguay Round, which was concluded in April 1994, produced changes in the international trading rules that were of importance for the EC's single market externally. The rules on preferential trade agreements were to be standardized, safeguard and anti-dumping actions were to be open to greater multilateral control and technical barriers to trade were to be limited. Market access to services was also included in the agreement and the EU made it clear that it would expect reciprocal treatment for its banking and financial services for non-EU access to that lucrative market. However, the General Agreement in Trade in Services (GATS) by no means solved the problems that had been foreseen over reciprocity (Milner and Allen, 1992).

In order to keep up the momentum of '1992' and to respond to the fears about the human costs of opening up the EC's market at a time when the business cycle seemed to be turning down, the Commission produced a White Paper in 1993 on growth, competitiveness and employment. This interventionist proposal foresaw investments across the EC in telecommunications, transport and energy, and environmental projects of some ECU 574bn by 2000 through a mixture of public and private financing, though member states prevented their financing through a new 'Eurobond' (Redmond, 1995: 56). After the emphasis on the market in the plans for '1992', the White Paper returned to another EC theme, that of solidarity 'between those who have jobs and those who do not ... between generations ... between the more prosperous regions and the poor or struggling regions ... in the fight against exclusion' (Bulletin of the EC, Supplement 6/93: 15).

The White Paper indicated those areas where the single market still had to be achieved and what the EC might do. In particular, this meant activity in *industrial and competition policy*, *commercial policy* and on *the free movement of labour*.

The EC/EU's approach to *industrial and competition policy* in the 1990s was pulled in two different directions. On the one hand, there was the desire that the EC/EU should be active in important industrial sectors (such as information technology, telecommunications and aerospace) and a recognition – as in the 1993 White Paper – that this may need massive investment, with some resources coming from Community funding. On the other hand, there was the drive to create competitive market conditions where particular firms were not favoured by subsidies but had to survive in the open market. The two drives were not necessarily contradictory, but sometimes they were bound to come into conflict.

During 1994 the Commission advanced an industrial competitiveness strategy with the aim of encouraging intangible investment, developing industrial co-operation, enforcing fair competition and modernizing the public authorities (Commission of the European Communities, 1994a), which again reflected the duality of industrial and competition policy. The EU itself had decided that support should be given to trans-European networks (TENs), which represented EU-wide webs of energy supply, transport and telecommunications, and which had received special attention in the Maastricht Treaty (Articles 129b-d TEU, 154–6 TEC). However, early attempts to develop the TENs were dogged by national disagreements over which ones should have priority and over the financing of such EU-wide efforts. By 1999 only three of the original planned 14 priority transport TENs were near completion, with six more expected to be complete by 2005 (Redmond, 1999: 73). The question of TENs financing has popped up again in *Agenda 2000*, the Commission's spending package for the start of the millennium (Galloway, 1999: 15). An area where the EU has given positive support is that of the Small and Medium-Sized Enterprises (SMEs – see p. 75), with the third multi-annual programme covering 1997–2000 and with ECU127m being accepted in November 1996. Another positive development was the acceptance of the notion of 'bench-marking' across industry, to identify and spread the best possible practices.

Article 113 of the TEU (now Article 133 TEC) set out the basis for a *common commercial policy*. Trade agreements and other aspects of the policy were to be negotiated by the Commission on the basis of a mandate set out by the Council. However, what constitutes a trade agreement has been defined in such a way as to exclude services and intellectual property where the EU and the member states share the negotiating responsibility, somewhat blurring the external view of the EU's common commercial policy.

Freer movement of labour should have been assisted when the Schengen Accord came into force in 1994. This should have abolished frontier controls between the 'core' states of France, Germany, the Benelux states, Spain and Portugal. However, almost as soon as it was implemented, France invoked safeguard clauses in order to re-establish frontier controls because of outbreaks of terrorism and the fear of drugs coming in from the Netherlands (see Chapter 8; Redmond, 1996: 45). Later Denmark, Sweden, Finland, Greece and Italy joined, with Norway and Iceland as associates, and the Treaty of Amsterdam brought the arrangement into the Treaty on European Union. The Commission has also advanced its plans to ease the free movement of workers within the EU labour market. These include the adoption of new rules to enhance the rights of job-seekers in a range of areas including residency, pensions, training, taxation and family situation; matching job vacancies and applications across frontiers by greater use of the internet and by co-operation among national employment services; greater involvement of national authorities in ensuring effective freedom of movement; and European Social Fund support for projects encouraging labour mobility (http://europa.eu.int/scadplus/leg/en/lvb/132027.htm).

In June 1997, at the time of the signing of the Treaty of Amsterdam, the Council also agreed on the Commission's Action Plan for the Single European Market. This represented an effort to tidy up those uncompleted parts of the SEM by the beginning of the single currency on 1 January 1999. It involved more effective SEM rules and their better enforcement and implementation; dealing with distortions created by the tax systems and by state aids; removing sectoral obstacles, especially in the service sector and improving the business environment; and delivering the benefits of the SEM to citizens by increased labour mobility, better information and 'an enhanced social dimension' (Redmond, 1998: 52). During 1999 the Commission pursued those states – principally France, Italy, Belgium and Greece – that had not transposed and implemented SEM rules. It simplified SEM legislation with the Simple Legislation for the Internal Market (SLIM) programme; pushed the liberalizing of the telecommunications, postal, and commercial communications (advertising etc.) sectors; set out broad guidelines for simplifying and increasing flexibility in public procurement; and set up a group to report on a more integrated financial services market (Redmond, 1999: 70).

In November 1999 the Commission set out its strategy for the internal market within the EU for the period to 2005 (update on the single market at the internal market and financial services homepage at http://europa.eu.int/comm/dg15/en/index.htm). Its four main objectives were:

- to improve citizens' quality of life by reviewing consumer legislation, improving the recognition of diplomas and professional qualifications and integrating environmental concerns;
- to enhance the efficiency of the EU's product and capital market, especially by completing the internal market for financial services;
- to improve the business environment by helping SMEs and streamlining public procurement policies;
- to exploit the achievements of the internal market in the world, especially by including representatives of the candidate states in the Commission's work.

A programme was accepted at the Lisbon European Council in March 2000 with the agreed strategic goal 'to strengthen employment, economic reform and social cohesion as part of a knowledge-based economy' (Presidency Conclusions, Lisbon European Council at http://ue.eu.int/en/info/eurocouncil/index.htm). The European Council also asked the Commission, the Council and the member states to set out by the end of 2000 'a strategy for the removal of barriers to services', in order to speed up liberalization of the utilities and to update public procurement rules (*ibid*.: point 17).

What remains to be done

From their beginnings in the Treaty of Rome, the plans for the internal market have largely been implemented. The European Union represents a single market – of sorts. There are still shortcomings, some of which have

been identified above. Some of the legislation has not been fully implemented. Other areas – such as utilities and public procurement – have
proved hard nuts to crack. Efforts at EU-wide action in the form of TENs or
the services side of the Common Commercial Policy have been resisted by
member states. Labour mobility is low compared with that of the United
States. Languages and cultures are themselves barriers to a single market,
although new technologies are overcoming these at a rapid pace.

Three important factors will affect the single market of the EU in the
twenty-first century. First, any enlargement of the EU will eventually have to
mean the extension of the SEM. However, most of the candidate members
are not as ready for the full force of the wind of competition provided by the
SEM, as the last group of states that joined the EU, the three EFTA
countries. Second, the activities of the World Trade Organization will
increasingly impinge on the EU (see Chapter 11). In order to do business in
the North American and Asian markets, the EU will have to adapt its own
rules and regulations to those of the WTO and will be part of the negotiating
process that agrees those rules. Finally, the main barrier to a truly EU-wide
market has always been the lack of a single currency. It is the efforts to
create such a currency, and the concomitant economic and currency union,
that will be covered in the following chapter.

References and further reading

Bulletin of the EC, Supplement 6/93, *White Paper on Growth, Competitiveness,
Employment, COM (93) 700*. Office for Official Publications of the European
Communities, Luxembourg.

Cecchini, P. (1988) *The European Challenge: 1992, The Benefits of a Single Market*.
Gower and the Commission of the EC, Aldershot.

Commission of the European Communities (1988) *Research on the 'Cost of Non-
Europe'. Volume 1 Basic Studies: Executive Summaries*. Office for Official
Publications of the European Communities, Luxembourg.

Commission of the European Communities (1992) *High Level Group on the
Operation of the Internal Market: The Internal Market after 1992. Meeting the
Challenge: Report to the EEC Commission*. Commission of the European
Communities, Brussels.

Commission of the European Communities (1994a) *An Industrial Competitiveness
Policy for the European Union, COM (94) 319*. Office for Official Publications
of the European Communities, Luxembourg.

Commission of the European Communities (1994b) *The Community Internal
Market*. Office for Official Publications of the European Communities,
Luxembourg.

Featherstone, K. (1990) *European Internal Market Policy*. Routledge, London.

Galloway, D. (1999) 'Agenda 2000: packaging the deal', in G. Edwards and G.
Wiessala (eds), *The European Union Annual Review 1998–1999*. Blackwell,
Oxford, pp. 9–35.

Grahl, J. and Teague, P. (1990) *1992: The Big Market*. Lawrence and Wishart, London.

Milner, C. and Allen, D. (1992) 'The external implications of 1992,' in D. Swann (ed.), *The Single European Market and Beyond: A Study of the Wider Implications of the SEA*. Routledge, London.

Milward, A.S. (1992) *The European Rescue of the Nation-State*. Routledge, London.

Monnet, J. (1978) *Memoirs*. Collins, London.

Moravcsik, A. (1991) 'Negotiating the Single European Act: national interest and conventional statecraft in the EC,' *International Organization*, 45 (1): 651–88.

Pelkmans, J. (1987) 'The new approach to technical harmonization and standardization', *Journal of Common Market Studies*, 25 (3): 249–69.

Pelkmans, J. and Robson, P. (1987) 'The aspirations of the White Paper,' *Journal of Common Market Studies*, 25 (3): 181–92.

Pinder, J. (1991) *European Community: The Building of a Union*, Oxford University Press, Oxford.

Redmond, J. (1995) 'Internal policy developments,' in N. Nugent (ed.), *The European Union 1994: Annual Review of Activities*. Blackwell, Oxford, pp. 51–62.

Redmond, J. (1996) 'Internal policy developments,' in N. Nugent (ed.), *The European Union 1995: Annual Review of Activities*. Blackwell, Oxford, pp. 43–62.

Redmond, J. (1998) 'Internal policy developments,' in G. Edwards and G. Wiessala (eds), *The European Union 1997: Annual Review of Activities*. Blackwell, Oxford, pp. 51–68.

Redmond, J. (1999) 'Internal policy developments,' in G. Edwards and G. Wiessala (eds), *The European Union: Annual Review 1998–1999*. Blackwell, Oxford, pp. 69–85.

Sandholtz, W. and Zysman, J. (1989) '1992: recasting the European bargain;' *World Politics*, 42 (1): 95–128.

Stirk, P.M.R. and Weigall, D. (eds) (1999) *The Origins and Development of European Integration: A Reader and Commentary*. Pinter, London and New York.

Thatcher, M. (1993) *The Downing Street Years*. HarperCollins, London.

Web sites

europa.eu.int/comm/internal_market/en/index.htm	Internal Market homepage
europa.eu.int/pol/singl/index_en.htm	EU Internal Market
europa.eu.int/scadplus/leg/en/lvb/160016.htm	European Social Fund
ue.eu.int/en/info/eurocouncil/index.htm	European Council

4 Economic and monetary union

Introduction

The previous chapter described how the EU has tried to create a single market among its members that would allow goods and services (the ends of economic production) as well as labour and capital (two of the main factors of production) to flow without any national let or hindrance. This would form one aspect of economic union – the single internal market side – but other policies would be needed in order to complete such a union. These would involve common rules on government intervention on economic matters and common budgetary authority and resources.

Monetary union is achieved when national currencies and exchange rates are permanently fixed, or replaced by a single currency, and when common financial and monetary regulations, devoid of national restrictions, and common institutions are in place. While creating a common market was a significant aim of the Treaty of Rome, economic and monetary union, as outlined above, was not part of those stated aims. However, there were sections of the 1957 Treaty that emphasized the desirability of co-ordinating national economic policies (Article 103 EEC). The need was stressed for member states to pursue economic policies that would 'ensure the equilibrium of the balance of payments' and to maintain confidence in the currencies while keeping a high level of employment and stable prices (Article 104 EEC). During the first dozen years of the EEC's existence, little more was done to co-ordinate economic policy except for meetings of the Governors of Central Banks and a Short-term Economic Policy Committee. Member states devalued and revalued their currencies for national purposes, often with sparse concern for the effects on their fellow EEC members.

Since the end of the 1960s, there have been three major attempts to move to EMU within the EC/EU, the first being in 1971, the next in 1978 and the most recent culminating in the establishment of the euro-zone on 1 January 1999. This last effort has been described by the Vice-President of the European Central Bank as 'the greatest achievement in modern European economic history' (Christian Noyer, January 2000, at the ECB's key speeches' web site), while one commentator has remarked that it could bring the EU and the USA closer to war (Feldstein, 1997).

Early moves

The Hague Summit in December 1969 is famous for opening the Communities' door to British membership. Point 8 of the Heads of State or Government communiqué contained another important aspiration – that of working out a plan in 1970 'with a view to the creation of an economic and monetary union' (cited in Stirk and Weigall, 1999: 228). The Council accepted the resulting report in October 1970 by the Luxembourg Prime Minister, Pierre Werner, and in a modified form in 1971. The Werner Report on Economic and Monetary Union (Stirk and Weigall, 1999: 229–30) made four main points about EMU:

- EMU would be achievable by the end of the 1970s if the member states had the political will;
- EMU would lead to main economic policy decisions being taken at the Community level, having been transferred from the national level, meaning a major shift in responsibilities with the creation of new institutions within the EC; thus EMU would act as a catalyst for the development of political union;
- EMU implied 'the total and irreversible convertibility of currencies', the ending of exchange rate fluctuations, the fixing of currency parity ratios and the free movement of capital; although 'national monetary symbols' could be kept, the adoption of a single currency would 'guarantee the irreversibility of the undertaking';
- in the final stages of EMU, a centre for economic policy-making – responsible to the European Parliament – and an EC system for the central banks would be indispensable.

This was a heady brew for the EC of the Six to face at the same time as the increase in their membership to include the United Kingdom, Ireland, Denmark and Norway.[1] Nevertheless, in adopting the plan, the EC's Council also decided, as a first step, to narrow the permitted margin of fluctuation between their currencies and the US dollar from 0.75 per cent to 0.6 per cent. This restriction in the freedom of movement of the European currencies placed greater pressure on national central banks to intervene sooner than before, should their currency near the new stricter limit.

However, the international economic conditions did not favour such a move. In August 1971, the US dollar, which had been the stable peg for other currencies since 1945, was devalued. The Smithsonian Agreement, reached among the Western states in December 1991, involved a widening of the permitted margin of fluctuation to 2.25 per cent above and below the value of the dollar. The EC's response in early 1972 was to set up a European system of exchange rates within which the gap between their strongest and weakest currencies was to be systematically narrowed. The EC's aim, set down at the Paris October 1972 Summit, was the completion of EMU by not later than the end of 1980. From 1 July 1972 the gap between any two EC currencies was to be limited to 2.25 per cent. The metaphor of the 'snake in the tunnel' was born. The snake was the slim body that encapsulated the new narrow movements of EC currencies against each other. This 'snake' could, however, move up and down against the dollar within the wider confines of the Smithsonian 'tunnel'. This flexible system provided a mixture of stability in currency terms with an ability for central banks to intervene if needed. However, it did require the EC central banks to intervene in order to keep their currencies within the narrow confines of the 'snake' as well as sometimes to adjust the position of the 'snake' within the wider 'tunnel' of international currencies, especially the dollar.

In July 1972 the 'snake' included the currencies of the six member states of the EC plus those of the four states about to join. However, the currency of one of those prospective members – the pound sterling – soon came under speculative attack and was 'floated', with its value being decided by the market. Its subsequent withdrawal from the 'snake' was followed by other EC currencies, especially the Italian lira and the French franc. By 1975 the 'snake in the tunnel' had collapsed and the notion of achieving EMU by the end of the decade disappeared like a mirage in the desert.

What had gone wrong? First, the international conditions were not right for even the most modest attempts at currency co-ordination. The devaluation of the dollar in 1971, the floating of the pound in 1972 and the oil crisis of late 1973 to 1974 were followed by recession in Europe accompanied by inflation and severe strains on a number of currencies.

Second, the Werner Plan had been simple and aspirational. It had not provided a detailed blueprint for EMU but had relied on 'political will'. Nor had it distinguished between the 'economic' and 'monetary' elements. As the West Germans had pointed out during 1972, closer monetary convergence was not possible as long as they enjoyed a low inflation economy while France and Italy endured high inflation.

Third, there was insufficient national political will to move towards EMU during the mid-1970s. The oil crisis caused the EC members to respond not only nationally, but also in ways that often beggared their neighbours.

Finally, the EC itself was hardly ready for such a move. As Werner had foretold, the march towards EMU would have to be accompanied by significant political change within the ranks of the European Communities. This scarcely seemed possible at a time when the EC had just increased its membership and, from 1 January 1973, three new members had to start adapting themselves to life within the EC. Also the EC had to adapt to them, which in the case of the United Kingdom became rather difficult after 1974 when the new Labour government decided that its priority was to renegotiate the terms of British membership.

However, this first Community excursion into monetary union had its uses. The member states learned the lesson that to achieve the ends they had to will the means, and that monetary union should be preceded not just by monetary co-operation but also by economic convergence. The opportunity soon arose for them to apply this new understanding.

The EMS

By the end of the 1970s the international economic climate – although with some ups and downs – had improved from the chaos of the 1971 to 1974 period. The French and German leaders – Giscard d'Estaing and Helmut Schmidt – had similar visions of how the EC might work and these included the provision of a stable economic and monetary framework for their respective economies (Gros and Thygesen, 1992). By 1977 the EC had recovered from the hiatus caused by the British 'renegotiation' and subsequent referendum in 1975, and a former British Chancellor of the Exchequer, Roy Jenkins, took over as President of the Commission. Jenkins advanced the case for monetary union in October 1977 and steered the idea through a divided Commission. The key point was the acceptance of the idea by Chancellor Schmidt of Germany in February 1978, mainly to help buffer Germany against further devaluations of the dollar (Jenkins, 1989: 183).

By the July 1978 Council, governments were in favour of a method of stabilizing the monetary situation and by March 1979 they had agreed on the European Monetary System (EMS). This differed from the 'snake in the tunnel' both in aim and method. The explicit aim of EMU by the end of 1980 was not mentioned; EMS was more a means to create a zone of monetary stability. It consisted of four elements:

- the Exchange Rate Mechanism (ERM);
- the European Currency Unit (ECU);
- the European Monetary Co-operation Fund (EMCF);
- other credit facilities.

Like the 'snake', the ERM provided a parity grid whereby the participating currencies would be bound together. Unlike the 'snake', there was a requirement for all states to intervene if exchange rates within the grid were under pressure, thus supposedly ruling out the unilateral action that had brought down the 'snake in the tunnel'. An innovation was the ECU, representing the value of a weighted basket of participating currencies. The value of the ECU would thus rise and fall as the value of the currencies in the basket changed, but as the rise in some currencies was likely to be matched by a fall in others, it was likely to be fairly stable compared with individual currencies.

The ECU also acted as the denominator within the ERM grid, providing its central rate, against which the divergence of the national currencies could be measured. The room for such divergence was fixed at 2.25 per cent on either side of the central ECU value. However, Italy – and the United Kingdom when it joined in November 1990 – were permitted a much wider 6 per cent movement on either side of parity. Should a currency fluctuate more than 75 per cent of the maximum allowable fluctuation, then the government and central bank of that country were expected to intervene in order to stabilize the currency's movement by intervention in the currency markets, by changing economic and monetary policy and by adjusting the interest rates.

The EMCF was based on the credit system for the 'snake', known as FECOM. The EMCF was a pool for 20 per cent of the gold and dollar reserves of the participating states; in return these countries would receive ECU deposits to settle debts arising from interventions to maintain the exchange rates.

Resource transfers from the stronger EC economies to the weaker ones were seen as vital if the latter were to stay in the ERM; Ireland and Italy made such transfers a precondition of their entry into the system. Thus both short- and medium-term loans were made available to allow states to prevent currency fluctuations.

Currencies were allowed to realign within the ERM and prior to 1992 there were 12 realignments, the last being that of the French franc in 1987. The EMS seemed to provide the necessary buffers for the EC to survive the massive oil price increases of 1979–80 better than expected. Indeed, the system attracted other non-EC states and by 1991 Norway, Finland and Sweden had linked their currencies to the ERM. Inflation rates in the ERM states declined after 1979, as did the differential between those rates. This was mainly because governments in Italy, France and the United Kingdom began to adopt the economic and monetary discipline that had been practised by the Federal Republic of Germany, which had helped provide it with a strong currency. Indeed, the D-mark dominated the system, especially without the presence of the pound sterling before 1990 and a relatively weak French franc. While the German example may have been a good one to follow, the strength of the D-mark tended to spotlight the weakness of other currencies, not least in the minds of speculators.

Exchange controls were still permissible when the EMS was established and these were used by countries that tried to protect their currencies. The free movement of capital had not been achieved as the plans for the single market were put in place during the latter part of the 1980s. The main barriers were market restrictions on capital movement and the lack of one currency within the EC. As one commentator wrote:

> ... the problem will emerge of the contradiction between full trade integration, complete mobility of capital, fixity of exchange rates, and as yet unchallenged national autonomy in the conduct of monetary policy ... the only solution to this contradiction that does not entail the undoing of the common market is to move toward a monetary union. (Padoa-Schioppa, 1988: 383)

It was this expression of the inevitability of spillover from one policy area to the next that led the Jacques Delors Commission, after its success in launching the single market project, to press for fully fledged economic and monetary union, the next step in what has been called 'the Russian doll' strategy (Ross, 1995: 20).[2]

Delors, TEU and EMU

After the Single European Act had been ratified and the SEM was well on its way to implementation, Jacques Delors – President of the Commission since 1985 – revealed the EMU Russian doll (Ross, 1995: 42). In June 1988 at the Hanover Council, he was appointed to chair a committee to report on EMU. Much to the dismay of the British government (see Thatcher, 1993: 740–2), and with reference to the commitment in the SEA to 'enhance the Community's monetary capacity with a view to economic and monetary union' (Article 20), this committee advanced a plan in 1989 that represented a blueprint for the achievement of economic and monetary union in three stages:

1. *Stage I* aimed to have all EC states as full members of the ERM, and for
    - the maximum permissible range of fluctuation for all the participating currencies to be 2.25 per cent;
    - free movement of capital to be achieved by the removal of exchange controls;
    - the Committee of Central Bank Governors to enhance their co-ordination of monetary policy;
    - the European Reserve Fund to be established with 10 per cent of the member states' foreign national reserves, in order to facilitate intervention in the currency market.

Stage I aimed to create a system of discipline for the EMS currencies, increase co-operation of monetary policies and bolster the ECU.

2. *Stage II* allowed for limited intervention within the ERM and for the establishment of the institutions of EMU, most notably the European System of Central Banks (ESCB), which would assume supervision of

national monetary policies. Member states would make sure that their central banks were independent, that is, free from direct political control, and the ESCB would also remain outside political interference. It would manage the ECU's exchange rate in relation to other currencies and would formulate monetary policy and issue ECUs.

3. *Stage III* would see the permanent fixing of exchange rates between the currencies of participating member states, and their replacement by a single currency. A European System of Central Banks would assume control of monetary policy and a European Central Bank would be established.

The Madrid Council of June 1989 adopted the Delors Committee's plan and designated 1 July 1990 as the start date for Stage I of EMU. The Commission outlined the benefits of a full economic and monetary union as follows:

- a single currency, under the conditions outlined in the Delors Committee, would achieve and maintain price stability, reduce speculation about exchange rate fluctuations and would eliminate the transaction cost of having different currencies within the single market; all this would lead to a more efficient economy;
- by using EMU as a way to reduce public debt and interest rates, it would be an effective platform on which to tackle inflation and unemployment;
- the single currency would be a more effective cushion against international economic events and would allow the EC to assume a strong world role in the international economy;
- it would necessitate the addressing of regional divergencies and underdevelopment within the EC by additional means to regional policy. The Commission argued that 'unduly large regional imbalances would pose an economic as well as a political threat to the Union ... the exchange rate can no longer be used by individual member states as a policy instrument to deal with a loss of competitiveness or to adjust to adverse economic shocks' (Commission of the EC, 1990: 25–6).

The Commission also pointed out that as '1992' neared and restraints were removed within the single market, it would become more difficult for the EMS to manage exchange rate fluctuations, especially as capital was allowed to flow more freely within the EC. In such a case, a quick move to one currency seemed more attractive than attempts to maintain the EMS. The Delors Committee's recommendation remained to be translated into hard-and-fast treaty obligation, thus avoiding the voluntary nature of the 'snake in the tunnel' and the EMS. An Inter-governmental Conference (IGC) of the states of the EC was called on this issue and, with the parallel

IGC on political matters, produced the Treaty on European Union (TEU or Maastricht Treaty), agreed in December 1991 and signed in February 1992.

The TEU had the move to EMU at its core. It was covered by a new Title VI (now Title VII) to Part III of the Treaty of Rome (Community Policies), consisting of four chapters (Articles 102a to 109m TEU, Articles 98 to 124 TEC) and a number of protocols, on the establishment of an economic and monetary union, including a single currency.

Article 102a (98 TEC) set out that both member states and the Community 'shall act in accordance with the principle of an open market economy with free competition, favouring an efficient allocation of resources ...'

Article 103 (99 TEC) detailed the responsibilities of the Council to supervise the period of convergence: in 103.1 members are to 'regard their economic policies as a matter of common concern and shall coordinate them within the Council ...', while 102.2 allowed the Council to formulate a draft for the 'broad guidelines of the economic policies' of members, and in 103.3 the Council is to monitor the consistency, with such guidelines, of member states' policies or to see whether they 'risk jeopardizing the proper functioning of economic and monetary union' (Article 103.4 TEU, 99.4 TEC). The Council could, by a qualified majority vote, decide to make its recommendations public. This suggested that all possible pressure would be used to bring recalcitrant members into line, though Article 103a (Article 100 TEC) did allow the Council to decide unanimously to grant financial assistance to a member state 'in difficulties or [which] is seriously threatened with severe difficulties caused by exceptional occurrences beyond its control ...'

Articles 104 to 104b (101–3 TEC) exhorted public institutions to behave prudently in their finances and 104c (104 TEC) stated that member states 'shall avoid excessive government deficits' with the Commission monitoring compliance in terms of a growing deficit as a ratio of Gross Domestic Product (GDP). The Council, acting on a qualified vote on a Commission recommendation, can decide whether a member state has such an excessive deficit. It can make recommendations on how to bring the situation to an end. If these are not implemented, it can then 'decide to give notice' to the member on measures to be taken within a given timeframe for deficit reduction as 'judged necessary by the Council in order to remedy the situation' (Article 104c.9 TEU, 104.9 TEC). If a state still fails to comply, then the Council can decide – by a two-thirds majority of the weighted votes with the member state concerned being excluded from the vote – on any measures to be taken. These include the request to the state to make a deposit with the Community until the Council considers the deficit has been corrected or the imposition of a fine (Article 104c.11 TEU, 104.11 TEC).

Articles 105 to 109 (105–11 TEC) dealt with monetary policy. A key sentence was in Article 105.1 (TEU and TEC), which stated that '(t)he primary objective of the ESCB shall be to maintain price stability'. Without prejudice to this aim the European System of Central Banks, the key institution, was to support the 'general economic policies of the Community' in order to help achieve its objectives. The stress on price stability has to be seen in the context of the late 1980s and 1990–91 when inflation was stoking up and EC members feared a return to the even higher inflation figures of 1973–75, which had destroyed early plans for EMU.

The tasks of the ESCB were set down: it was to define and implement the EU's monetary policy, to conduct foreign exchange operations, to hold and manage the official foreign reserves of member states and to promote the smooth operation of the payments system (Article 105.2 TEU and TEC). In other words it was to act like the controlling authority of a national central bank. The ESCB would be composed of the ECB and the national central banks; it would be governed by the decision-making bodies of the ECB (Article 106 TEU, 107 TEC). The ESCB thus had at its core the European Central Bank (ECB), which was to have 'legal personality' (Article 106.2 TEU, 107.2 TEC), with its decision-making bodies being the Governing Council and the Executive Board. The Governing Council of the ECB was to comprise the members of the Executive Board and the governors of the national central banks. The Executive Board was to have a President, a Vice-President and four other members appointed in common accord by the member states from those with professional standing in monetary and banking matters (Article 109a TEU, 112 TEC). The Governing Council was to adopt guidelines and make decisions according to the requirements of the Treaty, while the Executive Board would implement policy and prepare meetings of the Governing Council. The ECB was to have 'the exclusive right to authorize the issue of banknotes' within the EC (Article 105a TEU, 106 TEC). The ECB was to come into being in the third and final stage of the move to monetary union.

Articles 109e to 109m of the Maastricht Treaty (116–24 TEC) dealt with Stage II, the transitional stage. Member states were supposed to prepare for this stage by making sure that restrictions on capital movements among members were freed and that their economies were converging, especially 'with regard to price stability and sound public finances' (Article 109e.2a TEU, 116.2a TEC). Members were also to adopt more prudential public debt policies, to 'endeavour to avoid excessive government deficits' (Article 109e.4 TEU, 116.4 TEC) and to start the process leading to the independence of their central banks. Also a European Monetary Institute (EMI) was to be established as a forerunner to the ECB during the second stage. Its Managing Council would consist of a President and the governors of the national central banks; it would take over the tasks of the European

Monetary Co-operation Fund, facilitate the use of the ECU, monitor the EMS and co-ordinate between central banks. It would also prepare for the third stage by making ready the instruments and procedures for the third stage and would supervise the preparation of single currency banknotes.

Article 109j (121 TEC) set out the route to Stage III. The Commission and the EMI were to report to the Council on the progress made by member states towards the achievement of EMU during Stage II. This included the central banks' successful moves towards independence, but most importantly contained the four 'convergence criteria', which states had to meet in order to be considered ready for Stage III. These were:

- the achievement of a high degree of price stability with a rate of inflation during the previous year not exceeding that of the three best performing states by more than 1.5 percentage points;
- no excessive budget deficit according to a Council decision, meaning in effect that public debt should be less than 60% of the GDP;
- no movement of the currency outside the margins of the EMS and no unilateral devaluation during the two years before the evaluation;
- nominal long-term interest rates of no more than two percentage points higher than those of the three best performing states in the year before the examination (Article 109j.1 TEU, 120.1 TEC).

The Council, acting by a qualified majority on a Commission proposal, was then to assess whether each state would fulfil the criteria to adopt a single currency and whether a majority of member states would be in that position. The European Council, no later than 31 December 1996, would decide whether a majority of member states had fulfilled the qualification for a single currency, and 'whether it is appropriate for the Community to enter the third stage'. If so, it would set the date for the launch of the third Stage (Article 109j.3 TEU, 121.3 TEC). If a date had not been fixed by the end of 1997, then it would automatically start on 1 January 1999 with whichever states that were deemed to have fulfilled the criteria. Member states that were not deemed ready to adopt the single currency would be designated as 'Member States with a derogation' and these states would not have voting rights in the ESCB or ECB or in certain Council decisions (Article 109k TEU, 122 TEC). The member states without a derogation – those to be part of the single currency – would then activate the ESCB and appoint the ECB ready to work from the first day of Stage III. On that day the ECB and ESCB would take over from the EMI and the conversion rates for the participating currencies would be fixed against the single currency (the ECU, renamed the euro), which would become a currency in its own right. The Council could decide at a later date whether states with derogation could join the single currency and at what rate their currency would be fixed against the euro.

To complicate the question of participation in the single currency one protocol allowed the United Kingdom to stay out of Stage III, unless it notified the Council that it wished to join. Another protocol recognized that the holding of a referendum on the issue in Denmark meant that it could postpone any move to Stage III.

The Maastricht Treaty thus provided a balance between having strict qualifications for the move to a single currency and full monetary union, and the need to press ahead with such a union without the possibility of a reverse, as had happened with 'the snake in the tunnel'. The four convergence criteria were used to make sure that the single currency would not be the excuse for a spending spree on behalf of some members who would then expect others to pick up the bill. They spread to the EU the tight monetary policy exercised in Germany by its central bank, the Bundesbank. However, although these criteria seemed objective, the decision as to whether a state was deemed ready for the single currency was left with the Council, and was thus a political issue open to being affected by non-economic factors.

The whole arrangement meant that the EU would be divided into four possible groups by the move to a single currency (see Table 4.1): those states that were willing to join the currency from the start, and those that were able to do so. It was hoped that the willing and able would be a majority of EU members.

Table 4.1 *Examples of possible single currency membership, 1998*

	Willing	Not willing
Able	Germany	UK
Not able	Greece	Sweden

The euro and beyond

After the signing of the Maastricht Treaty – during 1992 and 1993 – the EMS was severely tested. In September 1992 the Finnish markka and the Swedish krona came under speculative attack and the Italian lira was devalued by 7 per cent, representing the first major realignment of EMS currencies since 1987. Speculators started to sell the pound, which led to its suspension from ERM membership together with the lira; by November 1992 a number of EMS members had re-introduced exchange controls and the Spanish and Portuguese currencies had been devalued. In January 1993 the Irish punt was devalued and in May 1993 it was the turn of the Danish krone and the French franc to face speculative pressure. By August 1993 the ERM was in a state of collapse but this was prevented by the adoption of 15 per cent fluctuation bands for all members, in effect allowing the currencies to find their own market level. All this occurred at a time when the Maastricht Treaty was facing severe difficulties in the ratification process and the progress of European integration was being challenged not just internally within the member states but also in the EC's inability to deal with the crisis in Yugoslavia.

One response to this Euro-depression was the claim that a single currency was needed more than ever as confidence in the half-measure represented by the EMS had been shaken. A Danish commentator (Thygesen, 1994: 25) wrote that 'the political microeconomic benefits of a common currency stand out more clearly now than in the heyday of confidence in a stable EMS in which many of those benefits could be claimed to have been already largely achieved'. It seemed unlikely that many of the EU members would be able to meet the convergence criteria in time. The recession of the early 1990s had increased government borrowing requirements and many of the currencies had devalued. The EMI reported that by the end of 1993 only Luxembourg and Ireland had fulfilled all four criteria, with some member states scarcely scoring on one.

With the ratification of the Maastricht Treaty, the Cohesion Fund came into existence (see Chapter 7) and the poorer countries of Spain, Portugal, Greece and Ireland were to benefit provided they stayed within budgetary limits. However, there was doubt whether this would bring about fundamental economic convergence (Scott, 1993). It seemed that the EU might be stuck at Stage II on the road to monetary union.

The general economic situation started to improve from 1994 onwards and in 1995 three new – and relatively rich – states joined the EU, with two of them, Austria and Finland, expressing a wish to be considered for participation in the single currency and to join the ERM. By the time the Council made its evaluation in 1998 of the member states' capacity to sustain monetary union, only Greece was deemed to be unable to join, though the United Kingdom, Denmark and Sweden maintained their unwillingness to participate from the beginning. The other states' economies were showing a high degree of convergence. A number of states deemed fit for Stage III of monetary union had public debts of over 60 per cent of their GDP and were only accepted because this debt was being reduced.

The move to the single currency went ahead on 1 January 1999 with 11 of the 15 EU states,[3] and with the ESCB assuming control over interest rates and exchange rate policy for those 11 states. By the beginning of 2002 participating national currencies would be phased out and replaced by the euro.[4] The ESCB and ECB replaced the EMI with the head of the EMI, Wim Duisenberg, becoming the first President of the European Central Bank. He is expected to retire halfway through his eight-year term of office in order to make way for Jean-Claude Trichet, the Governor of the Bank of France. The 11 states in 'Euroland' started to meet as the 'euro–11' before meetings of the 15 EU finance ministers (ECOFIN), much to the annoyance of the British.

In moving to Stage III, EU politicians were faced with achieving monetary union without tackling the need for greater macroeconomic policy co-ordination. Theo Waigel, the German Finance Minister, advanced the idea of a Growth and Stability Pact to supplement the Maastricht criteria, and this was accepted by the other EU states in June 1997. It was made clear that support would not be given to states that borrowed too much. Members should have balanced budgets and prudent fiscal policies, with non-compliance being met with the prospect of sanctions such as fines for states with deficits over 3 per cent but without special circumstances (Redmond, 1997: 56–7). Just before the third stage started, the 11 participating states agreed the 'Waigel declaration', by which

- they were committed to pursue budgetary balance as in the past;
- the Growth and Stability Pact was confirmed;
- the need to convert growth into employment was stressed;
- the need for structural reforms in both the labour and capital markets was emphasized, with special reference to more effective training and entrepreneurship and increased tax efficiency (Redmond, 1999: 72).

However, '(c)o-ordination between monetary and fiscal policy in Euroland is likely to be a problem for some time to come' (Buiter, 1999: 204). As Buiter points out, balancing monetary and fiscal policy is not easy even when there is a single fiscal authority (*ibid*: 205).

The United Kingdom in Euroland?

Membership of the single currency was a politically divisive issue for the British Conservative government of John Major from 1991 to 1997. Many cabinet ministers, including the then Chancellor of the Exchequer Kenneth Clarke, were sympathetic to the arguments for membership, but most of the Conservative members of parliament and voters were opposed.

After Tony Blair's Labour government came to power in May 1997, he quickly announced that the Bank of England would be made independent, thereby fulfilling one of the pre-conditions for adhesion to the single currency. He also said that a final decision on British membership would be made after a referendum on the issue. Meanwhile it seemed that the government was at least preparing for the eventuality of membership based on five economic tests (Gordon Brown, the British Chancellor of the Exchequer at www.euro.gov.uk in October 1997):

1. cyclical convergence: whether the British and Euroland business cycles were compatible;
2. flexibility to deal with problems arising;
3. investment: whether EMU would produce better conditions for investment in the United Kingdom;
4. financial services: the possible effects on British financial services;
5. employment and growth: whether membership would favour high growth, stability and a lasting increase in jobs.

The arguments for British membership can be placed under the following headings (see Zestos and New Europe web sites):

- There are substantial transaction costs savings to be gained by being part of the single currency as there would no longer be the expense of exchange from one currency to another. This is of particular importance for the United Kingdom if many of its competitors are already part of the single currency and no longer have to bear transaction costs.
- There would be a reduction in the uncertainty over the exchange rate. As could be seen from the British experience on 'Black Wednesday' in September 1992, when Britain fell out of the ERM, speculators can rock the pound sterling. As the euro has a larger reserve behind it, it is less likely be vulnerable to predatory speculators.
- Interest rates can be reduced because of the stability of the currency and the commitment to stable prices. Taylor (1995) estimated that the effect of the creation of the euro could be equivalent to a reduction of the average real interest rates of 1 to 1.5 per cent, and certainly the ECB managed to keep the rate for 'Euroland' well below that experienced in the United Kingdom. Also gold and foreign reserves could be reduced.
- Foreign investment and business confidence would increase. As long as the United Kingdom remained outside the euro, investors and business would have doubts about the long-term health of its economy. This is especially important as the UK receives about 17 per cent of the OECD's foreign direct investment, second only to the United States.

The points against membership reflect – and try to refute – those made above:

- It is a permanent experiment and there has never been an economic and monetary union that has lasted without political union. As the former Chancellor of the Exchequer, Nigel Lawson, said before he came to office: '... economic and monetary union implies nothing less than European government – albeit a federal one – and political union: the United States of Europe' (cited in Thatcher, 1993: 691).
- Even without a move to federal government, such an organization represents a severe curtailment of effective state sovereignty, insofar as it

takes from the hands of national governments the control of the currency used in their own country.

- There is a lack of true convergence between the economy of the UK and those of Euroland. Indeed, as shown above, some of those in Euroland could not even meet the rather artificial criteria created in the Maastricht Treaty.
- There is a lack of economic shock absorbers, especially as the Stability and Growth Pact has limited the budget deficit increase to below 3 per cent. The main method left to control the economy will be financing from the centre or from unemployment.
- In the future, unfunded pension liabilities in Germany, Italy and the Netherlands, in particular, will be unfairly funded by British taxpayers if the UK joins the euro. These liabilities will be 10 per cent of GDP in the UK by 2040, but 110 per cent of GDP in Germany.
- The conversion costs could be sizeable: it would mean scrapping the pound and changing all pricing to the euro.

These arguments – and many others – are bound to reverberate in the UK's debate about joining the euro. In the end, the decision will be a political one taken most likely on political grounds, rather than on cool economic calculations. However, it can be said that the move to monetary union and the euro was in itself undertaken for mainly political motives.

Notes

1 Norway, after an adverse referendum result in September 1972, stayed out of the EC.
2 One of the Delors team revealed the strategy to Ross: ' "You take the first doll apart," he said, "and then, inside it is another one, which leads to another and so on . . . until it is too late to turn back." ' (Ross, 1995: 39). For other views of the foundation of EMU see Youngs, 1999: 299–300.
3 The 11 were Austria, Belgium, Finland, France, Germany, Ireland, Italy, Luxembourg, the Netherlands, Portugal and Spain. Greece is to join from 1 January 2001. The Danish electorate rejected the adoption of the euro in a referendum on 28 September 2000.
4 The euro (€) replaced the ECU from 1 January 1999.

References and further reading

Buiter, W. (1999) 'Alice in Euroland', *Journal of Common Market Studies*, 37 (2): 181–209.
Calleo, D.P. (1999) 'The strategic implications of the euro,' *Survival*, 41 (1): 5–19.
Commission of the European Communities (1990) *Communication of the Commission on Economic and Monetary Union*. Office for Official Publications of the European Communities, Luxembourg.

Duff, A. (ed.) (1998) *Understanding the Euro*. Federal Trust, London.

Feldstein, M. (1997) 'The political economy of the European Economic and Monetary Union: political sources of an economic liability', *NBER Working Paper*, No. 6150.

Gros, D. and Thygesen, N. (1992) *European Monetary Integration: From the EMS to the EMU*. Longman, Harlow.

Jenkins, R. (1989) *European Diary 1977–1981*. Collins, London.

Padoa-Schioppa, T. (1988) 'The EMS: a long term view', in F. Giavazzi, S. Micossi and M. Miller (eds), *The European Monetary System*. Cambridge University Press, Cambridge.

Redmond, J. (1997) 'Internal Policy Developments', in N. Nugent (ed.), *The European Union 1995: Annual Review of Activities*. Blackwell, Oxford, pp. 53–71.

Redmond, J. (1999) 'Internal policy developments', in G. Edwards and G. Wiessala (eds), *The European Union: Annual Review 1998–1999*. Blackwell, Oxford, pp. 69–85.

Ross, G. (1995) *Jacques Delors and European Integration*. Polity Press, Cambridge.

Sandholtz, W. (1993) 'Choosing Union: monetary politics and Maastricht,' *International Organization*, **47** (1): 1–39.

Scott, A. (1993) 'Financing the Community: the Delors II package', in J. Lodge (ed.), *The EC and the Challenge of the Future*, 2nd edn. Pinter, London.

Shackleton, M. (1993) 'The Delors II Budget package', *Annual Review of EC Activities 1992*, 11–25.

Stirk, P.M.R. and Weigall, D. (eds) (1999) *The Origins and Development of European Integration: A Reader and Commentary*. Pinter, London and New York.

Taylor, C. (1995) 'EMU 2000? Some questions and answers,' *RIIA Briefing Paper No. 22*, Royal Institute of International Affairs, London.

Thatcher, M. (1993) *The Downing Street Years*. HarperCollins, London.

Thygesen, N. (1994) 'Why economic and monetary union is an important objective for Europe', *SAIS Review*, **14** (1): 17–34.

Weale, M. (1999) 'Monetary and fiscal policy in Euroland', *Journal of Common Market Studies*, **37** (1): 153–62.

Youngs, R. (1999) 'The politics of the single currency: learning the lessons of Maastricht', *Journal of Common Market Studies*, **37** (2): 295–316.

Web sites

www.cnu.edu/academics/busn/busn/ bber/union.htm	Zestos, G. Towards a European Monetary Union
www.ecb.int	European Central Bank
www.ecb.int/key/key.htm	European Central Bank: key speeches
www.euro.gov.uk	UK Treasury's euro page
www.new-europe.co.uk	Pro-Eu, anti-euro New Europe group
www.pitt.edu/ ~ wwwes/emu/guide.html	University of Pittsburgh virtual library EMU
www.sysmod.com/eurofaq.htm	EMU: euro FAQs

5 The social dimension

Introduction

The economic side of the EU has never been run on the basis of a crude unrestricted free market. The Common Agricultural Policy (see Chapter 6) is proof enough of that. While the aim has been to tear down restrictions on the markets that are nation-based, some of these have been replaced by market constraints at the EU level. It has also been the intention of those involved in the EC and the EU that the organizations' actions should reflect the aspect of European capitalism that emphasizes less the needs of the market and more the needs of the workers and citizens. As economic activity has become more regulated at EU level, so the effort has grown to create a body of EU legislation and action in the area of social welfare. The social dimension can be seen as part of the 'spillover' process in the creation of the European Union – as the 'Russian dolls' of the single market and EMU were exposed, so the necessity of having a social dimension became clear. However, this interpretation assumes voices within the EC/EU and within the member states that were willing to speak out for such policies at the Communities' level. Whilst such advocates have been strong, among Christian Democrat as well as the centre-left political parties, there has not always been unanimity as to the extent of EC/EU involvement in social policy.

The EC competence

The original Six EEC states had different social policies and there was little incentive for this aspect of policy to be included in the Treaty of Rome. However, the French government, which prided itself on its social provision, realized that the creation of a Common Market could be undermined if one country had a weaker national provision for welfare. This would mean a lesser burden in the form of taxation on industry and commerce to pay for such policies (Milward, 1992: 210–13). There would, therefore, be some need to address social policy, but that did not seem a priority in the negotiations leading to the Rome Treaty, where the French and German leaders did not allow such considerations to block a political agreement (*ibid.*: 214–15).

The Treaty of Rome included a number of social issues, mainly related to employment and the workplace; Title III of Part Three (Policy of the Community, now Title VIII) was entitled 'Social Policy'. Outcomes of the main points covered were that:

- the need 'to promote improved working conditions and an improved standard of living for workers' was agreed, and this was to be achieved by the functioning of the common market 'which will favour the harmonisation of social systems', by the Treaty itself and by the approximation of provisions (Article 117 EEC, 136 TEC);
- co-operation in the social field was to relate to employment, labour law and work conditions, vocational training, social security, prevention of occupational accidents and diseases, occupational hygiene, and the right of association (forming trade unions) and collective bargaining (Article 118 EEC, 137 TEC);
- the principle that men and women should receive equal pay for equal work was accepted (Article 119 EEC, 141 TEC);
- social security for migrant workers was a matter for common concern (Articles 51 and 121 EEC, 42 and 144 TEC);
- the European Social Fund was established with the task of 'rendering the employment of workers easier and of increasing their geographical and occupational mobility' within the EC (Article 123 EEC, 146 TEC).

The social provisions covered by the Treaty were tied closely to the prime aim of the EEC, economic integration: 'Social policy was essentially ancillary and corrective: its aim was to render more acceptable the occasionally harsh realities of market forces' (Moxon-Browne, 1993: 152). The other two Communities – Coal and Steel and Atomic Energy – also sought to improve the working and living conditions of employees in those industries, the former by supporting retraining and conversion projects as the European coal and steel industries faced decline, and the latter by addressing health and safety issues in the nuclear energy industry.

The Paris Summit of December 1972, in the lead-up to the first enlargement of membership, instigated a series of Social Action Programmes, the first of which was adopted in 1974. This was a response to the consequences of the slowing of economic growth in the early 1970s, as well as a partial fulfilment of the Treaty promises outlined above. The Social Action Programme covered a four-year period and aimed at providing more employment, improved living and working conditions, and increased participation by both sides of industry in EC decision-making. The Programmes centred on rigidities in the nature of the labour market and on unemployment. The first Programme extended the role of the ESF and created the Centre for the Development of Vocational Training, based in Berlin, and the European Foundation for the Improvement of Living and Working Conditions with its headquarters in Dublin (http://europa.eu.int/agencies.html).

The 1974 Social Action Programme was limited in its impact for a number of reasons. It was a non-binding Resolution; national governments and nationally based trade unions and management tended to resort to national measures when faced with the difficult social conditions of the 1970s in the wake of the 1973–74 oil price increases and dip in world economic growth. The Programme also depended on unanimity for acceptance of its legislative proposals in the Council, and thus tended to reflect the lowest common denominator rather than a strong Community programme (Wise and Gibb, 1993).

The SEA and social policy

With the relaunching of the EC project in the negotiations for the Single European Act during 1985–86, the creation of a single market by the end of 1992 was to be the core element. However, there was a realization that, in order to achieve this, institutional reform of the EC organizations would be required and that an economic market by itself was not enough. Other aspects needed to be addressed, not least the social implications of the freedoms of movement of goods, services, labour and capital. The SEA thus altered Title III of Part Three in the Rome Treaty, to strengthen the EC's standing in social matters:

- New Article 118a (138 TEC) committed member states to encourage improvements in the working environment 'as regards health and safety of workers', and the Council, using qualified majority voting, would adopt 'minimum requirements for gradual implementation' but would avoid imposing 'administrative, financial and legal constraints' that may hold back small and medium-sized undertakings, although any member states could introduce more stringent measures provided they were compatible with the Treaty.
- New Article 118b (139 TEC) exhorted the Commission to develop 'the dialogue between management and labour' (known as the social partners) at the EC level, which built on the more informal 'Val Duchesse' meetings of these partners, encouraged by the French presidency in 1985 to assist in achieving agreement in single market and technology legislation affecting both sides of industry.

The SEA also introduced a new section, Title V (now Title XVII), on Economic and Social Cohesion into the Treaty, reflecting, among other factors, the extension of membership of the EC to Greece in 1981 and to Spain and Portugal in 1986. The main points were that

- The EC should pursue action that strengthened 'its economic and social cohesion', in particular, 'reducing disparities between the various regions and the backwardness of the least-favoured regions' (Article 130a, 158 TEC).
- Economic and social cohesion would be pursued through the economic policies of the member states; the implementation of common policies and of the internal market; and by action taken through the structural funds, the European Investment Bank and other financial instruments (see Chapter 7).
- The European Regional Development Fund was to help in the structural adjustment of those regions lagging behind or where declining industries were being converted (Article 130c, 160 TEC).
- After the SEA came into force, the system of structural funds would be examined with reform in mind (Article 130d, 161 TEC).

The SEA brought in greater use of qualified majority voting in the Council, as well as the co-operation procedure, which allowed certain legislation to be fashioned by the Council and the Parliament (see Chapter 2). Over half of the '1992' legislation was covered by this procedure, as were both Article 118a (138 TEC) on health and safety at work and Article 130e (162 TEC) on decisions in the structural funds. This allowed greater parliamentary involvement in this social aspect of '1992' and at one stage in 1990 the Socialist group in the European Parliament threatened to hold up single market legislation unless progress was made on the social policy aspect (Grant, 1994: 85).

After the ratification of the SEA, the Commissioner for Social Affairs, Manuel Marin, outlined how the 'social dimension of the internal market' could be achieved. His 1988 report touched on the improvement of the free movement of labour by mutual recognition of qualifications and by the removal of discriminatory practices, the promotion of cohesion through programmes against poverty and an assistance to the handicapped. It also covered the reform of the structural funds, and employment and retraining measures with special projects for women, the long-term unemployed and for small enterprises. Training for the new technologies was encouraged through industry-university transnational cooperation (Comett scheme), the mobility of university students through the Erasmus programme and language training through Lingua. Changes were made in the structural funds to accommodate greater social element (see Chapter 7). However, the most contentious element in this new activity was the improvement of living and working conditions and the enhancement of the social dialogue through a social charter.

One of the origins of the idea of a social charter was the fear of Jacques Delors that the single market programme was becoming 'a mere cornucopia for capitalists' (Grant, 1994: 83). There was a concern that '1992' might lead to the phenomenon of social dumping, which meant that firms would choose to position their factories in those countries with poor social conditions, low wages and worker protection and thus low labour costs. Tackling social issues through the EC was, according to George Ross (1995: 43), Delors' 'Russian doll III' (the single market and the plans for EMU being the two other larger Russian dolls). On election to the Commission Presidency in 1985, he had turned to the three major Brussels organizations that represented the world of work throughout the EC – UNICE, the employers' confederation, ETUC, the European Trade Union Confederation and CEP, for the public sector – and asked them to work together to improve working conditions. With the move towards '1992', Delors and his Commission placed the emphasis on social legislation and in June 1989 presented the Madrid Council with a Social Charter. Ministers watered this down in the hope that when it was adopted at Strasbourg in December 1988, the United Kingdom would also subscribe to it. Despite references to working hours and minimum wages being cut from the text, the British government considered the charter unnecessary and even a way of 'introducing the Delors brand of socialism by the back door' in the words of Mrs Thatcher, then British Prime Minister (Thatcher, 1993: 751).

The 11 states that subscribed to the Charter, which was a 'Solemn Declaration', agreed to 30 rather general statements of the type that 'all employment shall be fairly remunerated' and that 'social consensus is an essential condition for ensuring sustained economic development'. This list included items covering

- health and safety at work;
- protection of children and the young;
- the rights of the disabled and the elderly;
- equal treatment for men and women;
- information, consultation and participation of workers;
- vocational training;
- freedom of association and collective bargaining;
- freedom of movement, employment and pay;
- the improvement of living and working conditions (Commission of the European Communities, 1989, President's Conclusions: 1.1.10).

The Commission advanced over 40 various pieces of legislation in the Action Programme arising from the Charter. The strongest line was taken in the areas of work conditions, freedom of movement, worker involvement, equal treatment of the sexes and health and safety issues, whereas non-binding recommendations and opinions were used in issues of wider social policy (Ross, 1995: 44).

In the period leading up to the ratification of the Maastricht Treaty, the EC made patchy progress on social issues. Little progress was reported in the area of living and working conditions for workers, with the European Parliament rejecting the Commission's proposal. In 1993 the Working Time Directive on minimum rest periods at work, shift work conditions, night work and health and safety was adopted under Article 118a EEC (health and safety) with the United Kingdom abstaining because it thought that such legislation was more about employment than health and safety. A controversial directive on the protection of young workers made slow progress through the institutions, with the fear being expressed that it would suppress traditional jobs for youngsters (such as newspaper delivery in the United Kingdom). A directive on establishing works councils was postponed until the Maastricht Treaty came into force. A European Agency on Health, Safety and Hygiene was agreed in principle and the Helios II Action Programme for the disabled was agreed (Commission of the European Communities, 1993).

Social policy in the Maastricht Treaty

Given the widespread acceptance of the Social Charter throughout the EC and the way that Delors had tied it to the single market and EMU, it seemed logical that the Treaty on European Union would have a 'Social Chapter' in it. However, the Conservative government in the United Kingdom refused to countenance such a move and this 'Chapter' was banished to a protocol that contained an Agreement on Social Policy by 11 countries (the EU membership minus the United Kingdom). Decisions based on this protocol could not bind the United Kingdom, but, although EU procedures and institutions were still used, the British were excluded from the decision-making process. What still became known as the Social Chapter had as its objectives:

> promotion of employment, improved living and working conditions, proper social protection, dialogue between management and labour, the development of human resources with a view to lasting high employment and the combating of exclusion. (Article 1 of Agreement)

To achieve these aims, it was agreed in Article 2 that the EU would 'support and complement the activities of the Member States' in the following:

- protection of workers' health and safety by improvement in the work environment;
- work conditions;
- information and consultation of workers;

- equal labour market opportunities and treatment at work for men and women;
- the integration of persons excluded from the labour market.

The Council was to adopt minimum requirements on these points, using the co-operation procedure (Article 189c TEU), and was to avoid extra burdens on small and medium-sized undertakings. However, the Council had to act unanimously in the following areas:

- social security and protection of workers;
- protection of workers whose contract is ended;
- representation of workers' and employers' collective interests;
- third-country nationals' employment conditions in the EU;
- support for employment promotion and job creation.

The provisions of Article 2 were not to apply to pay, the right of association (to form trade unions), the right to strike and the right to impose a lock-out by management. All these are fairly basic criteria to employment rights and conditions and their exclusion from the protocol partly indicated national differences in these areas, but also represented a vain attempt to persuade the British to subscribe to the protocol.

Article 3 indicated a continuation of the social dialogue within the Union, with management and labour being consulted by the Commission, and, under Article 4, the dialogue of the social partners could lead to contractual agreements at the Community level. Equal pay for equal work for male and female workers was entrenched in Article 6.

The TEU also replaced the Rome Treaty's Title III of Part Three with Title VIII on 'Social Policy, Education, Vocational Training and Youth'. Article 118a on health and safety (138 TEC) was to be subject to the co-operation procedure under Article 189c TEU. Article 123 (146 TEC) strengthened the ESF's role in facilitating labour mobility and easing adaptation to industrial change through vocational training. ESF decisions were to be adopted using the co-operation procedure. A new Chapter was added on education, vocational training and youth that espoused the development of a European dimension in education, mobility of students and teachers, youth exchanges and the development of distance education (Article 126 TEU, 149 TEC). The basis for an EU policy in vocational training was laid in Article 127 (150 TEC).

The treatment by the TEU of social policy at an EU level was scarcely satisfactory. It disappointed all around. First, the division between the British and the other EU members was written into the Treaty, or at least its protocols. This further complicated the EU decision-making process and opened up the prospect of, for example, Social Chapter matters being discussed in the European Parliament with British MEPs participating, although their ministers would not take part in Council discussions. Second, the Social Chapter itself fell short of the expectations of those who wanted the EU to have a strong social policy element. It ruled out important aspects of work relationship and was mostly concentrated on issues of employment, saying little on other social issues.

Furthermore, there were only two pieces of legislation that used the Social Chapter – the 1994 Works Council Directive (94/45/EC) and the 1996 Parental Leave Directive (96/34/EC).

The Amsterdam Treaty

The election of a Labour government in the United Kingdom in May 1997 resulted in the new administration announcing that it would subscribe to the Social Chapter. This led to the inclusion of the protocol containing the 'Social Chapter' to be incorporated into Title VIII of the Treaty of Amsterdam. This was done with only the smallest of changes. Qualified Majority Voting in the Council and the co-decision procedure was to be used in the case of equal pay and the Council was urged to adopt measures in this area (Article 119 TEU, 141 TEC). The Commission was to co-ordinate states' policies on employment, labour law, training, social security, the prevention of occupational accidents and diseases, occupational hygiene and the rights of association and collective bargaining (Article 118c TEU,140 TEC). While the inclusion of the United Kingdom tidied up the Union's profile on social policy, the changes made in the substance of the Social Chapter scarcely represented a major step towards running such a policy at an EU-level. The member states were anxious to avoid further expenditure in this area and seemed to want to keep control over the most important aspects of social policy.

As a result of being included in the Social Chapter, the United Kingdom also subscribed to the 1994 Works Council Directive and the 1996 Parental Leave Directive.

With some 18 million people out of work throughout the EU by the mid–1990s, Sweden – then one of the new members of the Union – placed on the IGC agenda the idea that there should be a new Chapter on full employment in the revised Treaty (Duff, 1997: 63). The subsequent debate on this question involved the Nordic members, the Irish and the new French socialist government pressing for a firm commitment to full employment. On the other hand, the British, Germans and Dutch wanted a greater emphasis on the competitiveness of the European economy, being convinced that this would lead to falling unemployment and more 'real jobs' in the long run. The compromise was a new Title VIa (VIII TEC) on employment, sandwiched between that on economic and monetary policy and that on common commercial policy, but the emphasis was more on high rather

than full employment. Indeed the aim of promoting 'a high level of employment' was added to the objectives of the Union in Article B TEU (2 TEC) and
'the promotion of co-ordination between employment policies of Member
States' was set down as an activity (3 TEC). This was reflected in the new
title by which the EU and the member states were to develop 'a co-ordinated
strategy for employment' and to promote 'a skilled, trained and adaptable
workforce and labour markets responsive to economic change ...' (Article
109n TEU, 125 TEC). Employment is thus placed in the wider economic
context.

The Council was to monitor the employment situation with the help of a
new Employment Committee established under Article 109s (130 TEC),
and could adopt incentive measures 'to encourage cooperation between
Member States' through information, analysis and advice (Article 109r, 129
TEC). It was, however, stated that such action must be based on 'an
objective assessment of their need' and of 'added value' at the EU level.
Employment issues would remain primarily the concern of national governments, though the Amsterdam Treaty placed an EU marker on the
subject.

The scope of policy

Over the years, the EC/EU has shown increased involvement in social
policy. The SEA built on the modest beginnings of the Treaty of Rome, and
the 'Social Chapter', exiled to the protocol section of the Maastricht Treaty,
has been brought into the body of the Treaty of Amsterdam. The EU now
covers a wide range of subjects that can be placed under the heading of
'social policy', but still the world of work dominates. The priorities are in
the Commission White Paper of 1994 on European social policy (http:/
/europa.eu.int/scadplus/leg/en/cha/c10112.htm), the 1995–97 medium-term
action programme (http://europa.eu.int/scadplus/leg/en/cha/c10113.htm),
and in the 1998–2000 social action programme (http://europa.eu.int/
scadplus/leg/en/cha/c10114.htm).

Labour and industrial relations

Early efforts which were made in the 1970s to protect the *rights of workers*
culminated in attempts to increase the social dialogue at the EC level and to
allow the workforce a voice in the running of firms. This was strongly resisted
by some governments (especially the British Conservatives) and by corporate
lobby groups, who resented the strengthening of trade unions at the transnational level and opposed any involvement in the management of firms (Butler,
1991; Rhodes, 1992). The Works Council Directive in 1994, which emerged
after a long debate, proposed the creation of works councils in enterprises
with at least 1000 employees and with 100 of these employed in two or more

member states. The form of the councils was to be negotiated by management and employee representatives. These councils had the right to be informed and consulted on matters of interest to the workforce. As Duff (1997: 72) points out, the former was not of much use when the French management closed a profitable Belgian plant without the necessary consultations.

By the mid-1990s the top priority was to be *jobs*, based on the 1993 Brussels Council's endorsement of the White Paper on growth, competitiveness and employment, though action on this priority was limited to the supervision of the situation and the encouragement of small and medium-sized enterprises (SMEs). Under the heading of 'investing in a world-class labour force', the Commission proposed to 'provide a Union-wide guarantee that no young person can be unemployed under the age of 18' with the EU's Youth Start initiative contributing to the achievement of this aim. Basic skills, entrepreneurship and wider apprenticeship schemes were to be encouraged, with money from the structural funds being used to support these ends.

Another aim has been to encourage *higher labour standards*. The 1993 Working Time Directive set the minimum standards for workers across the EC in that area: a maximum 48 hours working week, minimum daily rest periods and four weeks' annual paid leave, with comparable conditions for night and shift workers. Later the Commission started to tackle the rights of those in 'atypical forms of employment' (fixed-term, temporary and part-time work), and to examine the cases of those excluded from the Working Time Directive such as fishermen and junior doctors. The Commission had to tread carefully and it rightly pointed out that member states 'were divided in their opinion about the need for further legislative action on labour standards at European level' (http://europa.eu.int/scadplus/leg/en/cha/c10112.htm, 4). As the worldwide nature of markets and capital was realized, some governments – noticeably the United Kingdom Conservative government, in office until May 1997 – felt that too many European labour laws would hinder competitiveness in the face of less regulated American and Far Eastern firms.

Under the heading of building a *European labour market*, the Commission hoped to press forward with the mutual recognition of diplomas and other qualifications, and to enhance the co-ordination of social security schemes for those moving across frontiers to work. Some attention was also given to the status of migrant workers.

Equal opportunities

The commitment to equal pay for equal work in the Treaty of Rome (Article 119 EEC) was one that was difficult to implement in countries where, over the years, women had been paid less than men both generally and specifi-cally. A landmark case in 1961 (Defrenne v. SABENA) showed that there was the need for further legislation at the European level, but it took until the mid-1970s for the legislation to be passed. The three Directives address-ing equal opportunities were:

- equal pay for equal work for men and women (1975): this tried to put flesh on Article 119 EEC (141 TEC) by introducing the notion of equal pay for work of equal value and by producing a code of conduct on the effective implementation of the directive;
- equal entry to the labour market (1976) including vocational training, promotion and working conditions;
- equal treatment for statutory social security schemes (1978), although this did not cover the question of pensionable age, which was addressed by a later ruling from the European Court of Justice in its Barber judgment.

By the early 1990s the EC was being criticized for making little progress in the area of equal opportunities (Springer, 1992: 74), for 'ghettoization' of its women's policy and for the treatment of women as primarily economic agents, which served 'to reinforce rather than diminish the divide between the public and the private, and between paid and un-paid work, which remains so damaging to women' (Hoskyns, 1992: 22). Partly in response to such criticism, the Equal Opportunities Working Party of Members of the Commission examined the possible inclusion of gender dimension in all relevant EC programmes and policies. The Amsterdam Treaty tightened up the legal basis of equal opportunities; the Commission's medium-term action programme for 1996–2000 contained the principle to mainstream equal opportunities, that is, including in the definition and implementation of relevant policies at Community, national and regional levels (http://europa.eu.int/scadplus/leg/en/cha/c00006.htm, 2). In May 1998 the Commission proposed a five-year programme (Daphne) to combat violence against women and children (Redmond, 1999: 84). This was to be open to applicant states.

Relevant specific legislation introduced through the Equality and Social Action Programmes includes

- equal treatment in company social security and occupational schemes;
- equal treatment for self-employed women;
- equal participation in training and retraining schemes;
- the New Opportunities for Women (NOW) initiative to support the creation of small businesses and co-operatives run by women;
- child care, parental leave and reconciling family and work life.

Despite these initiatives, the Commission had to admit that, by the end of the twentieth century, women in the EU were more likely to be unemployed and to hold contingent jobs (where they could easily be made redundant) than men and that women made up the bulk of part-time workers (http://europa.eu.int/scadplus/leg/en/cha/c00006.htm, 1).

Health and safety, and public health

A long-standing EC involvement has been in the area of health and safety, covered by Article 118 of the Treaty of Rome with Qualified Majority Voting introduced for these issues by the SEA. Early legislation covered the risks posed by dangerous substances and the 1989 framework directive established general principles for health and safety 'at the workplace', irrespective of where that was. Detailed legislation has covered the use of protective clothing and equipment, the use of Visual Display Units (VDUs) and the issue of construction site safety. In 1995 agreement was reached to place the newly created European Agency on Health, Safety and Hygiene in Bilbao, Spain.

Public health activity by the EU has been most noted in three fields. First, the EU has entered the fight against cancer. Its Third Action Plan on Cancer, covering the period 1995–99, aims to disseminate knowledge about cancer and support early detection and screening, public information campaigns and funding for research programmes. As part of this fight, the EC attempted to ban tobacco advertising but action was continually postponed until 1998. Second, the EC/EU have supported co-operation, exchange of information and awareness campaigns on illegal drugs. Finally, the EU's 'Europe against AIDS' programme has been one of the main projects in the area of fighting communicable diseases.

Protection of children, the disabled and the elderly

The EC designated 1993 the European Year of the Elderly and of solidarity between generations, and followed this up with a decision to help meet some of the challenges of an ageing population at a EU-wide level.

Another area of interest has been that of working children. The Commission has tried to ensure the protection of child workers in order to ensure their schooling and proper training, as laid down in the Social Charter. A 'young person' is defined as anyone under the age of 18; an 'adolescent' is a person over the age of 15 not attending full-time education, whereas a 'child' is either a person under the age of 15 or one who is attending full-time education.

EC/EU action for the 10 per cent of their population that is disabled has been shaped through the Helios programmes, which aim to improve the 'social and professional integration' of the disabled by bringing together voluntary and non-governmental organizations and governments in awareness and information programmes. Recent emphasis has been on good practice and codes of conduct in industry.

Poverty

With the prospect of over 50m poor people in the EU-15, the acute problem of social exclusion represented by this number has required concerted action. The prime responsibility in policy-making for the poor lies with the member states, and the EU has also accepted that the best way to tackle poverty is through employment, growth and competitiveness. However, there has also been specific EC-wide anti-poverty programmes since 1995.

The EU has attempted to create a network of anti-poverty organizations and has undertaken an assessment of member states policies in this area. In 1992 the Council adopted a Recommendation of 'the basic right of a person to sufficient resources to live in a manner compatible with human dignity'. The follow-up to this Recommendation has been overshadowed by the insistence of member states that subsidiarity should be applied to this issue and to its close association with the state of the wider economy.

Migrant workers

From the beginning of the EC, non-EC nationals have in theory been subject to the free movement of labour within the EC. Migrant labour has been common in the EC, but national controls over the labour market and immigration policies have been dominant (Romero, 1993). By the early 1990s Community rules were 'not systematic in the protection they offer, or not, to "third country migrants" ' (Meehan, 1993: 14).

By the mid-1990s the EU was faced with an influx of migrant workers from Central and East European states as well as from countries of North Africa. This was seen partly as a problem for border control; it was also an area where national policies and traditions dominated. However, the Commission attempted to bring an EU perspective to the issue by ensuring that third-country nationals who were permanently and legally resident in one EU state could, for example, pursue job vacancies in another member state.

The Corfu European Council issued a statement condemning racism and xenophobia and efforts have been made to combat these attitudes at a Union-wide level by financing anti-racist projects and funding organizations whose programmes have a significant anti-racist element. During 1997 ECU3.2m was used in the European Year Against Racism to address greater public awareness, day-to-day racism, racism at work and the implementation of legislation (Redmond, 1998: 64).

Education, training, youth

The EU has developed a number of schemes that aim to give a European dimension to education and training and to encourage a greater mobility of youth and of those in education and training.

The European programme for education (called Socrates) aims to encourage a European dimension to education, improve knowledge of European languages, promote mobility and to encourage innovation. Its eight Actions cover schools (Comenius), higher education (Erasmus), adult education (Grundtvig), language teaching and learning (Lingua), and education and multimedia (Minerva).

The objectives of the vocational training programme (Leonardo da Vinci) are to improve the skills of those in initial vocational training, enhance the quality and access to continued vocational training and lifelong acquisition of skills, and to reinforce the contribution of vocational training to innovation in business. Improved mobility, pilot projects and transnational networks are used for these purposes.

The new youth programme aims to create greater solidarity, active involvement in the European ideal and a spirit of enterprise and initiative among Europe's young people. The Actions include mobility under the European Voluntary Service scheme, group exchanges and joint action with education and training (http://europa.eu.int/en/comm/education/newprog/index.html).

European Social Fund (ESF)

Before the TEU, the focus of the ESF was that of 'rendering the employment of workers easier and of increasing their geographical and occupational mobility' (Article 123 EEC). The Maastricht Treaty extended this to include workers' 'adaptation to industrial change and to changes in production systems, in particular through vocational training and retraining' (146 TEC). Since the mid-1990s the ESF has concentrated more on supporting programmes to help the socially excluded and to improve vocational training. Programmes have included NOW, which promotes women's engagement in enterprise; Horizon, which helps the handicapped in the labour market; and Ergo, which assists the long-term unemployed.

With the Commission's adoption of its Social Action Programme for 1998–2000, the ESF became 'the financial arm of the EU's strategy for employment', helping to reform labour market policies and practices (Redmond, 1999: 83–4).

Conclusions

The social policy of the EC/EU has clearly faced problems in its construction. From its modest beginnings, it was always tied to the creation of a common, then a single, market. Together with the dominance of the member states in wider social policy questions, this restricted its range. It has played a useful role in co-ordinating the policies of the member states, setting out good practice and defining minimum standards. Progress has been made in particular areas such as equal opportunities, where the European Court of Justice has also played an important role. As Majone (1993: 155–6) remarked at the start of the 1990s: 'in the field of social regulation ... the progress has been so remarkable that some recent directives exceed the most advanced measures in the level of protection they afford'.

However, EC/EU social policy is a patchwork quilt. It covers some areas well, such as work conditions, but others – those of welfare benefits – are left to the states and other welfare providers. At the core, the EU is not a welfare provider and that reality limits its effectiveness in social policy. Indeed, Majone called the EC a 'welfare laggard' (1993: 155), which is unfair as it has not the resources to play the welfare game. However, his praise of its progress in social regulation may need rewriting at the beginning of the twenty-first century as attempts to find a 'European social model' have floundered and the heightened activity that followed the Social Charter has calmed into the everyday activity of co-ordination, cooperation and information. Social policy-making has reflected the needs of the market and the requirement to keep Europe competitive. This can be seen in the Presidency Conclusions of the Lisbon European Council, 23 and 24 March 2000 (http://ue.eu.int/en/info/eurocouncil/index.htm), where 'modernising the European social model' is very much placed in the context of a 'competitive, dynamic and knowledge-based economy'. The emphasis is on benchmarking, best practice, public–private partnerships and the EU as a catalyst in the modernization process. This may help locate policy activity more in the member states, though not necessarily at the national governmental level (*ibid.*: sections 37–41).

EU social policy will face a number of challenges in the new century. First, the advent of EMU in a sizeable part of the EU could provide an incentive for greater co-ordination of welfare policies. The variation in costs of welfare provision will be easier to see and, again, the dangers of 'social dumping' may arise. Should the EU be faced with a period of recession, will the response be national or in a monetary union will there be the expectation that at least some welfare elements should be provided at the EU level?

Second, the population of the EU is ageing. There is a higher percentage of people leaving work and going into retirement. This 'greying' of the EU brings not only social challenges but also economic ones. If the balance of the population in work is dwindling and of those drawing pensions is increasing, where is the money to pay the pensions to be found? Will those countries that have made better provision for their pensioners be expected to share their resources with the less far-sighted EU members?

Third, the EU social policy will have to face up to enlargement. What will be the consequences of EU membership by states whose welfare provision and social legislation is not up to EU standards? Legislation can be changed, but the lack of resources for provision will require an act of welfare solidarity by the existing EU states. Will their governments and peoples be willing to countenance a shift of resources – however modest – from themselves to the new members?

As can be seen, these issues contribute to a number of question marks about the future of EU social policy.

References and further reading

Butler, F. (1991) 'Social policy and the EC: proposals for worker participation legislation', *Public Policy and Administration*, 6 (1): 72–9.

Commission of the European Communities (1989) *Bulletin of the European Communities*. Office for Official Publications of the European Communities, Luxembourg.

Commission of the European Communities (1993) *Background Report ISEC/B25/93. Application of the Social Charter: Second Report*. Commission of the European Communities, London.

Duff, A. (ed.) (1997) *The Treaty of Amsterdam: Text and Commentary*. Sweet and Maxwell, London.

Grant, C. (1994) *Delors: Inside the House that Jacques Built*. Nicholas Brealey, London.

Hoskyns, C. (1992) 'The EC's policy on women in the context of 1992', *Women's Studies International Forum*, 15 (1): 21–8.

Majone, G. (1993) 'The EC between social policy and social regulation', *Journal of Common Market Studies*, 31 (2): 153–70.

Meehan, E. (1993) *Citizenship and the EC*. Sage, London.

Milward, A.S. (1992) *The European Rescue of the Nation-State*. Routledge, London.

Moxon-Browne, E. (1993) 'Social Europe', in J. Lodge (ed.), *The European Communities and the Challenge of the Future*, 2nd edn. Pinter, London.

Redmond, J. (1998) 'Internal policy developments', in G. Edwards and G. Wiessala (eds.), *The European Union 1997: Annual Review of Activities*. Blackwell, Oxford, pp. 51–68.

Redmond, J. (1999) 'Internal policy developments', in G. Edwards and G. Wiessala (eds), *The European Union Annual Review 1998–1999*. Blackwell, Oxford, pp. 69–85.

Rhodes, M. (1992) 'The future of the "social dimension": labour market regulation in post-1992 Europe', *Journal of Common Market Studies*, 30 (1): 23–51.

Romero, F. (1993) 'Migration as an issue in European interdependence and integration: the case of Italy', in A.S. Milward, F.M.B. Lynch, R. Ranieri, F. Romero and

V. Sorensen, *The Frontiers of National Sovereignty: History and Theory 1945–1992*. Routledge, London.

Ross, G. (1995) *Jacques Delors and European Integration*. Polity, Cambridge.

Springer, B. (1992) 'Pay, gender and the social dimension to Europe', *British Journal of Industrial Relations*, 30 (4).

Thatcher, M. (1993) *The Downing Street Years*. HarperCollins, London.

Wise, M. and Gibb, R. (1993) *Single Market in Social Europe: The EC in the 1990s*. Longman, Harlow.

Web sites

europa.eu.int/agencies.html	EU agencies and bodies
europa.eu.int/en/comm/education/ newprog/index.html	*Education, training, youth, a new generation of programmes.* European Commission, Directorate General Education and Culture.
europa.eu.int/scadplus/leg/en/cha/ c00006.htm	*Equal opportunities for women and men: current position and outlook.* Europa, SCADplus.
europa.eu.int/scadplus/leg/en/cha/ c10110.htm	*Introduction. The protocol on social policy and the annexed agreement.* Europa, SCADplus.
europa.eu.int/scadplus/leg/en/cha/ c10112.htm	*Introduction. White Paper. European social policy: a way forward for the Union*, Europa, SCADplus.
europa.eu.int/scadplus/leg/en/cha/ c10113.htm	*Introduction. Medium-term social action programme (1995–97).* Europa, SCADplus.
europa.eu.int/scadplus/leg/en/cha/ c10114.htm	*Introduction. Social action programme (1998–2000).* Europa, SCADplus.
ue.eu.int/en/info/eurocouncil/index.htm	European Council

6 Agricultural and environmental policies

Introduction

Farming and fishing have always been very special economic activities, not least because of their dependence on the vagaries of climate and the availability of natural resources, and because of their central role in providing food for a population. Agriculture also has a special role within the EU and its predecessor, the EC. It has always taken a lion's share of Communities' resources and, even at the end of the twentieth century, accounted for over 40 per cent of the EU's expenditure. Agriculture was also the first true Community policy; it was an important factor in the political basis for the deal between Germany and France that formed the EC. Even now, the Common Agricultural Policy (CAP) and, to a lesser extent, the Common Fisheries Policy are key political elements in the EU, in terms both of domestic political support (and, in some cases, opposition) and the external relations of the Union.

Environmental policy was a relative latecomer as an area of EC competence, but has proved to be a subject for further EU engagement. It has provided an arena for the contest among a number of national and Union-based interest groups, including farming, industry, consumer groups and ecologists. It is also an area of EU external activity, especially in terms of international environmental agreements. The environment is likely to become an area of increased EU concern as new Central and East European countries (CEECs) approach membership.

The common agricultural policy

The CAP's Foundation

After the Second World War, the agricultural sector was a sizeable and important part of the economies of continental Western Europe. Farming had been badly disrupted by the war and the priority was to re-establish activity both to feed the population and to revitalize economic and social life in the still-strong rural regions of Western Europe. Farmers and their families also provided a crucial sector of political support for many of the governments in the region.

By 1950 it was recognized that the aims of stabilized prices, increased production, prosperity for farmers and surpluses for export – the general aims of national agricultural policies in Western Europe – could not be achieved in a purely national context. At a time when the European Coal and Steel Community was being constructed, French politicians in particular sought a supranational solution for agriculture akin to that provided for coal and steel by the Schuman Plan. A French delegate to the Council of Europe advanced the Charpentier Plan and the French government put forward the Pflimlin Plan. Both aimed at a 'Green Pool', a European agricultural community. However, they were opposed by the British who proposed the Eccles Plan, based on intergovernmental co-operation. By 1954 it was clear that the Six states of the ECSC – France, West Germany, Italy and the three Benelux states – could not agree with the United Kingdom on a common approach to agricultural policy.

The 'relaunching' of the Community idea by the Benelux governments in 1955 and the subsequent discussions about the creation of a European Economic Community placed the agricultural policies of the Six in a wider context. Their governments wanted a protected market for agriculture and outlets for their exports. This was necessary not only for political reasons but also for economic ones. By 1958 agriculture 'accounted for 10 per cent of GNP and 26 per cent of employment' in the Six (Pearce, 1983: 143), showing it still to be a large sector of the economy. Also, it was not always possible to decide where agriculture ended and industry started. This was not just the case of agricultural products entering the industrial process, something more common nowadays with frozen and processed foods. The cross-over was also evident in the increasing dependence of agriculture on industrial machinery and products such as artificial fertilizers and pesticides, and the effect of agricultural prices – not least through the cost of food – on industrial costs (Ackrill, 2000: Chapter 1).

While this situation pointed to the inclusion of agriculture in any plans for a common market, it did not mean that this sector would be treated in the same way as industry. Unlike industrial products, agricultural produce would need more than the reduction and abolition of trade restrictions between the six EEC member states. Prices would have to be fixed, exports subsidized and a system of buying surpluses created, if agriculture was to survive any major change. National measures would be transformed into Community ones. As there were differences in the pre-existing national measures, a transition period would be necessary, and this would match the period needed to create the common external tariffs for industrial goods (Ackrill, 2000: Chapter 1).

The creation of the CAP is often seen as a French victory, with it being insisted upon by French ministers as a *quid pro quo* for the industrial common market so desired by West Germany. This is too simplistic a view. While it is true that French farmers wanted an outlet for their surpluses, they would have been content with solutions other than that of the CAP (Milward, 1992: 309–10). However, it was not disputed that there should be a common agricultural policy within the EEC (Ackrill, 2000: Chapter 1) and its final form owed much to the determination of the Dutch Agriculture Commissioner, Sicco Mansholt (*ibid.* 1–2).

The Treaty of Rome thus included a sizeable section on the Common Agricultural Policy and its introduction. It stated that 'the common market shall extend to agriculture and trade in agricultural products' (Article 38, 32 TEC) and that the development of a common market for agriculture 'must be accompanied by the establishment of a common agricultural policy'. The objectives of such a common agricultural policy (CAP) were outlined in Article 39 (33 TEC):

- to increase agricultural productivity by promoting technical progress, the rational development of production and the optimal use of the factors of production, especially labour;
- to ensure a fair standard of living for those employed in the sector;
- to stabilize markets;
- to assure availability of supplies;
- to ensure reasonable prices for consumers.

Article 40.2 (34.1 TEC) outlined the forms of intervention: common rules on competition, co-ordination of national market organizations and the creation of a European market organization. The EEC Council meetings of the early 1960s developed three main principles for the CAP: *market unity*, with common rules and prices leading to a single market in agricultural policy; *community preference*, meaning that community produce would be sold in member states' markets with protection against cheaper produce from elsewhere; and *financial solidarity*, indicating that the costs of the policy would be shared by the member states.

Developing the CAP

The policy was to be managed mainly through the European Agricultural Guidance and Guarantee Fund (EAGGF, often known by the French acronym FEOGA). The Fund is a part of the general EU budget and, as the name suggests, has two major elements. The Guidance section supports structural improvements – improving farm buildings, upgrading markets, modernizing production methods – and, as a result of the general structural funds, has played an increasingly important role for areas under Objective 5 (see Chapter 7) and, more lately, Objective 1 regions.

The Guarantee section disburses money for price and market support. The most common methods used to guarantee the position of EEC agriculture were those of target, intervention and threshold prices for Community products. *Target prices* for a commodity, for example wheat, would be the best one that could be obtained on the market within the EC for that product. The Council would adopt that price for wheat for the year, thus providing producers with a reasonable and guaranteed return for their effort. The *intervention price* would be some 10 to 12 per cent lower than a target price. If an excess of supply over demand of a product brought its price below that intervention price, farmers could sell the product to the relevant intervention board, which would store it or dispose of it. A *threshold price* is the one set for an agricultural product imported into the Union and represents a price at which those imports do not undercut EU produce. Levies are placed on the imports to bring their price up to the threshold price. Subsidies for farmers who export produce are known as *export restitution*.

The creation of an internal agricultural market within the EC was adversely affected during the 1970s and 1980s by currency fluctuations. The CAP system had been set up in a period of relatively stable currencies in Western Europe, the early 1960s. From 1969 currencies became more vulnerable to market pressure and started to fluctuate more widely. The price for an agricultural product was expressed in Brussels in terms of the European Currency Unit (ECU) but the value to a farmer in France or Italy depended on the exchange rate of the franc or the lira. As these rates fluctuated more, governments decided to lower the element of risk for the farmer by fixing a 'green franc' and 'green lira' as the stable rate against the ECU for calculating their farm prices. However, these green rates soon got out of line with the 'real' currency exchanges. If the green rate was weaker than the real rate of the currency, then the farmers in that state benefited, though consumers would have to pay a higher price. If the green currency was stronger, then farmers lost out but the consumers got cheaper food. A system of levies and subsidies at the national frontiers, called Monetary Compensatory Amounts (MCAs) were created after 1971 in order to offset the distortions created by the green currencies. Hopes that this complex system would be dismantled with the creation of the single European market at the end of 1992 were dashed with the renewed currency turmoil in September 1992, and the structure was only dismantled with the move towards a single currency.

These processes have, over a period of some 40 years, helped to increase productivity in agriculture, have led to a better standard of living for those in the sector and have certainly led to a greater availability of supplies.

However, whether the system has been able to stabilize the EU agricultural market, and whether 'reasonable prices' have prevailed, is disputed. Soon after the CAP was established in 1965, it became clear that it would produce surpluses. By 1968 Sicco Mansholt was suggesting major reforms assigned to curb the rising CAP budget and to reduce the 'butter mountains' and 'wine lakes' created by produce that could not be sold through purchase by 'intervention boards' at an artificially high price. However, this system continued to create surpluses well into the 1980s. By then the cost to the rest of society was apparent: 'present price supports cost the taxpayer some 17bn ECU and the consumer some 38bn ECU. ... [F]or every 1 ECU received by the farmers, 1.4 ECU is contributed by the rest of society' (Harvey cited in Marsh, 1991: 37). The taxpayer dipped into his or her pocket to help pay for the CAP, while the consumer paid extra for food that could have been bought more cheaply on the world market. One estimate was that the inefficiency of the CAP cost the EC a dead-weight loss of around one per cent of the EC's Gross Domestic Product by the late 1980s (Demekas *et al.*, 1988: 126–7, 140).

Furthermore, support for Community agriculture meant that by the late 1980s the EC had become the second largest exporter in the global food market. Community preference was not only blocking exports of food products to the EC but was encouraging the EC to export to markets it had not reached before. The OECD estimated that in the 1979–81 period, EC beef and cereals were protected by as much as 70 per cent, dairy products by 267 per cent and skimmed milk powder by 247 per cent (OECD, 1987: 86). The EC and the USA clashed in the Uruguay Round of GATT about Community preference and the CAP: the pressure for change was coming from outside as well as from within the EC.

Reform of the CAP

Efforts were made from 1984 to 1988 to reform the CAP, mainly as a result of British prompting. Quotas were used to reduce output, especially of milk, and the real prices paid for a number of products were pegged or even reduced. The 'lakes' and 'mountains' were reduced, often being sold off for use by those in social need. By 1988 the amount of butter in storage had been cut by 1 million tonnes. Farmers were persuaded to 'set aside' some of their land from cultivation. To ease the financial burden of the CAP on the EC, member states co-financed some elements at the national level.

Major reform faced a formidable opposition. The CAP represented the one real Community policy of the EC and behind it was an 'accumulation of special interests, representing lobby groups, politicians and Community institutions' (Pearce, 1983). It was hard to imagine that the Agricultural Council, the Agriculture Committee or the sizeable agricultural directorate of the Commission might give up their dominant position within the EC, 'voluntary to retire to the wings where objectively they might be more properly located' (Fennell, 1987: 74).

However, the creation of a Single European Market ('1992') with the 1986 Single European Act, while not directly affecting agriculture, and the demands for reform of the EC's finances, led to an increased push for reform within the Commission. The emphasis was on the more flexible use of agriculture policy mechanisms, such as the intervention price, and on the move towards a more market-based system with producers bearing greater co-responsibility for their surpluses. The budgetary stabilizers in the Commission's 1988 budgetary package ('Delors I') involved the setting of Maximum Guaranteed Quantities (MGQs) for individual products. If production exceeded these MGQs, then support and guaranteed intervention was reduced. However, the MGQs were not set at punitive levels and the real effect was marginal (Commission of the European Communities, 1990).

The real impetus for reform came from outside – from the GATT Uruguay Round in the early 1990s. The inclusion of agriculture in these negotiations to cut trade protection worldwide provided strong support for the Commission's efforts to reform the CAP before the negotiations reached their climax (Warley, 1991–92). The Agriculture Commissioner Ray MacSharry introduced reforms which were accepted in 1992. He achieved a 29 per cent price cut for cereal prices, a 15 per cent cut for beef and 5 per cent for butter in the 'MacSharry II' reforms (http://europa.eu.int/pol/agr/newcap_en.htm). This package went further than simply cuts in price support: it also tried to overhaul the role of farming in the economic life of rural areas and to bring environmental protection and sustainability into the picture. The reforms encouraged farmers to move to more ecologically sound processes, supported afforestation of previous agricultural land, provided income replacement for set-aside land and offered incentives for farmers over 65 to retire (Butler, 1993). These reforms did not anticipate any major change in CAP expenditure, as they would cost money to implement. However, they meant that it was possible to keep the planned CAP spending in the Delors II budgetary package from rising beyond ECU40bn by 1999 from ECU38bn in 1993. By 1999 the Guarantee part of the CAP appropriated budget was €40.4bn, representing 41.7 per cent of the total EU budget[1] (47.0 per cent with the Guidance expenditure, which is now placed under the Structural Operations heading – see Redmond, 1999: 78).

Another major effort to reform the CAP came with the Commission's *Agenda 2000* plans. As the name of this publication suggests, it outlined the Commission's view of the way forward for the EU into the new millennium. It is also a response to the question of enlargement with the potential to double the EU's farm population and increase the agricultural area by more than 40 per cent (http://europa.eu.int/pol/agr/newcap_en.htm). In agriculture, the proposal was to continue the move away from supporting produce and towards greater support of the farmer and a rural lifestyle. The Commission proposed a 22 per cent price cut for cereals from 2000, 30 per cent for beef between 2000 and 2002, and a 10 per cent cut for dairy products by 2006, with compensation payments in all sectors. The quota system in milk was to be continued until 2006 (Redmond, 1998: 62–3).

Agricultural spending was affecting a whole series of EU reforms as well as the enlargement process and 'the circle of actors involved in agricultural policy formation' has consequently widened (Grant, 1997: 148). After the predictable campaign by those states that would have suffered most from these cuts, an agreement on future agricultural spending was agreed at the Berlin Council in March 1999. The overall milk quota was increased by 2.4 per cent. The main beneficiaries were Greece, Spain, Italy and Ireland; each had specific, and rather generous, quota increases for the 2000–02 period (http://europa.eu.int/comm/newcomm/hearings/answers/fischler.en.pdf). The intervention price in the dairy and cereals sectors would drop each by 15 per cent, by 2005–6 for dairy products and by 2002 for cereals. The intervention price for beef would be cut by 20 per cent with a 'safety net' intervention system established from 2002. Direct payments to farmers would save €6.2bn between 2001–06, of which half would go to rural development (*Eur-op News*, 1999: 6).

The Berlin meeting also provided some detail of the adaptation of the CAP for the applicant Central and East European countries (CEECs): €1.6bn is to be available for accession-related agricultural expenditure in 2002, rising to €3.9bn in 2006 (in 1999 prices). There was talk of a transition phase for farmers in the CEECs, during which time their structural problems would be addressed and they would not be eligible for the support experienced by the rest of the European Union (http://europa.eu.int/comm/newcomm/hearings/answers/fischler. en.pdf). The general aim to reduce the *price* support element in the CAP and to switch to stronger support of the farmers and aspects of their lifestyle would also mean a lesser burden once the CEECs' agriculture is fully included into the CAP. To help the acceding countries the EU has established a special instrument for agriculture and rural development (Sapard) which will provide about €520m a year for pre-accession help in these two areas (*ibid.*).

Two other key areas in the Berlin agreement on Agenda 2000, as it related to agriculture, were those of rural development and the environment. Environmental goals were broadly integrated into the CAP (see p. 123), and rural development policy became 'a second pillar of the CAP' with the aim of having a 'living countryside, where the local community is able to provide the infrastructure and services they [farmers] need' (*ibid.*: 17; see Chapter 7 for further details).

One major challenge to the CAP came in the form of BSE, a deadly disease affecting cattle (commonly known as 'mad cow disease'), which struck the United Kingdom herd in the 1980s. As soon as it became known that a similar disease called CJD might have resulted from cross-species infection (from cattle to humans), the domestic and foreign markets for British beef collapsed. The EU was faced with its member states placing unilateral bans on the import of British beef and, on the advice of its Scientific Veterinary Committee, it instituted a ban in March 1996 on the export of such beef. The issue became a source of conflict between the United Kingdom and the rest of the EU from March to July 1996, as the UK felt that the scientific evidence did not warrant such a harsh, blanket treatment of British beef products (Westlake, 1997: 11–36). This continues to be a difficult issue for the EU, especially in 2000 with the French government's refusal to lift their ban on the import of British beef.

Internationally, the EU's main concern over the CAP is the way it may be affected by world trade agreements and the World Trade Organization (WTO). The emphasis of that organization, which includes all the major trading countries except China, has been on free and fair trade. Successive US governments have used the WTO rules to open up world markets for their products and to prevent any protective measures that work against their interests. A major disagreement has arisen between the USA and the EU concerning the interpretation of WTO rules on the banning of agricultural imports on health grounds. This came to a head over two issues: those of hormones in beef and genetically modified food.

The EU has banned the import of beef treated with growth-inducing hormones since 1988 on the grounds that they could pose a health risk to consumers. In 1998 the WTO ruled that this risk had not been proved and that the ban was a restriction of trade. By May 1999 the United States, which was exporting such beef, asked the WTO to authorize retaliation against the ban (Guay, 1999: 78). The USA implemented such retaliation by banning carefully chosen EU exports; this resulted in sometimes violent demonstrations against US enterprises in France (Webster, 1999: 10). The USA and the EU also seem to have a different approach to genetically modified foods. This could lead to a stand-off every time such US foods are restricted for sale in the EU, should the EU take a 'no-risk' approach to such crop production (http://europa.eu.int/comm/newcomm/hearings/answers/fischler.en.pdf).

In December 1999 the WTO negotiations in Seattle broke up without any agreement (see Chapter 11). The EU's Agriculture Commissioner, Fritz Fischler, said that 'Seattle did not fail because of agriculture. Compared to the other sectors, the talks on agriculture made the most progress over the four days' (EU Agriculture and the WTO, http://europa.eu.int/comm/ dg06/wto/index_en.htm). However, during 2000 the WTO agriculture negotiations will have faced the differences between the main groupings, with the EU stressing the multifunctional aspects of agriculture: food safety, environment, the landscape and rural development. It also wants special treatment for the Least Developed Countries (LDCs). The USA and other states will have called for the elimination of export subsidies and sees many of the EU's concerns as being hidden barriers to freer trade.

The Common Fisheries Policy

As it covers a foodstuff, the Common Fisheries Policy (CFP) is associated with the CAP and is run by the same Commissioner. Fisheries products are deemed to be included in the term 'agricultural products' in the Treaty of Rome and are therefore covered by the requirement to have a common market in such goods (Articles 38.1 and 38.4 EEC, 32.1 and 32.4 TEU). In the first years of the EEC, however, the main development in the fisheries industry was the requirement to abolish internal tariffs among EEC states and to have a Common External Tariff, much to the disadvantage of the French fishermen, who previously had been protected by high tariffs. Between 1957 and 1966 fish imports into France rose threefold, and the French industry placed pressure on its government to back a CFP that might bring French fishermen the advantages that French farmers received from the CAP (Wise, 1984: 87–8). Once negotiations started with the applicants in 1970 – the UK, Ireland, Norway and Denmark (all states with sizeable fishing industries) – there was an incentive for the existing Six EEC states to fashion a CFP before the new members could block such a policy. Furthermore, Iceland was leading international moves to extend national control over traditional fishing waters that could exclude both new and old members of the EEC from traditional fishing grounds.

The CFP agreement reached in June 1970 had four main aspects:

- all EC vessels would have equal access to the territorial waters and exclusive fishing zones of EC member states, including the new members;
- the EC would provide structural aid in order to help make the fishing industry more efficient;
- a network of Producers' Organizations (POs) would have the main task of running the internal EC market in fish and would sustain a market intervention system, similar to that in agriculture;
- a reference price would be set for the import of major fish species, in order to ensure that their importation would not undercut the market within the EC (Wise, 1984: 102–5).

This policy caused problems in the accession negotiations in 1970–72 and in the end the applicants obtained adjustments to the June 1970 agreement. However, the Norwegian electorate did not deem these satisfactory and the CFP was one factor that led to the Norwegian electorate's rejection of EC membership in September 1972. The articles on fisheries in the Treaty of Accession restricted fishing in the six-miles zone around the EC's coast to vessels based in ports in the geographical coastal area and 'vessels which fish traditionally in those waters' (Article 100.1). This limit was extended to 12 miles in certain areas off Denmark, the Brittany coast of France, much of Ireland and parts of the United Kingdom.

With the prospect of fisheries limits being extended up to 200 nautical miles from January 1977, the EC's Hague Resolutions of November 1976 allowed the Commission to negotiate fishing access agreements with third countries and to adopt common conservation measures. In January 1983 a more stable basis for the CFP was adopted, based on five points:

- all the waters within the 200-mile fisheries zones of the EC member states were to be open to fishing by vessels from the member states, apart from a 12-mile coastal belt within which fishing was to remain restricted to the fleets of individual countries and those with traditional rights;
- the Council was to decide Total Allowable Catches (TACs) for species, with national quotas, on the basis of traditional fishing patterns, the needs of areas dependent on fishing and the requirement to compensate for losses of traditional fishing grounds in non-EC grounds, such as those off Iceland;
- endangered species were to be protected;
- other conservation measures were to be taken;
- the member states were to enforce EC rules within their national sectors on a non-discriminatory basis and under the general supervision of EC inspectors.

In addition the market organization was strengthened and agreements were signed with third countries such as Norway and Sweden.

The accession of Spain and Portugal offered challenges to the CFP, mainly because of the large size and structure of the Spanish fishing fleet. These two states doubled the number of fishermen in the EC, increased fishing capacity by 75 per cent, tonnage by 65 per cent and fish consumption and production by 45 per cent (http://europa.eu.int/pol/fish/info_en.htm). Each was given a long transitional period, which meant that access was restricted to specified waters while it restructured and reduced its fleet. Nevertheless, the activities of the Spanish fleet upset British fishermen, especially when Spanish fishing interests bought up British boats and quotas ('quota hopping').

Indeed the CFP has had to face the general problem of over-fishing, and to some extent has exacerbated this process. By the mid-1990s fisheries were in crisis, mainly from structural factors including overcapacity in the fleets, low productivity and inefficient commercial structures. The Council prevented attempts by the Commission in its 1992 review to reduce substantially the TACs. In 1993 the structural elements of the CFP were overhauled in an attempt to give the policy greater coherence by integrating certain elements with the Structural Funds, in order to improve control and monitoring and to reduce the number of boats.

In the context of the negotiations for Norway's entry into the EU, Spain and Portugal's integration into the CFP was brought forward from 2003 to 1996, further adding to the pressure on the policy. (In fact Norway, with its vast fisheries zone, did not join the EU.) Spanish presence was shown in the North Atlantic with the catch of Greenland halibut. This led to conflict with Canada in 1995 over the quotas, most of which was taken on the EU side by Spanish vessels. A similar dispute with Morocco restricted the outlet for Spanish boats there, especially at a time when the TACs and quotas for member states were being reduced by 20 per cent in 1996 (Redmond, 1996: 58). By May 1996 the Commission had proposed the Bonino Plan to cut fleets by 40 per cent over six years but this was rejected by the Council. In 1997 a compromise was reached in the Fourth Multiannual Guidance Programme (MAGP IV, covering 1997– 2001), which allowed for reductions of 30 per cent in fishing efforts of stocks threatened with extinction and of 20 per cent for overexploited stocks. National authorities were given some choice in how to achieve these cuts. In 1998 national quotas were introduced, for the first time, for six stocks in the North Sea. The Commission also proposed a ban on drift-nets (which threatened other species) in 1994 but the Council rejected it, and a partial ban was later agreed for 2002 onwards (Redmond, 1999: 82–3).

Environmental policy

Environmental policy was not mentioned in the Treaty of Rome but the issue was introduced at a European Council in 1972 after the impact of the Stockholm UN Conference on the Human Environment earlier that year. The first Environmental Action Programme (EAP) covered 1973–76 and established the principles concerning EC involvement in this area. These include the 'polluter pays' principle, individual governments being allowed to enforce stricter environmental regulations than those of the EC, and the importance of involving the different levels of government in policy formulation and implementation. The various EAPs since then (the fifth covered 1992 to 2000) have demonstrated the changing EC/EU concern over the environment, but, until the SEA, the Commission could only utilize the rather limited instruments provided by the Treaty of Rome in this area. This meant using the catch-all Article 235 or legislation based on trade distortion or restriction of movement of production factors (Vogel, 1993). Indeed, it was more the 'imperative of economic growth [that] determined the boundaries within which Community environmental policy was framed' (Baker, 1993: 10).

The SEA, in Title VII, gave environment policy a firmer footing in EC law. Article 130r laid down the objectives of EC environmental policy: the preservation, protection and improvement of the quality of the environment, the protection of human health and the prudent and rational use of resources. Article 130r.2 set out that EC action should be based on preventive action, the rectification of problems at source and on the 'polluter pays' principle, already accepted by the EC in 1972. Article 130r.4 confirmed that the EC would take action on environmental matters when the objectives 'can be attained better at Community level than at the level of the individual member states'. Indeed, Article 130f specifically permitted member states to maintain 'more stringent protective measures compatible with this Treaty', irrespective of EC action in that area. This was to allay the fears of those member states, such as Denmark and the Netherlands, that prided themselves on high environmental standards, that these would not be undermined by an EC policy pandering to the 'lowest common denominator'.

Maastricht confirmed the EU competence in environmental policy. Article 130r.2 (174 TEC) sets out the basis of EU environmental policy which

> shall aim at a high level of protection taking into account the diversity of situations in the various regions of the Community. It shall be based on the precautionary principles that preventive action should be taken, that environmental damage should as a priority be rectified at source and that the polluter should pay.

The Treaty of Amsterdam pressed home the centrality of the environment to other policies in Article 3c (6 TEC), which states that

> Environmental protection requirements must be integrated into the definitions and implementation of Community policies and activities . . . in particular with a view to promoting sustainable development.

Amsterdam also eases the path for states that wished to have more stringent environmental measures than those agreed within the EU. Article 100a.5 (95.5 TEC) states that such action must be based on new scientific evidence and that, in considering the derogation, the Commission must reassess the original EU measure (Article 100a.8 TEU, 95.8 TEC).

How has the EC/EU utilized the powers accumulated in environmental policy since the SEA was passed in 1987?

The scope of environmental policy and the limited resources within the EU for this area have meant that there has been much deciding on priorities.

One of the main aims has been to integrate environmental targets into other EU policies and Article 6 TEC was a culmination of that effort. The fifth EAP emphasized this integration and the development of partnerships with governmental and non-governmental institutions. The EU has been most active in the following areas:

- *Water quality*: the first and second EAPs introduced a number of Directives that laid down minimum quality standards for bathing water, drinking water and shellfish waters. The 'bathing waters directive' (COM 76/160/EEC) became contentious among the Commission, local authorities, environmental groups and privatized water authorities in, for instance, the United Kingdom over the cost and desirability of cleaning up such waters. An effort was made to restrict the discharge of dangerous substances such as cadmium, oil and mercury into EU waters. The EU participates in conventions which aim to reduce pollution in international waterways such as the Rhine, the North Atlantic, the North Sea, the Baltic Sea and the Mediterranean (http://europa.eu.int/pol/env/info_en.htm).
- *Atmospheric pollution*: EU legislation has reflected scientific and public concern in this area. Action ranged from 1970s legislation to limit emissions of sulphur dioxide and nitrous oxide (which contribute to acid rain) to 1980s Directives to limit vehicle emissions, encourage lead-free petrol and to require the fitting of catalytic converters on new cars with engine sizes below 2.0 litres. Restrictions on the use of chlorofluorocarbons (CFCs), reflecting concern over their effect on the ozone layer, have followed the transposition into Community law of international environmental agreements such as the 1985 Vienna Convention on the protection of the ozone layer and the subsequent Montreal Protocol of 1987. At the start of the 1990s the EC seemed to be making the running on the control of 'greenhouse gases', especially carbon dioxide, in the preparations for the UN Second World Climate Conference in November 1990. However, the EC/EU follow-up on the 1993 Framework Climate Change Convention – which set the EC the aim of stabilizing emissions of carbon dioxide in 2000 at 1990 levels – was less than perfect. A series of Directives aimed at energy efficiency – SAVE – produced modest results, as did renewable energy investments in the form of the ALTENER programme. Attempts to introduce a carbon/energy tax at the EU level were abandoned in 1994, leaving the EC strategy 'in shreds' (Grubb *et al.*, 1994: 25). At the Kyoto 'Earth Summit' in December 1997 on greenhouse gases, the EU proposed a 15 per cent decrease in the emission of three greenhouse gases by 2010 compared to the 1990 level, but accepted a target of an 8 per cent cut for six gases by the 2008–12 period (Redmond, 1999: 84).

- *Waste and recycling*: a number of Directives control the collection and disposal of some 2bn tonnes of waste every year within the EU. Measures have been taken to control the disposal and transportation of toxic waste, radioactive waste and the dumping of waste at sea.
- *Habitats and nature*: the EU has incorporated a number of international agreements including the 1973 Washington Convention on the Trade in Endangered Species (CITES) and the 1979 Bonn Convention on the conservation of migratory species. Cases concerning the non-implementation of the 1979 Wild Birds Directive, arising from Bonn, were subsequently taken against nine EC states. Some financial support is given to support the conservation of natural habitats.
- *Chemical products*: since the Seveso dioxin accident in Italy in 1976, increasingly stringent measures have been taken in order to counter the risks of manufacturing chemical substances. A June 1982 Directive obliges manufacturers in the EU 'to inform the authorities about substances, plants and possible location of accidents' (http://europa.eu.int/pol/env/info_en.htm).
- *Noise*: Directives have fixed maximum noise levels for cars, lorries, motorcycles, tractors, subsonic aircraft, lawnmowers and building-site machinery.

The EU has a number of instruments to implement environmental policy. These include:

- *The European Environment Agency*, based in Copenhagen and operational since 1994, aims to provide objective information about environmental protection policies; present technical, scientific and economic information in order to help prepare measures and laws; develop forecasting techniques; and to ensure that EU environmental data are incorporated into international environmental programmes (*ibid.*).
- *Environmental impact assessments* of the potential damage caused by individual projects have a procedure determined by an EU Directive. The public must be involved in the process.
- *The LIFE Regulation*, adopted in 1992, provides incentives for EU priority projects in the environmental field. This provided ECU96.6m for 201 new projects in 1998 (Redmond, 1999: 85). However, it should be remembered that environmental matters took only 0.2 per cent of the EU's budget in 1999 (Redmond, 1999: 78).

Environmental policy within the EU has been caught between the need to act globally on such matters, with a variety of international agreements being negotiated, and the requirement of certain states not to let their standards slip. Perhaps more than most policies, there has been a north–south divide in this area, with the Southern members receiving aid through the structural and cohesion funds (European Commission, n.d.: 14–24) in order to bring their environmental policies up to scratch. The enlargement of the EU to include some or all of the CEECs will place further stress on the inclusive nature of the EU's environmental policy.

Conclusions

The Common Agricultural Policy has traditionally provided substance to the EC. Together with the Common External Policy, it was the fruit of the efforts of the first Commission. The CAP helped to bind France and Germany together and provided a benefit, not always appreciated, for the stolid countryside of Western Europe. Its creation cost the taxpayers and the consumers of the EC; its surpluses undermined world markets. It was a source of conflict between the United Kingdom and most of the other EC members and has become associated with waste and fraud. Yet it still takes the lion's share of the EU budget and draws heavily on the resources of the Union's institutions.

The predominance of the CAP in the EU is being challenged from a number of sources. First, with the SEA, Maastricht and Amsterdam Treaties, the number of competencies of EU has grown. Time has to be spent on other policies and these are demanding a comparatively larger share of the budget. Also agriculture is becoming more integrated with other policies, in particular with structural and environmental ones.

Second, the CAP is being challenged internationally, especially through the WTO. Within the next decade the WTO will want to tackle the protectionist element in agricultural policies throughout the world and the EU will not be immune to this process. Most likely the WTO will be used by the friends of reform within the EU as an opportunity for change, just as the GATT negotiations were in the early 1990s.

Finally, the EU will have to decide on how the CAP and enlargement can be made compatible. Either the CAP will be fully extended to the CEEC candidate states, increasing the budget beyond present plans, or some of the CAP's elements that are particularly attractive to such countries as Hungary and Poland will be scaled down, which is the basic message of Agenda 2000. In this case, the new EU members may find that the much-vaunted benefits of joining are much less than their voters had thought.

A similar challenge is facing the environmental policy of the EU. To cite Agenda 2000: 'while the adoption of the Union's environmental rules and standards is essential, none of the candidate countries can be expected to comply fully with the *acquis* in the near future' (Avery and Cameron, 1998: 109). It is quite clear that the adaptation of the potential members is a long-term matter.

In all three policies discussed in this chapter, there are heterogeneous pressures. Co-financing in agriculture and the move to support the farmer is allowing the nation-state to play a greater role. The CFP has a regional element with separate rules for the Mediterranean states. Environmental policy suffers from a north–south divide and, with enlargement, will see an even greater east–west division. One of the EU's major challenges of the coming decade will be the maintainance of distinct common policies that are flexible enough to accommodate the differing needs and demands of an expanding membership.

Note

1 'Accompanying measures' – included in the Guarantee figure – represented some 2.7 per cent of the budget. In 1999 calculations were made in euros rather than its predecessor and equivalent, the European Currency Unit (ECU).

References and further reading

Ackrill, R. (2000) *The Common Agricultural Policy*, Contemporary European Studies 9. Sheffield Academic Press, Sheffield.

Avery, G. and Cameron, F. (1998) *The Enlargement of the European Union.* Contemporary European Studies 1. Sheffield Academic Press, Sheffield.

Baker, S. (1993) 'Environmental policy of the EC: a critical review', *Paradigms*, 7 (1): 8–29.

Butler, F. (1993) 'The EC's Common Agricultural Policy', in J. Lodge (ed.), *The EC and the Challenge of the Future*, 2nd edn., Pinter, London.

Commission of the European Communities (1990) *The Agricultural Situation in the Communities.* Commission of the European Communities, Brussels.

Demekas, D., Bartholdy, K., Gupta, S., Lipshitz, L., and Mayer, T. (1988) 'The effects of the Common Agricultural Policy of the European Community: a survey of the literature', *Journal of Common Market Studies*, 27 (2): 113–45.

European Commission (n.d.) *The Environment and the Regions: Towards Sustainability.* Office for Official Publications of the European Communities, Luxembourg.

Eur-op News (1999) No. 2. European Communities Publications Office, Luxembourg.

Fennell, R. (1987) 'Reform of the CAP: shadow or substance', *Journal of Common Market Studies*, 26 (1): 61–77.

Grant, W. (1997) *The Common Agricultural Policy.* Macmillan, Basingstoke.

Grubb, M. with H.O. Bergesen, J.C. Hourcade, J. Jaeger, A. Lanza, R.Loske, L.A. Svendrup and A. Tudini, with D. Anderson and D. Brack as editors for the second edition (1994) *Implementing the European CO_2 Commitment: A Joint Policy Proposal*, 2nd edn. The Royal Institute of International Affairs, London.

Guay, T. (1999) *The United States and the European Union: The Political Economy of a Relationship*, Contemporary European Studies 8. Sheffield Academic Press, Sheffield.

Marsh, J. (1991) *The Changing Role of the CAP: The Future of Farming in Europe.* Belhaven Press, London.

Milward, A. (1992) *The European Rescue of the Nation-State,* Routledge, London.

OECD (1987) *National Policies and Agricultural Trade: Study on the EEC.* OECD, Paris.

Pearce, J. (1983) 'The CAP: the accumulation of special interests', in H. Wallace (ed.), *Policymaking in the EC.* 2nd edn. John Wiley and Sons, Chichester.

Redmond, J. (1996) 'Internal policy developments', in N. Nugent (ed.), *The European Union 1995: Annual Review of Activities.* Blackwell, Oxford, pp. 43–62.

Redmond, J. (1998) 'Internal policy developments', in G. Edwards and G. Wiessala (eds), *The European Union 1997: Annual Review of Activities.* Blackwell, Oxford, pp. 51–67.

Redmond, J. (1999) 'Internal policy developments', in G. Edwards and G. Wiessala (eds), *The European Union: Annual Review 1998–1999.* Blackwell, Oxford, pp. 69–85.

Vogel, D. (1993) 'The making of the EC environmental policy', in S.S. Anderson and K.A. Eliassen (eds), *Making Policy in Europe: The Europeification of National Policy-making.* Sage, London.

Warley, T.K. (1991–2) 'Europe's agricultural policy in transition', *International Journal,* 67: 112–35.

Webster, P. (1999) 'Arrest hardens French action against burger chain', *Guardian,* 24 August, p. 10.

Westlake, M. (1997) 'Keynote article: "Mad cows and Englishmen" – the institutional consequences of the BSE crisis', in N. Nugent (ed.), *The European Union 1996: Annual Review of Activities,* Blackwell, Oxford, pp. 11–36.

Wise, M. (1984) *The Common Fisheries Policy of the European Community.* Methuen, London.

Web sites

europa.eu.int/comm/dg06/ag2000/index_ en.htm	Agriculture and Agenda 2000
europa.eu.int/comm/dg06/wto/index_ en.htm	EU agriculture and the WTO
europa.eu.int/comm/dgs/agriculture/ index_en.htm	Agriculture Directorate General
europa.eu.int/comm/dgs/environment/ index_en.htm	Environment Directorate General
europa.eu.int/comm/newcomm/hearings/ answers/fischler.en.pdf	EP hearings: Fritz Fischler
europa.eu.int/pol/agr/newcap_en.htm	EU agriculture policy
europa.eu.int/pol/env/info_en.htm	EU environment policy
europa.eu.int/pol/fish/info_en.htm	EU fisheries policy

7 Regional and structural policies

Introduction

The founders of the EC considered that the social and the geographical disparities of economic activity that existed in 1957 might be sharpened by the creation of a common market, but could be eased by Community policies and institutions. The European Social Fund (ESF) was created (see Chapter 5) but also, in a modest way, certain regional differences in wealth were also addressed. However, the EC had to wait until 1975 to have a *regional policy* and a European Regional Development Fund. Other funds have regional implications: both the Guidance and Guarantee Sections of the European Agricultural Guidance and Guarantee Fund (see Chapter 6) are of importance for the regions of the EC. Since 1988 the ERDF, the EAGGF and the ESF have been defined as *structural funds*, with the Financial Instrument of Fisheries Guidance (FIFG) joining the list in 1993. To complicate the situation, a *Cohesion Fund* was created in 1993 that had structural consequences, but was not part of the EU's structural funds. Much of the focus in the early sections of this chapter is on the creation of a regional policy and its consequences, but the wider context of structural policies will also be examined.

The idea behind regional and structural policies, whether at a national or Community level, is that if market forces are left to work unhindered, they will either create or perpetuate inequalities that are unacceptable. Whether these differences are between socio-economic groups or between geographical areas, it is the task of the state – or the EC – to ameliorate them. This principle that government or administrative agents have a role to play in the socio-economic or geographic distribution of economic activity is one that is contested by free-marketeers, but even the most liberal of governments usually undertakes some interventionist action, if more for political survival than for economic good. The motivation behind the EC/EU's regional, structural and cohesion policies has often been political insofar as these have been pay-offs for groups of states to accept other Community policies. By the end of the 1990s, some 40 per cent of EU expenditure supported structural measures, including the structural funds and the

Cohesion Fund. While this may have been a small amount in terms of national budgets, it was an extra source of income for many local authorities, regions and groups, and therefore represented an important political resource for the EU.

The development of EC regional policy

Both the Treaty of Paris, which established the Coal and Steel Community, and the Treaty of Rome included elements that aimed to assist the regions. State aids that distorted the market were seen as incompatible with the common market. However, an exception was made in the Treaty of Rome for aid to promote the economic development of areas 'where the standard of living is abnormally low or where there is serious underemployment' and to help the development 'of certain economic activities or of certain economic areas' (Article 92.3a and c EEC, 87.3a and c TEC). Thus a 'region' could refer to a geographically outlying part of the EC or to an area that has become economically marginal to the main economic centre of the EC and is noticeably more deprived than the average. Such regions were the recipients of national aid and the ECSC and the EEC contributed from the beginning to the assistance of backward regions. The ECSC's restructuring plans in the 1950s and 1960s for the coal and steel industries of the Six tried to alleviate the effects of decline in areas that had been dominated by those industries. Also, in the EEC, the European Investment Bank and the Common Agricultural Policy's EAGGF provided assistance to economically backward areas, especially Southern Italy, and to those regions otherwise disadvantaged, such as the parts of the Federal Republic of Germany that bordered on communist-run East Germany.

The merger of the institutions of the three Communities in 1967 saw the creation of a Commission Directorate General for regional policy (DG XVI), although there was little impetus to create a comprehensive policy. The membership of Ireland and the United Kingdom of the EC in 1973 produced a pressure to create a distinct regional policy. Ireland wanted to counteract the effect of being far from the centre of the EC and to modernize its infrastructure, whereas the British motivation seemed – at least at first – more to get back money from 'Brussels'.

The subsequent efforts to establish a regional fund became entangled with the 'renegotiation' of the British terms of entry into the EC promised by the new Labour government in 1974 but were enhanced by new governments in both France and Germany in the autumn. Pressed by the Irish and the Italians, France and Germany dropped their opposition to a regional fund and in March 1975 the European Regional Development Fund (ERDF) was established. The idea was that this fund would provide up to half the costs of regional development projects in particular areas with the

rest of the money coming from domestic sources such as national governments. From the beginning the intention was that help from the ERDF
'should not lead Member States to reduce their own regional development
efforts but should complement these efforts' (Commission of the European
Communities, 1975). This principle of 'additionality' – that ERDF money
should be additional to national support, not to replace it – was one that
caused much rancour between the Commission and national governments –
especially those of the United Kingdom – for another couple of decades. At
its beginning the ERDF only took a modest 5 per cent of the EC's total
budget. Its distribution was undertaken on a quota basis for the member
states (see Table 7.1), partly based on need. During the Fund's first decade
the major beneficiaries were the United Kingdom, France, Ireland and
Italy.

Table 7.1 *National distribution of regional and structural funds (per cent)*

	1975[a]	1985[b]	1994–99[c]	2000–06[d]
Belgium	1.5	0.90–1.20	1.31	1.00
Denmark	1.3	0.51–0.67	0.54	0.41
France	15.0	11.05–14.74	9.65	7.96
Germany	6.4	3.76–4.81	14.12	15.36
Ireland	6.0	5.64–6.84	4.07	1.69
Italy	40.0	31.94–42.59	14.29	15.51
Luxembourg	0.1	0.06–0.08	0.06	0.04
Netherlands	1.7	1.00–1.34	1.59	1.44
United Kingdom	28.0	21.42–28.46	8.26	8.52
Greece	–	12.35–15.74	10.12	11.41
Portugal	–	–	10.12	10.36
Spain	–	–	22.91	23.47
Austria	–	–	1.04	0.80
Finland	–	–	1.09	1.00
Sweden	–	–	0.85	1.03

[a]National quotas for the ERDF agreed in 1975; [b]ERDF distribution in 1985, lower
and upper limits; [c]Structural funds allocation 1994–99; [d]Structural funds allocation
2000–06.

Sources: (a) Bache, 1998: 56, 226; (b) De Witte, 1986: 425; (c) Bache, 1998: 85; (d)
IP/99/442, http://europa.eu.int/rapid/start/welcome.htm

Regulation 724/75, which set up the ERDF as the main funding body for
the EC's regional policy, also established a Regional Policy Committee of
national and EC representatives, which was to examine regional policy
programmes. However, from the start the member states showed that they
did not want to lose control of this important policy. An attempt by the

Commission to draw up a map of the regions within the EC was overruled and instead the various national definitions of regions had to be accepted.

Despite the creation of the ERDF, EC regional policy had considerable shortcomings. In 1975 regional assistance was limited to only two sorts of project: those that created or maintained employment in the industrial and service sectors, and those that created infrastructure investment for industrial needs or for remote areas. Thus other, perhaps needier, cases were excluded. Second, there was no agreement over the definition of a region. Some were defined politically, such as the German Länder, others – such as Ireland and Scotland – reflected national concerns, whilst regions such as North West England were based on national planning divisions. Third, the national governments were responsible for the process of sifting applications for regional funds and for sending details of those they wanted to be funded to the Commission, in order to ensure that they achieved their national quota of funds. This left the Commission with little scope to fund those projects not supported by governments, which it nevertheless may have felt to be more worthy than the government-promoted projects. Finally, it became clear that some governments, especially that of the United Kingdom, were not upholding additionality but were using EC money to replace their own national resources that otherwise would have been spent on regional projects (Hooghe and Keating, 1994: 389). The UK Department of the Environment was open about government intentions in a circular to local authorities: 'the Government would not feel able to authorise individual local authorities to undertake additional projects because of the availability of assistance from the Fund [the ERDF]' (Department of the Environment Capital Programmes Circular 66/76, cited in Bache, 1998: 49).

An attempt was made to reform the ERDF during 1977–79. The Commission wanted 13 per cent of the funds allocated without any quota, thereby giving it the ability to fashion a more Community-based policy. This was opposed by the French and the British; in the end only a 5 per cent non-quota was agreed and its distribution was subject to a unanimous vote in the Council. This sort of control was unsatisfactory and, after Greek entry to the EC, the Fund was overhauled again in 1984. As well as changes in the quota system, the Commission wanted more funds, greater co-ordination of national policies and the establishment of integrated development programmes. The agreement reached in 1984 set minimum and maximum shares that each member country would be guaranteed to receive upon condition of satisfactory applications (see Table 7.1). The 11 per cent left unallocated once the minimum shares had been added together could be spent on 'Community programmes' proposed by the national authorities in consultation with the Commission. In the end only a small increase was agreed for the Fund, bringing it to 7.5 per cent of the EC's budget in 1985, even after Greek admission. The supranational elements in the reforms had been 'hijacked by member states' (Mawson *et al.*, 1985: 56). However, some progress had been made from a Commission perspective. The allocation of the non-quota element (in reality the amount over and above the minimum shares) no longer needed Council unanimity. The concentration on programmes rather than on one-off projects led to the funding of Valoren, to develop and strengthen local energy sources; Star, to promote high technology and communications; Integrated Development Operations (IDOs) and Integrated Mediterranean Programmes (IMOs).

The SEA and structural policy

In recognition of the need for a more effective regional policy once the Single European Market (SEM, internal market or '1992') had been achieved, the Single European Act (SEA) both entrenched and revised the EC's regional aspect. The accession of Spain and Portugal in 1986, representing 'a doubling of the population of the least favoured regions' (Commission of the European Communities, 1989: 9), as well as the move towards the single market, provided an impetus to a reconsideration of the structural policies.

Community competence was clarified by the addition of Title V (now Title XVII TEC) recognizing the need for 'economic and social cohesion' and for action to strengthen both these elements. It was feared that without such cohesion, the creation of the SEM would further advantage the core of the EC and marginalize the poorer regions even more. Areas without a decent infrastructure – roads, ports and telecommunications – and without a trained workforce would be less able to compete in the enlarged market.

Article 130b (159 TEC) stated that the achievement of common policies and the internal market should take into account the overall harmonious development of the EC and the strengthening of its social and economic cohesion. Also the EC should support the attainment of those objectives through the structural funds (the Guidance element of the EAGGF, the ESF and the ERDF), the European Investment Bank and 'other existing financial instruments'.

Article 130c (160 TEC) maintained that the ERDF was intended 'to help redress the principal regional imbalances in the Community through participating in the development and structural adjustment of regions whose development is lagging behind and in the conversion of declining industrial regions'. Article 130d (161 TEC) required the Commission to submit a proposal to the Council to reform the structural funds and thereby to improve their ability to achieve their set aims.

This review was carried out in 1988 and the new regulations that came into force in January 1989 set out six uses or 'objectives' for the structural funds:

- Objective 1 dealt with the 'development and structural adjustment of regions whose development is lagging behind', to cite Article 130c; it covered Greece, Portugal and Ireland, and areas of Italy, Spain and the United Kingdom (Northern Ireland), as well as the French overseas departments. The criterion was that the GDP of these areas should be at least 25 per cent below the EC average. Up to 65 per cent of the structural funds were devoted to these backward areas (Hooghe and Keating, 1994: 377).
- Objective 2 covered regions seriously affected by industrial decline; it included parts of the northern members of the EC as well as areas of Italy and Spain. These regions suffered from structural unemployment, which meant that this was hardly touched by the ups and downs of the economy generally but was determined by the decline of industries such as coal mining and steel.
- Objective 3 aimed to counter long-term unemployment. This could exist anywhere but tended to be concentrated in particular areas.
- Objective 4 intended to encourage the integration of young people in the economy and was therefore aimed at a particular section of the population rather than at a geographical area or at a type of economic activity.
- Objective 5a aimed to reform the structure of the agricultural sector, and encompassed the Guidance element of the EAGGF.
- Objective 5b aimed to promote the development of rural areas, providing a regional aspect to the sector support of 5a.

As can be seen, Objectives 1, 2 and 5b all contained strong regional elements and were covered by the ERDF, as set out in Article 130c (Article 160 TEC). The other Objectives were covered by the Guidance section of the EAGGF (Objectives 1, 5a and 5b) and the ESF and EIB (Objectives 1, 2, 3, 4 and 5b). A fisheries fund established in 1993 assisted within Objectives 1 and 5a (see below for changes in the Objectives).

The Council agreed to a doubling in real terms of the three structural funds (ERDF, ESF and the Guidance element of EAGGF) between 1987 and 1993. Expenditure in 1993 represented about 25 per cent of the EC budget, compared with 9.1 per cent in 1987 (Marks, 1992: 194). The four principles that were to guide the funds were familiar ones:

- Additionality: the Commission insisted on this notion and promised to check that states were adding the extra aid to their existing national effort. However, the United Kingdom continued to resist the principle. By receiving a large amount of aid in 1988, the UK was able to circumvent the agreed formula that 'increases in the appropriation' should have a genuine added impact on the regions concerned by pointing to a decrease in appropriations in the following years (Bache, 1998: 75–9).

- Concentration: the Objectives outlined above allowed the Commission to concentrate efforts to meet regional and structural needs. As well as money allocated by these Objectives, about 9 per cent of the ERDF budget was used in Community Initiatives such as Resider, dealing with steel producing areas; Renaval, for converting shipbuilding regions; and Interreg, which assisted border regions through cross-border economic development (Commission of the European Communities, 1992: 8).
- Partnership: local government, development agencies, business groups and others were encouraged to join national governments in partnerships preparing, negotiating and implementing programmes. This was an attempt – albeit at second-hand and through the actions of national governments – to engage the regions in regional policy. In 1988 a Consultative Council of local and regional authorities was set up, drawing on the experience of the close relationship of the Council of Municipalities and Regions of Europe (CCRE) and the International Union of Local Authorities (IULA) with the Commission.
- Programming: multi-annual programmes acted as the basis for funds, thus providing greater coherence. The Commission drew up regional development plans based on national submissions, then provided a Community Support Framework (CSF) for each Objective and region that defined the priorities for joint action. The CSFs could be over a five-year period for Objectives 1 and 5b and three years for Objective 2. The CSFs were translated into Operational Programmes (OPs) by the member states; after Commission approval, these programmes were implemented at regional or national level and were overseen by monitoring committees (Commission of the European Communities, 1992: 7).

Co-financing by the ERDF could make up between 50 per cent and 75 per cent of the total costs of an Objective 1 project (80 per cent in the case of Greece, Ireland, Portugal and Spain), and between 25 per cent and 50 per cent of Objective 2 and 5b projects.

When East Germany became part of the Federal Republic of Germany in 1991 and thus was included in the EC, the five new Länder and East Berlin, which the old East Germany represented, were made eligible for EC assistance under Regulation 3575/90. A CSF for these regions was allocated about ECU3bn for the 1991–93 period, with half coming from the ERDF. This helps explain the increase in the structural funds at the start of the 1990s, from taking up 20.3 per cent of EC budget commitments in 1989 to

30.6 per cent in 1993 and 31.9 per cent in 1997 (Commission of the European Communities, 1992: 3; http://www.europarl.eu.int/).

The European Investment Bank (EIB) also has a strong structural and regional emphasis in its activities. The Bank, established in 1958, has been the main financial institution of the EC/EU that has provided loans to promote European integration. The 1998 Annual Report (European Investment Bank, 1998: 8) said that

> the Bank will continue to concentrate its efforts on developing the Union's peripheral economic areas or those experiencing structural difficulties, in accordance with its principle [*sic*] mission of supporting economic convergence and integration in Europe. These activities will focus primarily on the less favoured regions of the present Union.

In 1998 the EU's less-favoured regions received ECU12.2bn in the form of individual loans from the EIB, making up some 72 per cent of such loans. Also an estimated ECU4.4bn of the global loans went to the less-favoured areas. About 45 per cent of the individual loans for regional development went to Objective 1 areas, those lagging behind in their development. Of this, about 20 per cent went to Germany's Eastern Länder in 1998, while 54 per cent was directed to the Cohesion countries of Spain, Portugal, the island of Ireland and Greece. In these Objective 1 areas, priority was given to communications infrastructure and energy networks which together received two-thirds of the money, while 11 per cent of the loans went to the environment and quality of life, health and education, and the industrial and service sectors. The Bank placed its money – which represented about 38 per cent of EIB individual loans – mainly in transport, energy networks and environmental programmes in the Objective 2, 5(b) and 6 regions, those which were undergoing economic restructuring or which had a low population density (European Investment Bank, 1998: 13).

Maastricht and structural policy

The Maastricht Treaty, reforms of the structural funds carried out in 1993 and the new membership of Austria, Finland and Sweden brought about important changes in the EU's structural policies.

The Maastricht Treaty increased the emphasis put on the role of the structural policies to prepare states for a closer economic and political union. It also introduced the Cohesion Fund and the Committee of the Regions (see Chapter 2, pp. 57–8).

Title XIV of the TEU (XVII TEC), entitled 'Economic and Social Cohesion', built on Title V of the Single European Act. The new Article 130b (159 TEC) asked the Commission to report every three years to the Council, the European Parliament, the ESC and to the Committee of the Regions on the progress made towards economic and social cohesion. Article 130d (161 TEC) allowed the Council to group the structural funds.

This Article also established the *Cohesion Fund* in order 'to provide a financial contribution to projects in the fields of environment and trans-European networks in the areas of transport infrastructure.' This was a fund – separate from the other structural funds – that would benefit the 'Cohesion countries', those states with a GDP of less than 90 per cent of the EU average and which included Greece, Ireland, Spain and Portugal. The Spanish government had refused to accept the Maastricht Treaty without this extra financing which was justified on the grounds of preparing the Cohesion countries for EMU and for the closer political union contained in the Treaty. The Cohesion Fund differed from the structural funds in a number of ways. First, it supported projects rather than programmes and was therefore much more specific in its targeting. Second, it could provide up to 85 per cent of the money for the projects, rather than the 50 per cent allowed for Objectives 2, 3, 4 and 5b and the 75 per cent of total cost for Objective 1. Third, the principle of additionality and partnership were substantially relaxed (Bache, 1998: 90). In particular, it was recognized that if the Cohesion states had to match these funds, this would weaken their ability to meet the 'Maastricht criteria' (see Chapter 4, p. 90) for achieving the final stage of monetary union (European Commission, 1998: 22).

The Cohesion Fund was implemented in May 1994, with a temporary arrangement in operation from April 1993. The Fund's budget from 1993 to 1999 was ECU15.5bn at 1992 prices and the allocations were divided among the four states, as noted in Table 7.2.

Table 7.2 *National shares of Cohesion Fund allocations 1994–99 (per cent)*

Country	Percentage share
Greece	18
Ireland	9
Portugal	18
Spain	55
Total	100

Source: Commission of the European Communities, 1996: 147

The 1993 reforms of the rules for the structural funds made a number of important changes for the 1993–99 period (Bache 1998: 83–8), which can be seen under the heading of the four principles used for the 1988 review, together with a new one:

- *Additionality:* the Commission tightened up the implementation of the additionality principle with the insistence that each member state, for each Objective, must keep its structural expenditure at least at the same level as that of the previous programming period, taking into account a number of other factors (Commission of the European Communities, 1993: 25). The idea was that member states would not be allowed to replace their national expenditure on programmes with that provided from the structural funds.
- *Concentration:* in order to concentrate more on the areas of greatest need, changes were made in the Objectives:
  - Objectives 3 and 4 were merged to form a new Objective 3 that aimed to ease the integration 'of those threatened with exclusion from the labour market' (Commission of the European Communities, 1993: 11);
  - a new Objective 4 aimed to help workers adapt to industrial change and to change in the production system;
  - the Financial Instrument of Fisheries Guidance (FIFG) was added to Objective 5a in order to help the fisheries sector;
  - Objective 5b was slightly revised in order to help the 'development and structural adjustment of rural areas' (Commission of the European Communities, 1993: 11);
  - an Objective 6 was to be added with the addition of new members in 1995 (see below).
- *Partnership*: the economic and social partners (such as trade unions and employers' representatives) were specifically included as collaborative partners, though it was left up to the individual states to decide how these might be involved.
- *Programming*: the five-year programme was replaced by a six-year one to coincide with the broader EU 'financial perspectives', although Objectives 2 and 4 were to have two three-year phases. The Edinburgh Council meeting in December 1992 agreed on an increase in the structural funds to ECU27.4bn by 1999, almost doubling the previous amount committed.
- *Environmental protection:* after the 1992 Rio conference on the environment, the EC was even more committed to protection of the environment. The new structural funds regulations, issued in July 1993, stipulated that the regional development plans submitted by member states should contain an assessment of the environmental impact of proposed measures and the steps taken to involve the relevant environmental authorities in the programming (European Commission, 1998: 14).

Bache (1998) has outlined how the above principles, especially partnership and additionality, were implemented differently in the member countries.

He also noted (*ibid.*: 103) that the partnership principle meant 'the formal involvement in decision-making of subnational actors' (such as regional and local governments). In the case of additionality the practice of member states varied widely, with the United Kingdom still using ERDF money 'to displace its own spending in the regions' (Bache, 1998: 107).

The issue of regional funds arose during the discussion about the entry of the Nordic and Alpine states into the EU during 1994. Although Austria fitted into the continental pattern with its borders to Germany and Northern Italy, the three Nordic applicants – Finland, Norway and Sweden – presented new problems. Each had vast, sparsely populated northern territories that depended on primary products from agriculture, fisheries and forestry. These areas received generous state aids and the farming population was heavily subsidized, especially in Norway. During the membership negotiations, a new Objective 6 was created that allowed support for these northern regions on the basis of their low population density. Areas such as Lapland in Northern Finland would be able to receive grants on a basis similar to Objective 1 areas, and other regions could also receive support under Objective 2 and 5b criteria. However, the Norwegian electorate rejected membership, so Objective 6 only covers the northern areas of Finland and Sweden. It should be noted that Austria, Finland and Sweden are net contributors to the EU funds.

The challenges of EMU and enlargement

The Treaty of Amsterdam included a title on employment (Title VIII TEC), although the changes in this area have been described as 'fairly cosmetic' (Duff, 1997: 65). Nevertheless, the emphasis on the 'employability' of the workforce provided a context within which any changes to the structural funds had to be placed.

The ending of the 1994–99 programme period, and the publication of a Commission report on economic and social cohesion since the establishment of the EU, meant that the structural policies of the EU had to undergo reconsideration by the end of the 1990s. Added to this internal requirement were the external pressures of preparation for Economic and Monetary Union (EMU) and for the possible admission of new members. EMU could mean that countries that had previously tried to gain an advantage over their competitors through currency devaluation could no longer do so. Many areas in the applicant countries had a GNP per capita well below that of even the poorest regions of the current EU. Faced with these challenges, the Commission published its blueprint for the future called 'Agenda 2000: For a Stronger and Wider Union' (Commission of the European Communities, 1997). In this report the Commission proposed a budget for the 2000–06 structural and Cohesion funds of ECU275bn (in 1997 prices) compared with the 1993–99 budget of ECU200bn. ECU45bn of the new budget was to be earmarked for the new member states in such instruments as Sapard (Support for Pre-Accession Measures for Agriculture and Rural Development) and ISPA (Instrument for Structural Policies for Pre-Accession).

The Commission also proposed a consolidation of the structural funds with the seven Objectives being reduced to two regional ones and another for human resources. The new Objective 1 would cover a smaller proportion of the EU and eligibility would be limited to those regions with a per capita GNP less than 75 per cent of the EU's average. The new Objective 2 would help regions, whether urban or rural, that needed major economic and social restructuring. The new Objective 3 would cover areas not included in Objectives 1 and 2 and would help regions to update education, training and employment. As well as a continued concern for the environment, the four principles of additionality, concentration, partnership and programming were to remain but a further principle – efficiency – was to be added. The Commission wanted to retain 10 per cent of the structural funds as 'efficiency' money to be used to reward those regions that performed well. The Commission planned that the Cohesion Fund would remain with its existing aims and with a 2000–06 budget of ECU3bn for the current members. While the amount going to structural and Cohesion funds would increase, the share of EU GNP that this funding represented would remain the same. However, the resources earmarked for new members would mean a decrease in the funds for existing members.

The Commission proposals were attacked on a number of grounds. The Dutch thought that the proposed expenditure was too high, while the Spanish considered that their share was too little. Each member state opposed changes in the Objectives that would see their share of the funds fall although they were more sympathetic to changes that benefited them. The applicant countries did not consider that the amount dedicated to them would be enough.

At the March 1999 Berlin European Council meeting a deal was struck that allocated €213bn of structural funds to be spent in the 2000–06 period (Galloway, 1999: 26–7). There would be three objectives:

- *Objective 1:* regions lagging behind, with inclusion to be decided on the basis of the eligible population, regional prosperity and severity of structural problems, especially unemployment. Those regions currently in Objective 1 but no longer in the new list would be allowed a transition period.
- *Objective 2:* 'converting regions', those seriously affected by industrial decline, to be defined by criteria similar to those of Objective 1.
- *Objective 3:* combating long-term unemployment, with the allocation being made on the grounds of eligible population, the employment

situation and the severity of social exclusion, as well as on education and training levels and the participation of women in the labour market (http://europa.eu.int/scadplus/leg/en/s60000.htm).

The acceptance of this deal allowed the EU to continue its structural policies into the twenty-first century and to prepare for the membership of new states. However, it was clearly a political compromise between those who were net contributors to the EU and the main recipients of the funds; the deal may have to be reconsidered once new members join the EC and voice their demands for a larger share of the structural cake.

Conclusions

Have the structural policies worked? Have they assisted the poor regions and narrowed the gap between these and the richer regions of the EU? As required by the Maastricht Treaty, the Commission (1996) published a report, mentioned above, on Economic and Social Cohesion that brought out a number of facts:

- From 1983 to 1995 economic disparities within the EU narrowed with the four Cohesion countries of Greece, Ireland, Spain and Portugal making the greatest progress and their average income per capita increasing from 66 per cent to 74 per cent of the EC/EU average over the period.
- Income per capita rose in all the regions during this period, leaving the difference between the richest and the poorest regions unchanged. However, regional income differences within states increased in all member states except the Netherlands.
- Since their 1988 reform, the structural funds' redistributive effect had been 'significantly increased' in favour of the less prosperous states and regions (Commission of the European Communities, 1996: 9–10).
- The four Cohesion states were those most vulnerable to the negative repercussions of trade liberalization such as tariff cuts.
- While unemployment in the 1983–93 period fell in the 25 regions with the lowest unemployment, in the 25 regions with the highest unemployment it rose from 17.2 per cent to 22.4 per cent, with the young, women and the poorly educated particularly badly hit.

This report – perhaps the most comprehensive on the practicalities of the structural funds and policies – paints a mixed picture. It is difficult to generalize as to whether the plight of the regions has lessened. They have made absolute gains and the Cohesion states have improved their relative position, but the poorer regions within member states still find their richer neighbours doing better and the disadvantaged groups of society have not seen an improvement in their comparative position. Furthermore, it should be recognized that the EU contribution to regional and structural policies is small compared with the national input. The structural and Cohesion funds of the EU only account for 0.46 per cent of the EU GNP. A much wider-scale distribution is undertaken within each member state through a greater range of policies financed by taxation. Nevertheless, the structural policies and funds of the EU are likely to become more important within the organization with the admission of new Central and East European and Mediterranean members. Whether it becomes more effective remains to be seen.

References and further reading

Bache, I. (1998) *The Politics of the European Union Regional Policy: Multi-Level Governance or Flexible Gatekeeping*, Contemporary European Studies 3. Sheffield Academic Press, Sheffield.

Commission of the European Communities (1975) Preamble to Regulation (EEC) No. 724/75 of 18 March 1975 establishing a European Regional Development Fund, *Official Journal L73, 21/3/75*.

Commission of the European Communities (1989) *Guide to the Reforms of the Community's Structural Funds*. European Communities, Brussels and Luxembourg.

Commission of the European Communities (1992) *Info Background. Report 'The ERDF in 1991'*. European Commission, Brussels and Luxembourg.

Commission of the European Communities (1993) *Community Structural Funds 1994–99: Revised Regulations and Comments*. European Communities, Brussels and Luxembourg.

Commission of the European Communities (1996) *First Report of Economic and Social Cohesion*. European Commission, Brussels and Luxembourg.

Commission of the European Communities (1997) Agenda 2000: for a stronger and wider union, *Bulletin of the European Union, 5/97*.

De Witte, B. (1986) 'The reform of the European Regional Development Fund', *Common Market Law Review*, 23: 419–40.

Duff, A. (ed.) (1997) *The Treaty of Amsterdam: Text and Commentary*. Sweet and Maxwell for the Federal Trust, London.

European Commission (1998) *The Environment and the Regions: Towards Sustainability*. Office for Official Publications of the European Communities, Luxembourg.

European Investment Bank (EIB) (1998) *1998 Annual Report*. EIB, Luxembourg.

Galloway, D. (1999) 'Agenda 2000: packaging the deal', in G. Edwards and G. Wiessala (eds), *The European Union: Annual Review 1998–1999*. Blackwell, Oxford, pp. 9–35.

Hooghe, L. and Keating, M. (eds) (1994) 'The politics of the European Union regional policy', *Journal of European Public Policy*, 1 (3): 367–93.

Marks, G. (1992) 'Structural policy in the European Community', in A. Sbragia (ed.), *Euro-Politics: Institutions and Policymaking in the 'New' European Community*, Brookings Institution, Washington, DC, pp. 191–224.

Mawson, J., Martins, M. and Gibney, J. (1985) 'The development of the European Community Regional Policy', in M. Keating and B. Jones (eds), *Regions in the European Community*. Clarendon Press, Oxford, pp. 20–59.

Web sites

europa.eu.int/comm/dgs/regional_policy/ index_en.htm	Regional Policy Directorate General
europa.eu.int/pol/reg/index_en.htm	EU regional policy
europa.eu.int/rapid/start/welcome.htm	Commission's RAPID press service
eib.eu.int/	European Investment Bank
europa.eu.int/scadplus/leg/en/s60000.htm	Agenda 2000
www.europarl.eu.int/	European Parliament
www.rural-europe.aeidl.be/rural-en/ index.html	EU rural development policy

8 Justice and the citizen

Introduction

This chapter will consider the structures that administer the relationship between EU citizens – and between citizens wanting access to the EU – and authorities, both in the Union and in its member states. What the EU and its predecessors have had to say about this relationship has altered significantly. Generally, the EEC was only concerned with the citizen as an economic entity – as a worker or a commercial entity. As the economic borders came down within the EU and as free movement of labour became more than just an aspiration, so the authorities of a number of EC states started to co-operate more closely in order to deal with some of the implications of this integration. They tried to stop free movement of drugs and criminals. They also tried to deal with the implications of a freer movement of persons within the EC on national immigration and asylum laws. With the creation of a European Union, the idea of an EU citizenship arose and co-operation on matters of justice and on what was called 'home affairs' was included as the Pillar III of the Union. This was a recognition that the policies covered by the Union went beyond those of the economic life of citizens and that the EU, in the context of a post-Cold War world, should espouse certain values beyond those of freer markets. The Treaty of Amsterdam reaffirmed the basis of the relationship between the authorities within the EU and the citizen; it also adapted many of the issues previously covered by Pillar III into the Community structure. A brief overview of key parts of the treaties charts this development.

The Union and the citizen

The Preamble of the Treaty of Rome set out the determination of the EEC founders 'to lay the foundations of an ever closer union among the peoples of Europe'. The means to do this were primarily economic and social – the establishment of a 'common market', by which economic barriers between the member states would be removed, and of an element of social progress to match the expected economic advancement. The original Six were thus resolved to pool 'their resources to preserve and strengthen peace and liberty' (Preamble, Treaty of Rome).

The Maastricht Treaty, written in the context of greater public engagement in the process of European integration and the upsurge of popular opinion in Central and East Europe that had rejected Communist regimes, had more to say about the relationship of the European Union and its citizens. The Preamble contained a number of relevant phrases. The signatories

> Confirming their attachment to the principles of liberty, democracy and respect for human rights and fundamental freedoms and of the rule of law . . .
> Resolved to establish a citizenship common to nationals of their countries . . .
> Resolved their objective to facilitate the free movement of persons, while ensuring the safety and security of their peoples, by including provisions on justice and home affairs in this Treaty . . .
> Have decided to establish a European Union . . .

Article B of the Common Provisions asserted that two of the Union's objectives were

> to strengthen the protection of the rights and interests of the nationals of its Member States through the introduction of a citizenship of the Union; to develop close cooperation on justice and home affairs . . .

Article F responded to the criticism that, while the EC had implicitly been based on the democratic system, this had not been set down in the founding treaties:

1. The Union shall respect the national identities of its Member States, whose systems of government are founded on the principles of democracy.
2. The Union shall respect fundamental rights, as guaranteed by the European Convention for the Protection of Human Rights and Fundamental Freedoms signed in Rome on 4 November 1950 and as they result from the constitutional traditions common to the Member States, as general principles of Community law . . .

The Treaty of Amsterdam further refined the relationship between the Union and the individual by replacing the objectives in the TEU's Article B on co-operation on justice and home affairs with the more detailed and balanced objective

> to maintain and develop the Union as an area of freedom, security and justice, in which the free movement of persons is assured in conjunction with appropriate measures with respect to external border controls, immigration, asylum and the prevention and combating of crime.

It also made Article F.1 more specific:

1. The Union is founded on the principles of liberty, democracy, respect for human rights and fundamental freedoms, and the rule of law, principles which are upheld by the Member States.

Furthermore, a section was added at the end of Title 1. This allowed the European Council acting unanimously, but without the vote of the country concerned, to determine the existence of 'a serious and persistent breach by a Member state of the principles mentioned in Article F (1)'. It could then, acting on a qualified majority, decide whether to suspend certain of the EU treaty rights as they affected that state, including its voting rights in Council. This addressed the question of what the Union might do about a member state that violated the very principles on which the Union was based (European Commission, 1999: 13–14).

A federalist view would see the above changes as inexorably leading towards something resembling the constitution of a European Union which would provide all its citizens with equal rights testable in a court, in criminal as well as civil law. At the moment, the European Court of Justice's jurisdiction only stretches to those parts of the treaties of the EU that allow for its intervention, basically what became known in the Maastricht Treaty as 'Pillar I', those aspects dealt with by the Community institutions. The role of the ECJ was severely limited in Pillar II, the Common Foreign and Security Policy, and in Pillar III, Justice and Home Affairs. The federalist might see the transfer of many subjects from Pillar III to Pillar I in the Treaty of Amsterdam as part of the gradual move to a United States of Europe.

An intergovernmentalist interpretation would not agree. This would more probably explain the above changes in more pragmatic terms. Such changes have been incremental and only as the need arose. The customs posts and immigration counters that were abolished between member states as the freedoms of movement of labour, capital, goods and services were achieved have merely been moved to the periphery of the EU. Furthermore, their management is undertaken primarily by an essentially intergovernmental method and is reversible by national decision.

A more neofunctionalist approach would see the inevitability of closer integration in justice and citizenship matters. As the four freedoms of movement were accepted with the Single European Market, it became almost inevitable that the governments of the member states would have to re-arrange not just customs frontiers but those concerned with immigration and asylum. If the EU wanted to portray its closeness to people by the creation of an EU citizenship, then this would have certain consequences. The granting of United Kingdom citizenship to only a few from the former colony of Hong Kong was compared to a more generous handing out of citizenship by Portugal to those from its former colony of Macao (just next door to Hong Kong in South China). The new Portuguese citizens could travel to get work in the United Kingdom while many of those who had served the British crown in Hong Kong could not do so. The logic of a common citizenship was a move towards common policies on who should be a citizen and who might be excluded. Furthermore, it could be argued that if criminals were to be allowed to move more easily across frontiers within the EU, then they should not be able to move outside the arm of the law.

Whichever view is taken, it has to be admitted that the EU is now more active in this field than the EEC or EC ever were. The main developments in these areas will now be tracked.

Background

During the 1970s the member states of the EC developed the habit of meeting together at the highest level – that of heads of government or state – on a regular basis. Although a member of the Commission was present, these meetings could, in the form of European Political Co-operation (see Chapter 2, p. 47), discuss matters that were outside the remit of the EC treaties, and they frequently touched on foreign affairs (see Chapter 9). Another phenomenon of the 1970s was the rise of terrorism, a matter that also came on to the EPC ministerial agendas. From 1975, ministers of the interior and justice met intergovernmentally in the so-called Trevi Group to discuss possible reactions to terrorism and serious crimes (Benyon 1994; den Boer and Walker 1993).

As the move towards a Single European Market gathered pace in the mid-1980s, another aspect of free movement began to concern ministers. The increase in unemployment during the 1970s and early 1980s had not abated and there seemed to be no return to the days when Western European states had encouraged immigration from outside the area to fill job vacancies. By the mid–1980s most EC states had tightened up their immigration laws, although there were differences between the laws in force. With the prospect of easier movement between member states on the horizon, the British EC Presidency in 1986 took the initiative in calling an intergovernmental meeting of ministers and their officials. A Working Group on Immigration was established which later led to the 1990 Dublin Asylum Convention.[1] However, there was a marked reluctance on behalf of most EC states for such issues to be brought into the EC decision-making procedure. They were regarded as being central to the order of the state and therefore not subject to outside control. Mrs Thatcher, the British Prime Minister throughout the 1980s (1993: 555), 'derived most satisfaction' from the inclusion of a general statement in the record of the IGC, leading to the Single European Act that confirmed

Nothing in these provisions shall affect the right of member states to take such measures as they consider necessary for the purpose of controlling immigration from third countries, and to combat terrorism, the traffic in drugs and illicit trading in works of art and antiques.

Implicit in this was the belief that these activities should remain primarily in the hands of the member states since they could manage these matters satisfactorily. But there was a recognition that the 'informal intergovernmentalism' of the various ad hoc bodies needed Co-ordination and in 1988 the European Council established a Group of National Co-ordinators that was responsible for the Palma document setting out the measures necessary for the free movement of persons (Kostakopoulou, 1998: 889). In the end, issues such as immigration and terrorism were to become the concern of the EU although the role of the member states was still to weigh heavily in policy-making in these areas.

Schengen

The view cited above of Mrs Thatcher, then Prime Minister of the United Kingdom, demonstrates the reluctance of some EC members to have the Communities involved at all with the issues mentioned. However, other EC states would at least consider closer co-operation on free movement within the borders of the Communities. In June 1984 the Fontainebleau European Council had agreed to abolish, in principle, customs barriers within the EC and in the following month the Germans and French had decided at Saarbrücken to move towards this end.

In June 1985 France and Germany were joined by Belgium, the Netherlands and Luxembourg in signing the Schengen Accord or Agreement, which aimed to abolish border checks between these countries and to allow free access for those travelling among them. In June 1990 these five states signed a more detailed agreement – the Convention of Application – setting out the conditions for such open frontiers and later that year Italy joined them. In November 1991 Spain and Portugal joined, and later Greece and Austria. The United Kingdom and Ireland – without any land frontiers with the rest of the EC – did not participate; neither did Denmark. Italy and Greece postponed application of the system to a later stage and in 1995 France utilized the safeguard clauses to re-establish national controls over its frontiers because of action by terrorists and drug-trafficking. Denmark, Finland and Sweden, together with the Nordic EEA states of Iceland and Norway – which together had formed the Nordic passport union from the 1950s – had an association arrangement with the Schengen states (Kostakopoulou, 1998: 886).

The aims of the Schengen Agreement, as set out in Title II, were:

- an end to frontier controls between members and the transfer of such controls to their external frontiers;
- to fight against international crime and to establish the right of pursuit for the police;
- the harmonization of legislation and regulations concerning drugs and arms;
- the harmonization of visa policies and the conditions of entry to national territories;
- easing customs procedures (Parlement Europeen, 1996: 6).

The 1990 Convention included a wide range of rules on these matters but only came into force in March 1995. It set up the Schengen Information System (SIS), which allowed the authorities to exchange passport information although a later report described this as being 'constantly the object of criticism' (*ibid.*). Schengen was included in the Amsterdam Treaty (see pp. 156–9).

The Treaty of Maastricht

The establishment of Schengen, Trevi and a number of other networks of co-operation meant that by the time of the draft Maastricht Treaty, issues such as immigration, asylum and police and judicial co-operation were taking place on a regular, though often fragmented, basis among EC members. The prospect of the creation of a Single European Market from 1992 brought into question the arrangement for the free movement of labour within the EC and a number of related issues. These included the free movement of all persons within the new Union, the entry of non-EU citizens into the Union and the more general relationship between the Union and its citizens. The Maastricht Treaty attempted to deal with these issues but the form in which they were treated reflected the sensitive nature of these subjects in relation to the member states of the EU.

As mentioned in the Introduction, the Preamble to the Maastricht Treaty saw the member states 'resolved to establish a citizenship common to nationals of their countries'. Article 8 of Maastricht set out the details.

1. Citizenship of the Union is hereby established.
    Every person holding the nationality of a Member State shall be a citizen of the Union.
2. Citizens of the Union shall enjoy the rights conferred by this Treaty and shall be subject to the duties imposed thereby.

This was a careful balance between a Union-wide right (citizenship of the Union) and the dominance of the member states in this area (Union citizenship being dependent on prior citizenship of a member state). The rights of citizens of the Union (Articles 8a–d, 18–21 TEC) are:

- to move and reside freely within the territory of the member states, subject to certain limitations;
- to vote and stand as a candidate in local and European Parliamentary elections, for citizens residing in member states of which they are not a national, subject to certain conditions;
- to have protection in a third country in which one's own state does not have diplomatic representation, by the diplomatic authorities of any member state, subject to agreed rules;
- to petition the European Parliament and to apply to the Ombudsman.

With the exception of the rights concerning petition, all the others were conditional, if only because they depended on the members working out the details. The list is clearly meant to be additional to those rights that a citizen would expect in his or her state and is in no way a replacement for such rights. A European Parliament report concluded that the Treaty had '*not yet produced measures conferring really effective rights*: the citizen enjoys only *fragmented, incomplete* rights which are themselves subject to *restrictive conditions*' (European Parliament 1996a: 9, emphasis in original).

In policy terms, the matters dealt with by Trevi, Schengen and other ad hoc arrangements were placed within Pillar III (Title VI) under the heading of 'Provisions on cooperation in the fields of justice and home affairs'. Article K.1 enumerated nine issues that were of common concern, not least for the purpose of achieving the free movement of persons:

1. asylum policy;
2. rules about the controls on people crossing the external borders of member states;
3. immigration policy for nationals of third countries, including their conditions of entry, and movement into member states' territory, their conditions of residence therein, and the combating of unauthorized immigration;
4. combating drug addiction;
5. combating fraud on an international scale;
6. judicial co-operation in civil matters;
7. judicial co-operation in criminal matters;
8. customs co-operation;
9. police co-operation to prevent and combat terrorism, drug trafficking and serious international crime, including the organization of an EU-wide information exchange system within the European Police Office (Europol).

These matters had to be dealt with in the context of the 1950 European Convention for the Protection of Human Rights and Fundamental Freedoms and the 1951 Convention relating to the Status of Refugees, and would not affect the responsibility of states 'with regard to the maintenance of law and order and the safeguarding of internal security' (Article K.2, 30 TEU).

Further initiatives could be taken to adopt joint positions or joint action, or to recommend conventions to member states. These initiatives could come from either a member state or from the Commission in the case of areas 1 to 6 listed above, but only from member states in the more sensitive cases of 7 to 9.

A Co-ordinating Committee of senior officials was established under Article K.4 (now Article 32 TEU) to advise the Council. This 'K4 Committee' took over from the Group of National Co-ordinators, and the Commission is also a member, being fully associated with Justice and Home Affairs (JHA) matters under Article K.4.2 (now 32.2 TEU). This did not give the Commission the right to initiate policy in this area that it had for Community policies (Pillar I). Article K.6 (now 34 TEU) allowed the European Parliament to be informed and consulted on JHA matters and to question the Council or make recommendations in this area, with a debate on the issues to be held annually.

There was one area of related business that was not included in the JHA title but that was placed in Pillar I, the Community pillar, this related to visas. The Council, acting on a Commission proposal and after consulting with the European Parliament, was to determine which third country nationals had to possess visas when entering the EU. This procedure could be extended to the matters covered by 1 to 6 in the above list, but it needed a unanimous Council decision, a remote possibility (den Boer, 1996: 13).

The vast range of issues covered by Pillar III meant that once the Maastricht Treaty came into force, there was the potential for a wide range of policies, conventions and actions.

Three Steering Groups were established (den Boer, 1996: 12). Steering Group I, on immigration and asylum, covered

- migration
- asylum
- visas
- external frontiers
- forged documents
- the Centre for Information, Reflection and Exchange on Asylum Matters (CIREA) and the Centre for Information, Reflection and Exchange on Crossing of Borders and Immigration (CIREFI).

Steering Group II dealt with police and customs co-operation and included

- terrorism

- police co-operation
- drugs and serious organized crime
- customs
- an ad hoc Europol group

Steering Group III covered judicial co-operation, that is,

- extradition
- international organized crime
- criminal and Community law
- driving licence withdrawal
- the transfer of trial documents
- the application of the Brussels Convention

A number of working groups dealt with issues ranging from more flexible extradition to the fight against corruption. However, a number of conventions and the establishment of Europol became entangled with disputes about the role of the European Court of Justice as well as with the United Kingdom and Spain's disagreement about the status of Gibraltar. Nevertheless, the EU agreed on a harmonized application of the term 'refugee', on minimum guarantees for asylum seekers and on simplified extradition procedures, taking it closer to what seemed to be a more restrictive view of entry to the EU area (Kostakopoulou, 1998: 891).

The Council Act of July 1995 drew up the Convention for the establishment of a European Police Office (Europol), with aims to improve member states' effectiveness in preventing and combating terrorism, unlawful drug trafficking and other forms of serious international crime. Each state was to establish a national unit to co-ordinate with Europol. The organs of Europol, with its headquarters in The Hague, are the management board, consisting of representatives of the member states; a director, appointed by the Council, and assisted by deputies; a financial committee; and a financial controller. Because of the continued disputes over the link between Europol and the European Court of Justice, which the British government opposed, it was first established by a ministerial-level agreement in 1994. The Europol Convention was ratified in 1998 and the organization was activated in July 1999. The Europol Drugs Unit (EDU) was set up by ministers in 1995 and acted as an information exchange not only on drugs but also on nuclear and radioactive materials, the movement of illegal vehicles, and illegal immigration networks, effectively becoming an interim core for Europol until the Convention was ratified. In the first year of its existence the EDU helped police and customs authorities in over 700 cases (European Parliament 1996b: 13). Europol and the EDU is supported by the European Computer System (TECS) (http://www.europol.eu.int/content.htm?facts/en.htm).

The Treaty of Amsterdam

The system established by the Maastricht Treaty to cover Justice and Home Affairs matters clearly had its weaknesses. From the viewpoint of those wishing to strengthen the Community element in the EU, Pillar III represented a bastion of member states' power in an area where many of the problems – drugs, immigration and criminality – were Union-wide. The only sensible solution from that viewpoint was to include Pillar III issues into Pillar I and allow them to be handled by the Community method. This was entirely opposed by the United Kingdom and Denmark, whose politicians considered that Pillar III went far enough and that any transfer of responsibilities should be on a case-by-case basis, with unanimous consent and with the possibility of opt-outs. Either way the arrangement in the Maastricht Treaty seemed to be interim and the Amsterdam Treaty of 1997 allowed for a reconsideration of the whole matter.

The Amsterdam Treaty attempted to rationalize the unsatisfactory situation described above but in effect shifted the lines of division between what was dealt with under Pillar I, the Community method, and old Pillar III, intergovernmental action. Title VI – Pillar III – is renamed 'police and judicial co-operation in criminal matters' and contains those elements under 7, 8 and 9 under the K.1 list (see p. 153). The other matters, broadly covering immigration and asylum, moved to the main Community body of the Treaty.

The new Article K.1 (29 TEU) sets out the aims of providing citizens 'with a level of safety within an area of freedom, security and justice' by developing common action in police matters and judicial co-operation 'and combating racism and xenophobia'. Article K.2 (30 TEU) lays down the areas for police co-operation; these include:

- detection and investigation of criminal offences;
- exchange of information, including that on suspicious financial transactions, subject to data protection;
- initiatives in training, secondments and research;
- the common evaluation of techniques to investigate serious organized crime.

Article K.3 (31 TEU) deals with judicial co-operation in criminal matters including:

- enforcement of decisions;
- facilitation of extradition between member states;
- adherence to the compatibility of rules to facilitate such co-operation;
- prevention of conflict of jurisdiction between member states;
- establishment of minimum rules for acts and penalties for organized crime, terrorism and drug trafficking.

Article K.6 (32 TEU) is the old Article K.3 on co-operation, somewhat revised and streamlined into framework decisions, second-tier decisions and conventions (Duff, 1997: 42). Article K.7 (35 TEU) deals with the role of the European Court of Justice which is now allowed 'to give preliminary rulings on the validity and interpretation of framework decisions, and decisions on the interpretation of conventions established under this Title and the validity and interpretation of measures implementing them' (Article K.7.1, 35.1 TEU). This makes the Court available for such decisions. Paragraph 2 of the same Article allows any member state to accept this jurisdiction for preliminary rulings. Paragraph 3 allows states to specify that courts and tribunals, under particular circumstances, may request a preliminary ruling from the ECJ on police and judicial co-operation in criminal matters, as covered by Title VI. Later in the Article it is noted that the ECJ has no jurisdiction to review 'the validity or proportionality of operations' under-taken by police or other law officers or over internal security matters. However, it does have jurisdiction to review the legality of decisions on the grounds of lack of competence, infringement of procedures or misuse of power (in cases brought by member states or the Commission) and to rule on the dispute among member states on the interpretation of acts adopted under K.6.2 (34.2 TEU: common decisions, framework decisions, other decisions and conventions).

Thus the ECJ has its foot in the door for Title VI. It does not have the same standing as the Community element of the EU, and the European Parliament and individual citizens are excluded from the process in this case. Nevertheless, it has entered what was previously almost a 'no-go zone' for it.

Police and judicial co-operation is to be managed by the K8 Committee (the renamed K4 Committee). The members are represented in international organizations and conferences by the Presidency and they are obliged to uphold common positions there (Article K.9, 37 TEU). Article K.11 (39 TEU) enhances the standing of the European Parliament in this area compared with Maastricht by extending the range of matters on which it should be consulted – rather than just informed – from principle issues to legislation and conventions.

Article K.12 (40 TEU) outlines how a number of EU states may co-operate on police and judicial matters and replaces the former flexibility article of K.7. Article K.13 (41 TEU) 'strengthens the ties that bind the remaining third pillar to the first' (Duff, 1997: 45) by extending the powers of the Ombudsman transparency and budgetary scrutiny by the Parliament to these areas.

The Schengen Agreement (see pp. 151–2) in effect allowed a majority of the EU states to advance their co-operation on the removal of internal borders, the strengthening of external borders, visa regulations, the move-ment of third country nationals, police co-operation, baggage control, asylum requests, assistance in criminal matters, extradition, drugs, and on firearms. They can do this without being held back by the United Kingdom, Ireland or by the weaknesses in the administrative structure of some of the Southern European members such as Italy and Greece. The Treaty of Amsterdam now incorporates the Schengen Agreement and its *acquis* (the backlog of its agreements, decisions, declarations and acts). However, in the words of Duff (1997: 53), the Agreement 'was glued in an ungainly manner on to both the first and the third pillars'. The executive committee that ran Schengen has evolved into a Council of the 13 members of Schengen, although the United Kingdom and Ireland can apply to join at a later date. Furthermore, the full Schengen acquis has to be accepted by those states wishing admission to the EU.

Issues 1–6 on the Maastricht K.1 list – asylum, visas, immigration, drugs, fraud and civil judicial matters (see p. 153) – were transferred from Pillar III to the Community part of the Amsterdam Treaty. A new Title IIIa (Title 4 TEC) outlines how measures should be taken to 'establish progressively an area of freedom, security and justice' (Article 73i TEU, 61 TEC), but at the same time recognizes that these measures should be at least at 'the same level of protection and security' as Schengen. Article 73j (62 TEC) aims to create free movement of persons (not just of labour or even of EU citizens) within the EU after a period of five years. The member states are also given five years to bring into force measures on asylum, refugees and immigration (Article 73k, 63 TEC). Co-operation on civil matters with cross-border implications is to be improved (Article 73m, 65 TEC). All this is subject to the rule of unanimity within the Council, although Article 73o (67 TEC) allowed this rule to be changed after five years and without the need for another IGC. Furthermore, all Title IIIa (IV TEC) did not apply to the United Kingdom and Ireland, who might, however, opt into any discussion and measure they desired. Likewise it did not apply to Denmark, which has six months to decide whether to accept directives from this Title. The attempted tidying up process of Amsterdam has thus produced a very untidy package. To cite two authors on the subject, it has produced both 'reform at the price of fragmentation' (Monar, 1998) and 'more complexity despite Communitarisation' (den Boer, 1997).

Once the Amsterdam Treaty had been signed in 1997, much was needed to be done to prepare for its implementation. In July 1998 the Commission advanced an 'Action Plan on how best to implement the provisions of the Treaty of Amsterdam in an area of freedom, security and justice' (Commission of the European Communities, 1998), which was adopted by the Justice and Home Affairs Council in December 1998. It clarified the concept of an 'area of freedom, security and justice'. Freedom goes beyond free movement across frontiers to mean 'freedom to live in a law-abiding environment'. Security is given a limited meaning at the EU level, stressing common action in police and criminal justice matters, but leaving law and order as being primarily a state responsibility. The Plan states that the Treaty aims to give citizens 'a common sense of justice throughout the Union'. In the section on priorities and measures, an overall migration strategy is promised, as is the examination of Europol's access to data (Monar, 1999: 167).

Since the implementation of the Amsterdam Treaty in 1999, gradual progress has been made in the areas covered by this chapter. The Commission has even instituted a 'scoreboard' on governments' progress in the home affairs field. The Eurodac Convention, which would establish a database of the fingerprints of refugees in order to prevent them from applying to several states for asylum, has been frozen because of the question of whether it should be subsumed under the main body of EU law (European Voice, 1999a). Greek efforts to become a full Schengen member have advanced but Spain voiced concerns about the United Kingdom's involvement with some aspects of Schengen, especially the SIS. This relates to the British requirement for access to some but not all information, and also reflected the dispute between Spain and the United Kingdom over the status of Gibraltar (European Voice, 1999b). In April 2000 a settlement of outstanding issues between the two countries allowed progress with a number of Schengen-related activities (European Voice, 2000: 2). There has been continued disagreement between member states as to whether the Charter of Fundamental Rights planned for late 2000 should represent merely a summary of existing rights or should be the basis of a constitutional document similar to the US Bill of Rights.

Conclusions

The links between the European Union, the legal systems of the member states and the citizens within the EU are complicated ones. These have developed from the early days of the EEC, when regard was given to the economic rights and duties of the workers, to the concerns in the Amsterdam Treaty to set out the democratic and human rights basis of the Union and to provide some indication as to which of those rights might be pursued through the Union. It is recognized that the member states have the prime responsibility for law and order and security within their own frontiers. However, there is also a reflection of the need for member states to act collectively in the face of common challenges, such as numbers of refugees, asylum seekers and immigration, and of common threats, such as those posed by illegal drugs and international criminal gangs.

What has been shown in this chapter is the disagreement between those states that believe that such collective action is best pursued through the Community method and those who prefer the more intergovernmental method. Spillover of the need for co-operation in one area thus demanding greater common action in another has provided pressure for more Community-based action, but this has been resisted by some northern states, with a number of southern states also finding it difficult to implement agreements. It is likely that the mere complications of the present system – the student that finds it confusing has perhaps understood it well – will lead to further rationalization.

Note

1   The Dublin Convention on Asylum came into force on 1 November 1996 but was superseded by the section in Schengen on asylum.

References and further reading

Benyon, J. (1994) 'Policing the European Union', *International Affairs*, 70 (3): 497–517.

Bieber, R. and Monar, J. (eds) (1995) *Justice and Home Affairs in the European Union: The Development of the Third Pillar*. Interuniversity Press, Brussels.

Commission of the European Communities (1998) *Action Plan on How Best to Implement the Provisions of the Treaty of Amsterdam in an Area of Freedom, Security and Justice, COM (1998) 459*. Office for Official Publications of the European Communities, Luxembourg.

den Boer, M. (1996) 'Justice and home affairs cooperation in the European Union: current issues', *EIPASCOPE*, 1996 (1): 12–16.

den Boer, M. (1997) 'Justice and home affairs cooperation in the Treaty on European Union: more complexity despite Communitarisation', *Maastricht Journal of European and Comparative Law*, 4 (3): 310–16.

den Boer, M. and Walker, N. (1993) 'European policing after 1992', *Journal of Common Market Studies*, 31 (1): 3–28.

Duff, A. (ed.) (1997) *The Treaty of Amsterdam: Text and Commentary*. Sweet and Maxwell for the Federal Trust, London.

European Commission (1999) *The Amsterdam Treaty: A Comprehensive Guide*. Office for Official Publications of the European Communities, Luxembourg.

European Parliament (1996a) *Secretariat Working Party Task Force of the International Conference: Briefing on European Citizenship*, JF/sm/186/96. Secretariat of the European Parliament, Luxembourg.

European Parliament (1996b) *Secretariat Working Party Task Force of the International Conference: Briefing on Europol*, JF/bo/195/96. Secretariat of the European Parliament, Luxembourg.

European Voice (1999a) 'Justice and Home Affairs Council', *European Voice*, 5 (40): 16.

European Voice (1999b) 'Athens set for full Schengen membership', *European Voice*, 5 (43): 7.

European Voice (2000) 'In brief', *European Voice*, 6 (16): 2.

Kostakopoulou, D. (1998) 'Is there an alternative to "Schengenland"?', *Political Studies*, 46: 886–902.

Miles, R. and Thranhardt, D. (eds) (1995) *Migration and European Integration: The Politics of Inclusion and Exclusion in Europe*. Pinter, London.

Monar, J. (1998) 'Justice and home affairs in the Treaty of Amsterdam: reform at the price of fragmentation', *European Law Review*, 23 (4): 320–35.

Monar, J. (1999) 'Justice and home affairs', in G. Edwards and G. Wiessala (eds), *The European Union: Annual Review 1989/1999*. Blackwell, Oxford, pp. 155–68.

Parlement Europeen (1996) *Groupe de Travail du Secretariat General Task Force 'Conference Intergouvernementale': Fiche thematique sur la CIG et la convention de Schengen*. JF/bo/217/96. Secretariat of the European Parliament, Luxembourg.

Thatcher, M. (1993) *The Downing Street Years*. HarperCollins, London.

Wallace, R. (1996) *Refugees and Asylum: A Community Perspective*. Butterworth, London.

Web sites

europa.eu.int/comm/justice_home/ index_en.htm	Justice and home affairs Directorate General
europa.eu.int/pol/justice/index_en.htm	EU policies: justice and home affairs
www.europol.eu.int/content.htm?facts/ en.htm	Facts about Europol

9 Common Foreign and Security Policy

Introduction

From the start the European Communities had a strong political element tied to their mainly economic activities. The Coal and Steel Community can be seen as a 'peace project', aimed at ensuring that France and Germany would be incapable of conducting war with each other. The Economic Community sought to strengthen Western Europe not just economically but also diplomatically. As the Communities grew in membership, co-operation on foreign affairs among the member states grew and was institutionalized in the European Union. However, the governments of the EU states have shown a degree of reluctance in allowing Community institutions – rather than intergovernmental ones – to be central in the formation and implementation of foreign and security policy. In particular, they have wanted to keep defence in their own hands or to pursue international security through the Euro-Atlantic institution of NATO. However, the Treaty of Amsterdam has provided another step towards greater Union competence in all these sensitive areas. This chapter will trace the institutional development of the EC/EU's political role, will examine the evolution of EC/EU involvement in foreign and security matters and will consider the emerging role of the European Union in defence issues.

As with developments outlined in Chapter 8, these developments have to be seen through the wider lens of theories of integration. Those stressing the federalizing nature of the process – whether they are in favour of it or not – will see the Common Foreign and Security Policy (CFSP) as a stepping stone to a unified European foreign and defence policy with a EU diplomatic corps and, eventually, army. Those stressing the role of intergovernmental institutions within the EU could point to the CFSP as an area where these are still dominant and are likely to remain so. However, a more neofunctionalist view (see Chapter 1, pp. 30–3) would maintain that, while this might be the case currently, the pressures of integration in adjacent areas – the defence industry, the EU's commercial policy – as well as other factors, such as possible disagreements with the USA or more direct threats to the EU, will make closer CFSP integration more likely.

Early days

The Introduction (pp. 8–11) has explained how the European Coal and Steel Community (ECSC) came about in a period when wartime hostilities were still smarting but had been muted by the newly perceived threat to Western Europe from the Soviet bloc. The ECSC thus had political as well as economic implications, with one of its founders, Robert Schuman, aiming to make 'any war between France and Germany ... not only unthinkable but materially impossible' (Hallstein, 1962: 10). Also the onset of the Korean War, not long after the announcement of the Schuman Plan, led to a fear that this could be the feint in the Far East hiding preparations for a more serious Soviet attack on Western Europe. The French Prime Minister René Pleven took up the idea of a European army and incorporated it into his proposal for a European Defence Community (EDC) in October 1950. This aimed at 'the creation, for our common defence, of a European Army tied to political institutions of a united Europe' (Pleven, cited in Vaughan, 1976: 56), which also needed a political authority – the European Political Community – to give guidance to the EDC as well as to the ECSC.

The six ECSC states – the Federal Republic of Germany, France, Italy, Belgium, the Netherlands and Luxembourg – signed the EDC Treaty in May 1952. The death of Stalin in 1953, the end of the Korean War in 1954, British and American criticism and the vagaries of French politics all contributed to the rejection of the EDC (Fursdon, 1980). The replacement for the EDC – the Western European Union (WEU) – was not a Community institution; instead it represented co-operation in the defence field, included the United Kingdom and eschewed a common policy with common institutions created by the Six.

President de Gaulle, who came to power in France in 1958, opposed the development of supranational institutions for the newly founded Communities, and stressed national decisions, especially in the vital areas of foreign and security policy. He maintained a strong Franco-German relationship and also advanced the idea of regular meetings of heads of state and government in order to co-ordinate foreign policies and to deal with other political problems in the six Community countries. This notion, together with the proposal for a small secretariat in Paris to service the meetings, was rejected by the Dutch, who thought that it would rule out the creation of a common political union with its own foreign policy.

In 1961 the six EEC states established the Fouchet Commission in order to examine these sensitive political questions, but its report only served to demonstrate the difference between the French and the other five states. Fouchet proposed a European political union which would consist of a council of the heads of state or government or of foreign ministers, a European Parliament and a European Political Commission made up of the senior officials of the foreign ministries of the Six. The aims were to bring about a common foreign policy; to ensure close co-operation in the scientific and cultural fields; to contribute to the defence of human rights, fundamental freedoms and democracy; and to adopt a common defence policy (Vaughan, 1976: 173–8). Although these proposals may seem far-reaching, they would have placed power in the hands of governments, with even the European Parliament being a shadow of the set-up agreed for the ECSC, EEC and Euratom. Fouchet's proposals were rejected, especially by the Benelux states, which feared domination of the system by the larger states.

Enlargement and EPC

The EC's Hague Summit of December 1969 decided both to broaden the membership of the Communities and to deepen their activities. The ministers confirmed that the EC's activity 'also means paving the way for a united Europe capable of assuming its responsibilities ... and of making a contribution' (para. 3 of communiqué, cited in Vaughan, 1976: 181). They reaffirmed 'their belief in the political objectives which gave the Community its meaning and purport' (para. 4, *ibid.*: 181) and they instructed their foreign ministers to study how best to make progress 'in the matter of political unification, within the context of enlargement' (para. 15, *ibid.*: 183).

In response to this, the foreign ministers produced the Luxembourg Report in 1970. In this it was agreed that member states should consult each other on foreign policy issues, but should use the intergovernmental approach rather than EC institutions. In what became known as the Davignon Procedure, it was proposed that foreign ministers should meet twice yearly and that a Political Committee of senior foreign ministry officials should meet at least four times annually with a general mandate to undertake work on tasks allotted them by ministers. The EC Commission could make its views known on matters of overlapping competence, such as when trade matters were involved (Commission of the European Communities, 1971: 52).

The EC foreign ministers' Copenhagen Report of 1973 refined the process of foreign policy co-ordination. A system of 'correspondents' from each member states' foreign ministry would keep in contact with each other and would implement decisions; meetings between the foreign ministers and the Political Committee were to be more regular and a telegram system between the ministries – called COREU – was established. This intergovernmental co-operation was not part of the Communities' institutions, although the Commission was to be invited to political co-operation meetings and it was emphasized that both the EC and political co-operation was directed towards European unification. Following the Copenhagen Report, the Political Committee established working groups on subjects such as the

Conference on Security and Co-operation in Europe (CSCE), the Middle East and Asia (Ginsberg, 1989: 49).

The 1974 Paris Summit tidied up this institutional network. The meetings of the EC heads of state and government were to take place three times a year and were called the European Council (not to be confused with the Council of Europe, sitting in Strasbourg). It would deal with both EC and political co-operation matters, co-ordination being facilitated by foreign ministers and EC Commission members. Meetings of the Conference of Foreign Ministers, under what was to be known as European Political Co-operation (EPC), would be collocated with those of the same ministers meeting as the Council of Ministers of the European Communities, although the institutional framework of the EPC and the EC would remain separate.

The recommendation of the Tindemans Report on the European Union in 1976, that the EPC be fully integrated into the EC institutions, was not accepted, but the Genscher–Colombo Proposals of 1981 proved more acceptable. They came from, respectively, the German and Italian foreign ministers, which helped to raise the standing of the Report among their colleagues. They wished the EPC to be underwritten in a treaty and for the European Council to be the highest form of decision-making in the EC. They also wanted greater use of majority voting in the Council of Ministers and that security issues be considered in the EPC.

The 1981 London Report suggested buttressing the work of the European Council and the EPC by introducing a troika system whereby the member state currently holding the Presidency of the Council should be assisted by officials and ministers of the immediate previous and forthcoming post-holders. The Presidency of the European Council would be rotated on a six-month basis (see Chapter 2, p. 47). The Report emphasized the need for consultation before any international initiative, before and during international conferences and in dealings with third countries. It proposed a system of crisis management, whereby a Conference of Foreign Ministers could be convened at 48 hours' notice, and stressed the value of the 'Gymnich Formula' of keeping the USA informed of EPC activities. In 1983 the heads of state and government agreed on a Solemn Declaration on European Union which committed them to 'joint action' on major foreign policy issues, prior consultation in the field of foreign affairs and co-ordination in the economic and political aspects of security. Nevertheless, the EPC was seen as 'a private club, operated by diplomats, for diplomats' (Nuttall, 1992: 11) with few of its activities being discussed in the wider political public.

The Single European Act

The 1986 Single European Act (SEA) brought together a number of the strands mentioned above. Title II amended the treaties establishing the EC;

Title III provided treaty provisions for the EPC; and Title I included common provisions and linked the EC and EPC together with the common aim of progressing towards European unity.

The SEA set out the institutions of the EPC:

- the European Council of the heads of state or government of the member states, together with foreign ministers and two Commissioners;
- meetings – at least four times annually – of foreign ministers and a member of the European Commission;
- the Presidency of the EPC, being the same country as that presiding over the EC and being responsible for initiating action and representing EPC positions to third countries;
- the Political Committee consisting of the Political Directors – senior officials of the member countries – with the task of maintaining EPC continuity and preparing ministerial discussions;
- the European Correspondents Group of civil servants responsible for the monitoring and implementation of EPC;
- Working Groups, as established by the Political Committee (SEA, Title III, Article 30.10);
- a Secretariat, set up in Brussels to assist the Presidency and to carry out administrative tasks.

The SEA also clarified the intended content of the EPC. There was to be information and consultation on 'any foreign policy matters of general interest' before members adopted their final position (Article 30.2). The external policies of the EC and EPC 'must be consistent' (Article 30.5). A readiness was expressed to co-ordinate more closely positions 'on the political and economic aspects of security', and to maintain the technological and industrial conditions for security, although this was not to impede security co-operation of members within the WEU or NATO (Article 30.6). Members would endeavour to adopt common positions at international conferences and towards third countries, and would intensify co-operation between the diplomatic representation in such countries (Articles 30.7; 30.8; 30.9).

The aim of EPC was 'jointly to formulate and implement a European foreign policy' (Article 30.1). It was not to create a *common* foreign policy but wished to exercise the combined influence of the member states, to draw together their positions and to implement joint actions. This was an attempt to provide a wider framework for the pursuit of national foreign policies.

The EPC, as set out in the SEA, was separate from the EC and its institutions. The roles of the European Parliament and the Commission were limited and the European Court of Justice was excluded altogether. The institutions established were different from those of the EC, with the intergovernmental aspects preserved, although by placing the EPC and the reform of the EC together in the Single European Act, the parallel nature of these institutions was stressed.

The context for Maastricht

The basis of EPC was established in 1973 and formalized in 1986 with the SEA. Still, the objectives of the EPC were more concerned with *how* foreign policy should be conducted – by consultation, co-ordination and common actions – than with *what* that policy should be. Evaluations of EPC tended to stress the ability of EC members to remain united in the field of foreign affairs rather than the content of any joint policy or its potential effectiveness on the world stage. A 1988 report on the EPC claimed that 'in measuring progress in EPC, what matters is the degree of co-operation on substance and cohesion in action' (EPC Statements 1988; 1989: I:25). By the mid-1980s members were starting to use the EPC not just for consultation but also for co-ordination and common action. There was even the emergence of an 'EC interest', apart from the sum of the various member interests (Ginsberg, 1989: 89), although this was ill-defined.

By the time of the 1991 Maastricht meeting, the EPC had faced a number of challenges and had shown certain weaknesses. The EC ministers' Venice Declaration of 1980 on the Middle East was virtually ignored by the Arab states and was rejected by Israel. The EPC immediately condemned the invasion of Kuwait in August 1990 by Saddam Hussein, and it called for an Iraqi withdrawal. The EC supported UN sanctions on Iraq, but members could not always agree on the mix of diplomacy and force that should be used against the Iraqi leadership. The British pressed for full support of the US-led effort to build up a force capable of evicting Iraq from Kuwait, while France and Germany showed greater willingness to search for a diplomatic solution (Cooley 1991: 137–8). In retrospect, Jacques Delors (1991: 99) stated that the Gulf War, which prised Kuwait back from the Iraqis, 'provided an object lesson – if one were needed – on the limitations of the European Communities'.

A further example of the weakness of the EPC was provided from the summer of 1991 up to the signing of the Maastricht Treaty in February 1992 and beyond with the crisis in Yugoslavia (see Chapter 10, pp. 204–6), when the system proved ineffective in attempts to contain the growing conflict in that region.

It was with this background of the inadequacies of the EPC that the CFSP element of the Maastricht Treaty was negotiated. There was a determination that the new system would be an improvement both in form and in substance, although there was some disagreement as to how this could best be done (de Schoutheete de Tervarent, 1997). However, the CFSP had much in common with the EPC – it still allowed member states to go their own way in key foreign policy areas – and it was not put in place until the Treaty on European Union came into force on 1 November 1993.

The Maastricht Treaty and the CFSP

The Treaty on European Union (TEU), negotiated in Maastricht in December 1991 and signed on 7 February 1992, established a European Union that enveloped the European Communities supplemented 'by the policies and forms of co-operation established by the Treaty' (TEU, Title I, Common Provisions, Article A). One of the objectives of the Union is 'to assert its identity on the international scene, in particular through the implementation of a common foreign and security policy which shall include the eventual framing of a common defence policy' (*ibid.*: Article B). According to Article C, the Union

> shall in particular ensure the consistency of its external activities as a whole in the context of its external relations, security, economic and development policies. The Council and the Commission shall be responsible for ensuring such consistency. They shall ensure the implementation of these policies, each in accordance with its respective powers.

Foreign and security policy

Maastricht set out the aim of a *common* foreign and security policy rather than just greater co-ordination and co-operation of national policies. It also provided the framework for a Union to have a defence competence. How were these objectives to be achieved?

The Provisions on a Common Foreign and Security Policy (Title V) set out the objectives and the mechanisms. In short, the five objectives (Article J.1.2)[1] were:

- to safeguard the values, interests and independence of the Union;
- to strengthen the security of the Union and its member states' in all ways;
- to preserve peace and strengthen international security in accordance with the UN Charter and the CSCE's Paris Charter;[2]
- to promote international co-operation;
- to develop and consolidate democracy and the rule of law, and respect for human rights and fundamental freedoms.

The implementation of these general aims was to be pursued by two routes.

First, according to Article J.2, the member states 'shall inform and consult' with one another on foreign and security matters to ensure 'their combined influence is exerted as effectively as possible' (as in SEA, Article 30.2a), but 'by means of concerted and convergent action'. This is the co-operation route familiar from the EPC and SEA, except that mutual information and consultation is made obligatory. In Article J.2, the Council is allowed to define a *Common Position*, when it deems this necessary, and member states are to ensure that their 'national policies conform to the common positions' (Article J.2.2), with these positions being upheld in international forums and conferences. This was an advance from the SEA, where the common position was merely 'a point of reference' which members would 'endeavour to adopt' in international forums (SEA, Articles 30.2c and 30.7a). Also the Maastricht Treaty's Common Provisions (Article C) state that there should be consistency between action taken under the Community part of the treaty and that taken under the CFSP, relating to 'external relations, security, economic and development policies'.

Article J.3 allowed for the adoption of *Joint Action* in foreign and security policies. The Council, normally consisting of the foreign ministers, would decide – on the basis of guidelines from the European Council (consisting of heads of state and government) – that a matter should be a subject for Joint Action. The Council would lay down the principle, scope, objectives, duration and means of Joint Action and, acting unanimously, would define those matters on which a qualified majority could take decisions. Member states declared that where a qualified majority existed, they would try to avoid preventing a unanimous decision. Joint Actions committed member states 'in the positions they adopt and in the conduct of their activity' and thus represented a step down the road of a common policy. Member states could still take their own action in the case of 'imperative need arising from changes in the situation and failing a Council decision', although such measures should have regard to the general objectives of joint action and must be reported to the Council (Article J.3.6).

Article J.4 declared that the Common Foreign and Security Policy 'shall include all questions related to the security of the European Union, including the eventual framing of a common defence policy, which might in time lead to a common defence' (Article J.4.1). The consequences of this Article are examined in the section below.

Policy-making and policy implementation

Article J.4 also covered the role of the Union's institutions in foreign and security policy. The Presidency of the Council was to be responsible for implementing common measures and for representing the Union in foreign and security matters; it would be assisted by the previous and following states in that office, collectively known as 'the Troika'. The Commission was to be associated with this work, could suggest initiatives but is not 'responsible for implementing policy or representing the EU on CFSP issues' (Hurd, 1994: 425).

A common defence policy

After the failure of the EDC in 1954, the European Communities had little to do with the defence policies of their members. International security was included in the intergovernmental co-operation of EPC. Trade and financial sanctions involved the EC, but neither the EC nor the EPC concerned themselves with the military aspects of security represented in defence policies. Whilst the main perceived threat to Western Europe was the possibility (however remote) of a massive Soviet attack, then NATO and the WEU, which tied, respectively, the United States and the United Kingdom to the defence of continental Western Europe, seemed the best defence option for most Western European states.

By the end of the 1980s and start of the 1990s, the security situation had changed radically (see the Introduction, pp. 16–19). The easing and then ending of the superpower confrontation in Europe was followed by a number of new security challenges, ranging from nationalist wars in the Balkans to the perceived threat of mass migration.

The Single European Act had formalized the EPC's involvement in security matters, but it specifically ruled out any competition with NATO and WEU (Article 30.6c). With the end of the Cold War and the collapse of the Soviet Union, the security dimension was taken up with greater vigour within EPC, as was the possibility of defence co-operation. The President of the EC's Commission, Jacques Delors, made it clear that he expected the EU to develop a defence competence (Delors, 1991: 106–9).

Article J.4 fudged the issue. As noted above, it included in the CFSP 'all questions related to the security of the Union, including the eventual framing of a common defence policy, which might in time lead to a common defence' (Article J.4.1). Integrationists were cheered by defence being admitted as a matter for consideration by the main institution of Western European integration and the reference to 'the security of the Union' rather than to that of the member states. However, the framing of a common defence policy was to be 'eventual' and a common defence 'might in time' be achieved. This represented a compromise between those states – France and Germany – that wished to press for a greater defence competence for the EU and those – such as the United Kingdom and the Netherlands – that were concerned that this increase might interfere with NATO's prime role in European defence.

The Union was to request the WEU, 'which is an integral part of the development of the Union, to elaborate and implement' decisions with defence implications, and then the Council – in agreement with the WEU – would adopt the practical arrangements (Article J.4.2). Issues with defence implications were not subject to 'joint action' procedures set out in Article J.3 (Cameron, 1999: 25).

Paragraphs 4 and 5 of Article J.4 showed the desire not to have policy incompatible with that established within the NATO framework (J.4.4) and not to prevent co-operation within NATO and the WEU (J.4.5) (Cameron, 1999: 25).

The WEU was identified as the temporary operational vehicle for 'decisions and actions of the Union which have defence implications' (J.4.2). Of the 12 members party to the Maastricht Treaty, three – Denmark, Greece and Ireland – were not members of the WEU[3], but the rest were willing to develop the WEU as the defence component of the European Union 'as a means to strengthen the European pillar of the Atlantic Alliance'. To this end they proposed to formulate concrete European defence policy and to advance its implementation. They advanced ideas on how to develop closer relations between the EU and NATO, as well as on the enhancement of their operational role (Treaty on European Union, 1992, Declaration on Western European Union, para. 2).

The context for Amsterdam

In preparation for the implementation of the CFSP, the Lisbon European Council, in June 1992, set out the objectives for joint actions:

- strengthening democratic principles and institutions and the respect of human and minority rights;
- promoting regional political stability;
- contributing to the prevention and settlement of conflicts;
- more effective international co-ordination in dealing with emergencies;
- strengthening co-operation in such areas as international terrorism, arms proliferation and drug trafficking (Commission of the European Communities, 1992: 19).

The basis for joint action was the existence of important interests in common, and in defining these it was suggested that geographical proximity, interests in the stability of a region and the existence of a threat to the security of the Union be taken into account (*ibid.*). Particular regions designated for joint action in the short term were Central and Eastern Europe, including the former Soviet Union and the Balkans; the Mediterranean and the Mahgreb; and the Middle East. The immediate security issues identified were: the CSCE/OSCE process, arms control and disarmament, nuclear non-proliferation and the economic aspects of security, including the transfer of military technology to third countries (*ibid.*: 20–1).

The October 1993 Brussels European Council adopted five *joint actions* in preparation for the CFSP:

1. the Balladur initiative on stability and peace in Europe, whereby democratic processes in Central and East Europe would be strengthened, frontiers secured and the rights of minorities guaranteed;
2. support for the Middle East peace process between Israel and the Palestinians and Arab countries;
3. support for the democratic development of South Africa, including help with the first all-race elections in April 1994;
4. support for the peace process and humanitarian relief in former Yugoslavia;
5. support for the democratic process in Russia, including the sending of observers to the December 1993 parliamentary (Duma) elections (Commission of the European Communities, 1993a: 8).

Since then, the EU has taken a number of further Joint Actions covering issues such as the appointment of a High Representative in former Yugoslavia, engagement in the Nuclear Non-Proliferation Treaty Renewal Conference, work towards an agreement to ban anti-personnel mines, and attempts to bring peace and stability to the Great Lakes region in Africa. Common Positions have been taken on embargoes of military exports to a number of countries, including Afghanistan and Sudan; economic sanctions against states such as Iraq and former Yugoslavia; and the detailing of relations with third countries such as Albania and Cuba.

At the December 1993 European Council, six important elements of the CFSP were outlined:

1. it should be active, not reactive, thus DG1A, within the Commission, was expanded to assist the systematic appraisal of policy;
2. it should have unity and coherence externally, thus the working practices of the Council and EPC were merged with Coreper's Political Committee preparing material for the Council meetings;
3. all aspects of security were involved, with the Commission having a role in co-ordination between the EU and the WEU;
4. joint actions should be taken in line with Article J.3 of the TEU (see the list above);
5. there should be visibility in the world arena, with more missions established in third countries;
6. there should be efficiency in decision-making with majority voting avoided for the time-being (Commission of the European Communities, 1993b: 12–13, 125–31).

Following on the third point, the WEU Secretariat moved from London to Brussels in order to be in closer contact with the EU and NATO, and a small

WEU planning cell was established there. The Independent European Programme Group and the committees of the Eurogroup, two defence institutions previously associated with NATO, were absorbed into the WEU. Work was undertaken on how the Combined Joint Task Forces, initiated under NATO auspices, might be used by the WEU. The WEU also established its own Forum of Consultation with the Central and East European states, in effect making them associate partners of the organization.

Nevertheless, the escalation of conflict within former Yugoslavia, especially during 1994 and 1995 (see p. 205), and the apparent rift between most EU states and the United States, backed by the United Kingdom, over use of force against Iraq in 1994 demonstrated the military and diplomatic weaknesses of the EU, even using the instruments of CFSP. The issue of the WEU's status in view of the fiftieth anniversary of its founding document (the 1948 Brussels Treaty) in 1998 was used in Article J.4.6 as an opportunity to re-examine Article J.4 after 1996. Furthermore, the admission in January 1995 to EU membership of Austria, Finland and Sweden – three states that were neither NATO nor WEU members – both encouraged and complicated a closer examination of the security role of the Union. The CFSP and its working practices, including the defence aspect, were to be matters of contention at the Inter-governmental Conference (IGC) leading to the Amsterdam Treaty.

The Amsterdam Treaty and the CFSP

Clearly one of the reasons for the 1996–97 IGC was to strengthen the CFSP part of the Union and to deal with the questions surrounding a common defence policy left open by the Maastricht Treaty. The need to rely on the national responses of mainly France and the United Kingdom and on US force within NATO had become obvious in the various Balkans crises before and during the IGC. However, there was little agreement on how the defence and military aspects of the EU might be improved. Once again the final document reflected a compromise between those who wanted a more integrated answer and those who started from the nation-state as the basis for any EU defence action.

Treaty developments

The Treaty adjusted the list of objectives of the CFSP (Article J.1, 11 TEU – see p. 168) so that the second was changed from 'to strengthen the security of the Union and its Member States in all ways' to 'to strengthen the security of the Union in all ways'. Significantly, the first indent had an extra element attached to it: this subsequently read that the first objective was 'to safeguard the common values, fundamental interest, independence *and integrity* of the Union in conformity with the principles of the United Nations Charter' (emphasis added).

The addition of 'and integrity' suggested that the EU was committed to defending itself against any attack on its territory, although there was no elaboration of the consequences. The third indent was altered so that 'to preserve peace and strengthen international security, in accordance with the principles of the United Nations Charter as well as the principles of the Helsinki Final Act and the objectives of the Paris Charter' had added to it 'including those on external borders', perhaps strengthening the indent mentioned above.

The aspiration that the member states 'shall work together to enhance and develop their mutual political solidarity' was also added to this Article, in the second paragraph.

The area where most change was made to Pillar II, the CFSP, was in the implementation of policy, where there was an attempt to simplify the maze left by Maastricht. The Union was to pursue its objectives, according to Article J.2 (12 TEU), by defining the principles of and general guidelines for the CFSP, deciding on common strategies, adopting joint actions and common positions, and strengthening co-operation between member states in conducting policy (see Table 9.1 below).

Article J.3 (13 TEU) set down that the European Council will define the 'principles and general guidelines' for the CFSP, 'including for matters with defence implications', and that it will decide on common strategies to be implemented in areas where the members have 'important interests in common'.

Article J.4 (14 TEU) on Joint Actions reflected what was J.3 of the Maastricht Treaty, calling for such actions to 'address specific situations where operational action' by the EU was required. Common positions under Article J.5 (15 TEU) 'shall define the approach of the Union to a particular matter of a geographical or thematic nature'.

According to Article J.8 (18 TEU), the Presidency continued to represent the Union in CFSP matters and was responsible for the implementation of common measures, with the Commission being 'fully associated' with these tasks. The Presidency was also to be assisted by the Secretary-General of the Council exercising the function of High Representative for the CFSP. During 1999 the retiring Secretary-General of NATO, Javier Solana, was appointed both to this post of 'Mr CFSP' and also as Secretary-General of the WEU in November 1999. He thus became a powerful player in the implementation not only of the EU's diplomatic initiatives but also of any defence initiatives. According to Article J.16 (26 TEU), he was also to help the Council in the preparation and formulation of the CFSP. The new CFSP Troika consisted of the Presidency (of the Council), the Secretary-General and the Commission (see Table 9.2). Unless these three institutions can work closely together, the external face of the CFSP is likely to have three facades rather than one, with resulting confusion.

Both the Commission and member states could refer CFSP matters to the Council and, in the case of an emergency, the Presidency could call an extraordinary Council meeting at short notice (Article J.12, 22 TEU). Although unanimity remained the dominant form of decision-making in CFSP, the opportunity to use qualified majority voting (QMV) was increased. The Council was able to use it to adopt decisions on the basis of a common strategy or decisions to implement a Joint Action of Common Position (J.13.2, 23.2 TEU). Furthermore, there was the possibility of 'constructive abstention' under J.13.1 (23.1 TEU), with a state that made a statement of such an abstention not obliged to apply that decision, although it should not impede consequent EU action. Under J.13.2 (23.2 TEU), a state could declare that 'for important and stated reasons of national policy' it would oppose a decision taken by QMV and that a vote should not be

Table 9.1 *CFSP instruments*

- Definition of the **principles** of and **general guidelines** for CFSP are made by the European Council.
- **Common Strategies** are adopted by the European Council for areas where the members share important interests, and may also cover Pillar I and III matters as well as CFSP issues. Common Strategies have been adopted on Russia, Ukraine, the West Balkans and the Mediterranean Region.
- **Common Positions** are taken by the Council in order to clarify the EU position about a situation without taking specific action, but they are legally binding acts. Between 1994 and 1998, 66 Common Positions were adopted.
- **Joint Actions** are decided by the Council and are legally binding operational actions with financial means attached to them (see p. 169). Between 1994 and 1999 over a hundred were adopted, with many referring to former Yugoslavia.
- **Concluding international agreements** are negotiated by the Presidency, assisted by the Commission and are given Council authorization in CFSP matters.
- **Declarations** give expression to a position, request or expectation of the EU regarding an international issue or a third country. There were 163 in 1998.
- **Contacts with third countries** may take place by the EU holding a 'political dialogue' with a group of countries on an issue. A démarche (normally a diplomatic complaint about an issue) may be undertaken with third countries by the EU in order to try to solve matters usually related to human rights or democracy.
- **Systematic co-operation**, including information exchange, co-ordination and convergence of national action.

Sources: CFSP – Common Foreign and Security Policy, http://europa.eu.int/comm/external_relations/cfsp/intro/index.htm; The Council of the European Union and the Common Foreign and Security Policy, http://ue.int/pesc/pres.asp?lang = en

Table 9.2 *CFSP structure*

- **The European Council** (heads of state/government and Commission Presidency): meets at least twice a year to provide broad guidelines for EU policies, including CFSP.
- **Council of Ministers** (EU foreign ministers and External Relations Commissioner): meets at least monthly as General Affairs Council to decide on CFSP and other external affairs issues.
- **Committee of Permanent Representatives** (Coreper – ambassadors of EU states and Commission Deputy Secretary-General): meets weekly to prepare Council meetings, including that of General Affairs Council.
- **Political Committee** (Political Directors of the EU states and Commission): meets about twice monthly to monitor international affairs and CFSP implementation and report to General Affairs Council.
- **European Correspondents** (member states and Commission officials): assist Political Directors, co-ordinate daily CFSP business, and prepare Political Committee meetings and CFSP aspects of General Affairs Council and European Council.
- **CFSP Working Groups** (experts from EU states and the Commission): meet on geographical (i.e. area) and functional (i.e. topic) lines to elaborate policy documents and options for the Political Committee.
- **CFSP Counsellors** of EU states (based in the permanent representations of those states in Brussels) and Commission officials examine problems of the CFSP, especially legal, institutional and financial aspects.
- **The Commission** is fully associated with the CFSP and can refer questions and submit proposals to the Council on CFSP issues (but does not have the sole right to do so, as in Pillar I matters). It can request an extraordinary Council meeting, and make suggestions to the Policy Planning Unit (see below). The Commission implements the CFSP budget and, with the Council, is responsible for ensuring the overall consistency of EU external activities.
- **The High Representative** is the Council Secretary-General who will assist the Council and the Presidency of the Council in CFSP matters and in the external representation of the EU. Mr Javier Solana was appointed to this post in October 1999.
- **The Troika**: the Council Presidency represents the EU in CFSP matters and is responsible for the implementation of decisions. It is assisted by the High Representative and the Commissioner for External Affairs, making up the three elements of the Troika. However, the next member states to hold the Presidency may also be involved.
- **Policy Planning Unit**: a Policy Planning and Early Warning Unit (PPEWU) is under the responsibility of the High Representative within the Council secretariat. It is to co-operate with the Commission to ensure full coherence with EU trade and development policies. It is to monitor, analyse and assess international events, and to draft policy options for the Council.

Source: CFSP – Common Foreign and Security Policy, http://europa.eu.int/comm/external_relations/cfsp/intro/index.htm

taken. In this case the matter would be referred to the European Council for a unanimous decision. The QMV provisions did not apply to decisions having 'military or defence implications'. The roles of the European Parliament in the CFSP were those of consultation and information (Article J.11, 21 TEU), though it had a greater say on the financing of the CFSP.

Amsterdam and defence

As mentioned on p. 70, there was disagreement over the development of a defence vocation for the EU. Broadly, the United Kingdom and Denmark wished to place the emphasis on the compatibility of any EU defence role with NATO; Germany and France wanted the WEU integrated into the EU; while the alliance-free states of Austria, Finland, Ireland and Sweden wanted their special security position recognized. Article J.7 (17 TEU), which took over from J.4, attempted to satisfy all parties. Its essential elements are that:

- The CFSP was to include 'all questions relating to the security of the Union, including the progressive framing of a common defence policy . . . which might lead to a common defence, should the European Council so decide' (Article J.7.1, 17 TEU). Thus the 'eventual' framing of this policy in Maastricht became 'the progressive framing' and the vague 'which might in time lead to a common defence' of J.4.1 changed in J.7.1 to place the responsibility for change on the European Council.
- The WEU was an integral part of the development of the EU, 'providing the Union with access to an operational capability'. It was to support the EU 'in framing the defence aspects' of the CFSP. A protocol was included, requesting the EU and WEU to draw up arrangements for enhanced co-operation between the two. Closer relations were to be fostered with the WEU 'with a view to the possibility of the integration of the WEU into the Union' – clearly a sop to France and Germany – 'should the European Council so decide' – thus providing the break for those opposing such integration.
- The progressive framing of a common defence policy would be supported, where seen as appropriate, by co-operation in the field of armaments (J.7.1, para. 4, 17.1, para. 4 TEU). This was a novel aspect but, in the words of Fraser Cameron (1999: 67), was 'not formulated in very strong terms'.
- At the behest of non-NATO members Finland and Sweden, Article J.7.2 (17.2 TEU) included the Petersberg Tasks of the WEU.[4] What might be covered by 'combat tasks in crisis management, including peacemaking' remains to be seen, although the Kosovo crisis (see Chapter 10) provided an early test.

- The Union was to avail itself of the WEU 'to elaborate and implement decisions' with defence implications (Article J.7.3, 17.3 TEU). When these were Petersberg tasks, all states of the Union (not just those members of the WEU) were to be entitled 'to participate fully in the tasks'. This was included at the insistence of the unaligned states, who feared that they might be faced with a decision to participate in such tasks on a 'second-class citizen' basis, that is, by contributing troops but having no say in the WEU.

Assessing Amsterdam

The section on CFSP in the Amsterdam Treaty is a measure of most member states' reluctance to allow key elements of their foreign policy and, certainly, of their defence policy to slip out of their hands. It also reflects the preference of most EU members to maintain their current security orientations with the emphasis of pursuing these through either NATO or alliance-free policies. In the words of one EU official and commentator, 'the Amsterdam treaty did not alter the character of the CFSP. The reforms were of an incremental character and designed to make the existing CFSP structures work better' (Cameron, 1999: 68). This seems to do little to close what Christopher Hill has called the 'capabilities–expectations gap' – the difference between what the EU delivers and what is expected of it (Hill 1993; 1998). Another writer has remarked that '(i)f the political outcome was disappointing, the procedural negotiations were byzantine' (Duff 1997: 124). As with many EU instruments, the institutions of the CFSP allow the EU to be as active or passive in international affairs as its member states wish it to be.

The small, cautious moves towards a Common European Security and Defence Policy (CESDP) reflect a recognition that the pursuit of national interests through national means and NATO had left Europe with a faltering voice in the various Yugoslav crises (see Chapter 10), and that this under-representation would continue in future crises if the EU states were seen to be ineffective as a collective group. Simon Duke (1999: 2) wrote that the Kosovo crisis in 1999, one in a continuing line of consequences of the collapse of Yugoslavia, would either 'rejuvenate the Common Foreign and Security Policy (CFSP) and give practical effect to a common defence policy and common defence, or it will leave the security of the region largely in the hands of the US ... '. At least the possibility has been left open for closer defence co-operation within the EU context, underpinned by a new structure-in-the-making.

After Amsterdam

The Treaty of Amsterdam was signed in 1997, but only came into force in May 1999. Nevertheless, while it was possible for member states and the Commission – troubled as it was by its resignation and changeover – to make some preparations in the intervening period for the new provisions in the CFSP field, the world did not stand still during this time. New challenges were issued to the EU both in the field of foreign policy and in defence and security; the EU had to find fitting institutional responses.

The idea of a *Common Strategy*, introduced by the Treaty, was that the EU should take a more long-term view of its foreign and security policy and that there should be a number of agreed priorities. The first Common Strategies were set out under the German and Finnish Presidencies of 1999. At the top of the list was a Common Strategy towards Russia – which was reviewed in the light of Russia's conflict in Chechnya at the December 1999 Helsinki summit – and this was followed by one on the Ukraine. A Common Strategy on the West Balkans played an important part in the EU's response to the Kosovo conflict and its aftermath; the development of a Common Strategy on the Mediterranean region reflected the EU's continued involvement in that area (see the Helsinki European Council, Presidency conclusions, 11 December 1999, paras 56 and 57, http://presidency.finland.fi/netcomm/news/).

The Policy Planning and Early Warning Unit (PPEWU), allowed for in a Declaration in the Treaty of Amsterdam and established under the High Representative for the CFSP, is an attempt to provide the EU with something more than the input of the foreign ministries of the member states. Its tasks are:

- monitoring and analysing developments in areas relevant to the CFSP;
- providing assessment of the EU's CFSP interest and identifying future areas of focus;
- providing 'timely assessments and early warning' of events that could have significant repercussions for the CFSP;
- producing option papers containing analyses, recommendations and strategies for the CFSP (*ibid.*).

The *WEU* had ten full members by the time Amsterdam had been ratified – Belgium, France, Germany, Greece, Italy, Luxembourg, Netherlands, Portugal, Spain, and the United Kingdom – with Austria, Denmark, Finland, Ireland and Sweden as observers. The six European countries that are NATO members but not yet part of the EU – the Czech Republic, Hungary, Iceland, Norway, Poland and Turkey – are associate members, while seven Central and East European states – Bulgaria, Estonia, Latvia, Lithuania,

Romania, Slovakia and Slovenia – are associate partners. While the associates, observers and associate partners may involve themselves in WEU activities, they do not have the mutual security guarantee of the full members.

The WEU has recourse to 'Forces Answerable to WEU' (FAWEU), consisting of a number of national forces plus the multilateral Eurocorps, which is made up of French, German, Spanish, Belgian and Luxembourg troops. An opportunity to use the WEU when Albania descended into chaos in April 1997 was not taken up and, instead, a multilateral ad hoc force of some 7000 European troops was dispatched (International Institute for Strategic Studies, 1998: 100). In 1996 a Joint Armaments Co-operation Structure (OCCAR) was set up as a forerunner to a European armaments agency. However, any such organization has an unenviable task, given the competition in the European market from the US-based armaments industry and the fragmented and national-based nature of the European industry (Molas-Gallart, 1999).

The issue of the relationship between NATO and the WEU has been a thorny one since 1994 when NATO called for a European Security and Defence Identity (ESDI), leading to plans to strengthen the institutional links. These allowed for NATO's 'separable but not separate' assets to be available for the WEU's use. The Combined Joint Task Forces (CJTF), including both NATO and WEU forces, could embark on joint operations under a single commander, but forces could also act under WEU direction. This meant close co-operation between the institutions and personnel of WEU and NATO (http://www.weu.int/eng/welcome.html).

Two significant events in the later part of 1998 were of relevance to the development of the Common European Security and Defence Policy (CESDP), the EU version of ESDI. In October 1998 Tony Blair, the British Prime Minister, brought up the defence issue at the informal European Council at Pörtschach and this was followed by a first-time meeting of EU defence ministers. These meetings discussed the questions of EU–WEU relations, the European armaments market and the institutions and procedures for CESDP (Cameron, 1999: 76–82). Already there was a good deal of harmonization and co-operation between the EU and WEU, with joint meetings and exchanges of information. The second major event – in November 1998 – was a Joint Declaration on European Defence between France and the United Kingdom at St-Malo. This recognized the importance of achieving the 'full and rapid implementation' of the CFSP provisions in the Amsterdam Treaty, and the need for the Union to have 'the capacity for autonomous action, backed up by credible military forces, the means to decide to use them, and a readiness to do so, in order to respond to international crises'. It went on to say that for the EU to take decisions and approve military action where NATO as a whole is not engaged, the Union must be given appropriate structures and a capacity for analysis of situations, sources of intelligence, and a capability for relevant strategic planning, without unnecessary duplication, taking account of the existing assets of the WEU and the evolution of its relations with the EU ... the European Union will also need to have recourse to suitable military means .... (Joint Declaration on European Defence, 4 December 1998, http://www.ambafrance.org.uk)

The Vienna European Council endorsed this declaration in December 1998. In June 1999 the Cologne European Council decided, in response, on the following:

- regular meetings of the General Affairs Council (which includes the foreign ministers) to be held with defence ministers present, if need be;
- the establishment of an EU military staff with a Situation Centre;
- a Political and Security Committee to be formed in Brussels, consisting of representatives with the necessary political and military expertise;
- an EU Military Committee to be set up of military representatives, making recommendations to the Political and Security Committee;
- other resources, such as a Satellite Centre and an Institute for Security Studies, to be founded.

The Council wanted the EU to be able to take military action outside NATO's control, but was faced with the reality that most of the national assets – armed forces and equipment – had been traditionally organized within a NATO context, that NATO's command structure was formidable and that it was dominated by the USA. To operate outside it would require a situation where the USA was content that European forces take such action but did not itself want to participate. Without the USA – as had been shown in former Yugoslavia – the European states did not necessarily have the wherewithal for effective action in the full spectrum of military operations. This was the impetus behind the St-Malo Declaration and the quickened pace towards defence co-operation within the EU since 1997. On the future of the WEU, the Cologne Summit talked about the inclusion into the EU 'of those functions of the WEU which will be necessary for the EU to fulfil its new responsibilities in the area of the Petersberg tasks' and left open to the end of 2000 the decision about the continued existence of the WEU. Later in 1999, Javier Solana, already appointed 'Mr CFSP' by the EU, was named as the next Secretary-General of the WEU, thus demonstrating the seriousness of intention to bring the defence element within the EU. The 1999 Helsinki European Council set 'headline goals' whereby by 2003 member states would be able to deploy military forces of up to 60,000 personnel within 60 days to undertake the Petersberg tasks. The June 2000 Feira European Council confirmed this aim, identified means for EU–NATO co-operation, and set out plans for members to have up to 5000 police officers ready for international civilian crisis management by 2003 (http://www.portugal.ue-2000.pt/rtffiles/file2329.rtf).

Despite its advances, the move towards a CESDP within the Union raises a number of difficult questions:

- What will be the relationship between any European defence capability and that within NATO? More precisely, what will be the US attitude towards the EU going its own way on defence? Should this be allowed to affect the EU defence effort?
- What will be the relationship between the national and the Union element? Will the Union's defence element in reality be a combination of various national efforts or will there be an attempt to define EU requirements that the member states will then be requested to fulfil? What will happen to the nuclear elements of the United Kingdom's and France's defence?
- What will be the division of labour on defence and security issues within the EU? Will the French and the British still be expected to provide a large share of the troops and equipment for any operation? To what extent will the EU alliance-free states be engaged? How will contributions from non-EU states be accommodated?
- What institutional arrangement will be made for the WEU? Will it survive or be included into the EU? What institutions will link the CESDP with NATO and the OSCE?
- When will European forces be used? Will it be in response to the Petersberg Tasks or will they be sent 'in harm's way' into enforcement action? For what cause will politicians and the electorates decide these troops can die, if need be?

The final two chapters will deal with the relations of the EC/EU with the rest of Europe and the wider world, including those through the EPC and CFSP. In many cases, the record of achievement has been mixed, to be generous. Especially over former Yugoslavia, EPC and CFSP have both proved ineffective in providing solutions, though this has reflected more the lack of will by those wielding these instruments than the faults in the systems themselves. As Geoffrey Edwards (1997: 193) wrote, 'If individual Western democracies are constrained in what they can do, it is unlikely that the European Union will be less so'.

Notes

1   The CFSP was the Pillar II of the Maastricht system, represented by Articles J.1 to J.18 under Title V of the Treaty. The renumbering of the Treaty articles brought about by the Amsterdam Treaty reconfigures some of these articles and renumbers them as Article 11 to Article 28 of the Treaty on European Union

section (TEU, as opposed to the following section, the Treaty Establishing the European Community – TEC) of the Treaty of Amsterdam.

2   The Conference on Security and Co-operation in Europe (CSCE) became the Organization for Security and Co-operation in Europe (OSCE) after its meeting in Budapest, Hungary, 1994.

3   Greece later joined and Austria, Finland and Sweden, which joined the EU in 1995, were not WEU members.

4   The Petersberg Tasks are 'humanitarian and rescue tasks, peacekeeping and tasks of combat forces in crisis management, including peacemaking' (see WEU Council of Ministers, Petersberg Declaration, 19 June 1992, http://www.weu.int/eng/comm/92-petersberg.htm).

References and further reading

Algieri, F., Janning, J. and Rumberg, D. (eds) (1996) *Managing Security in Europe: The European Union and the Challenge of Enlargement*. Bertelsmann, Gütersloh.

Allen, D. and Smith, M. (1998) 'The European Union's security presence: barrier, facilitator or manager?' in C. Rhodes (ed.), *The European Union in the World Community*. Lynne Rienner, London and Boulder, CO.

Cameron, F. (1999) *The Foreign and Security Policy of the European Union: Past, Present and Future*, Contemporary European Studies 7. Sheffield Academic Press, Sheffield,

Commission of the European Communities (1971) *Bulletin of the European Communities Commission*, 4 (6), Office for Official Publications of the European Communities, Luxembourg.

Commission of the European Communities (1992) *Bulletin of the European Communities Commission*, 25 (6), Office for Official Publications of the European Communities, Luxembourg.

Commission of the European Communities (1993a) *Bulletin of the European Communities Commission*, 26 (10), Office for Official Publications of the European Communities, Luxembourg.

Commission of the European Communities (1993b) *Bulletin of the European Communities Commission*, 26 (12), Office for Official Publications of the European Communities, Luxembourg.

Commission of the European Communities (1998) Common Foreign and Security, Policy, *Bulletin of the European Communities Commission*, 31 (3), Office for Official Publications of the European Communities, Luxembourg.

Cooley, J.K. (1991) 'Pre-war Gulf diplomacy', *Survival*, 33 (2): 125–39.

Delors, J. (1991) 'European integration and security', *Survival*, 33 (2): 99–109.

de Schoutheete de Tervarent, P. (1997) 'The creation of the Common Foreign and Security Policy', in E. Regelsberger, P. de Schoutheete de Tervarent and W. Wessels (eds), *Foreign Policy of the European Union: From EPC to CFSP and Beyond*. Lynne Rienner, London and Boulder, CO, pp. 41–63.

Duff, A. (ed.) (1997) *The Treaty of Amsterdam. Text and Commentary*. Sweet and Maxwell, London.

Duke, S. (1999) 'From Amsterdam to Kosovo: lessons for the future of CFSP', *EIPA SCOPE*, **2**: 2–15.

Durand, M.-F. and de Vasconcelos, A. (1998) *La PESC Ouvrir l'Europe au monde*. Presses de Sciences Po, Paris.

Edwards G. (1997) 'The potential and limits of the CFSP: the Yugoslav example', in E. Regelsberger, P. de Schoutheete de Tervarent and W. Wessels (eds), *Foreign Policy of the European Union: From EPC to CFSP and Beyond*. Lynne Rienner, London and Boulder, CO, pp. 173–95.

Eliassen, K.A. (ed.) (1998) *Foreign and Security Policy in the European Union*. Sage, London.

EPC statements 1988, 1989. Ministerio de Asuntos Exteriores, Madrid.

Fursdon, E. (1980) *The European Defence Community: A History*. Macmillan, London.

Ginsberg, R.H. (1989) *Foreign Policy Actions of the European Community*. Lynne Rienner, Boulder, CO.

Grant, C. (1996) *Strength in Numbers: Europe's Foreign and Defence Policy*. Centre for European Reform, London.

Hallstein, W. (1962) *United Europe*. Oxford University Press, London.

Hill, C. (1993) 'The capabilities–expectations gap, or conceptualizing Europe's international role', *Journal of Common Market Studies*, **31** (3): 305–28.

Hill, C. (ed.) (1996) *The Actors in Europe's Foreign Policy*. Routledge, London and New York.

Hill, C. (1998) 'Closing the capabilities–expectations gap?', in J. Petersen and H. Sjursen (eds), *A Common Foreign and Security Policy for Europe*. Routledge, London and New York, pp. 18–38.

Holland, M. (ed.) (1997) *Common Foreign and Security Policy: The Records and Reforms*. Pinter, London and Washington, DC.

Hurd, D. (1994) 'The European Union: the immediate priorities', *International Affairs*, **70** (3): 421–8.

International Institute for Strategic Studies (IISS) (1998) *Strategic Survey 1997/98*. Oxford University Press for IISS, London.

Molas-Gallart, J. (1999) *The European Missile Industry*, CRIS Paper 1. Centre for Research in International Studies, Manchester.

Nuttall, S. (1992) *European Political Co-operation*. Clarendon Press, Oxford.

Petersen, J. and Sjursen, H. (eds) (1998) *A Common Foreign and Security Policy for Europe*. Routledge, London and New York.

Regelsberger, E., de Schoutheete de Tervarent, P. and Wessels W. (eds) (1997) *Foreign Policy of the European Union: From EPC to CFSP and Beyond*. Lynne Rienner, London and Boulder, CO.

Regelsberger, E. and Jopp, M. (1997) 'Und sie bewegt sich doch! Die Gemeinsame Aussen- und Sicherheitspolitik nach den Bestimmungen des Amsterdamer Vertrages', *Integration*, **4**: 255–63.

Rhodes, C. (ed.) (1998) *The European Union in the World Community*. Lynne Rienner, London and Boulder, CO.

Salmon, T. (1992) 'Testing times for European political co-operation: the Gulf and Yugoslavia, 1990–1992', *International Affairs*, **68** (2): 233–53.

Schake, K., Bloch-Lainé, A. and Grant, C. (1999) 'Building a European defence capability', *Survival*, **41** (1): 20–40.
Stirk, P.M.R. and Weigall, D. (eds) (1999) *The Origins and Development of European Integration: A Reader and Commentary*. Pinter, London.
Vaughan, R. (1976) *Post-War Integration in Europe*. Edward Arnold, London.
Whitman, R. (1998) *From Civilian Power to Superpower? The International Identity of the European Union*. Macmillan, London.
Zielonka, J. (ed.) (1998) *Paradoxes of European Foreign Policy*. Kluwer Law International, The Hague, London and Boston.

Web sites

europa.eu.int/comm/external_relations/ index.htm	EU's External Relations Directorate
europa.eu.int/pol/cfsp/index_en.htm	EU CFSP
presidency.finland.fi/netcomm/news/	Finnish EU Presidency news site
ue.eu.int/pesc/pres.asp?lang = en	The Council of the EU and CFSP
www.ambafrance.org.uk	French Embassy, London
www.europarl.eu.int/dg4/factsheets/en/ 6_1_1.htm	European Parliament's factsheet on CFSP
www.nato.int/	NATO
www.osce.org/	OSCE
www.portugal.ue-2000.pt/rtffiles/ file2329.rtf	Presidency Conclusions, Santa Maria da Feira European Council, 19 and 20 June 2000
www.weu.int/eng/comm/92-petersberg.htm	WEU Council of Ministers, Petersberg Declaration
www.weu.int/eng/welcome.html	Western European Union

10 The EU and the rest of Europe

Introduction

As the ECSC and EEC evolved into the EC and the EU, 'Community Europe' expanded from the original six members to nine in 1973, 12 after the Mediterranean enlargement in the 1980s and then 15 with three EFTA members joining in 1995. The EU number will continue to grow and what is defined as 'the rest of Europe' will shrink. This chapter will examine the evolving relationship between 'Community Europe' and the other countries in the continent.

A layer of relationships

The EU orders its relations with other European states in a way that reflects, to some extent, past links, and that increasingly influences the expectation of future relationships, especially that of membership. It is against this standard that other states' 'proximity' to the EU can be measured.

The EFTA states[1] have formed an inner ring of rich, traditionally democratic states, most of which had or would have little trouble in becoming full members of the EU with a relatively short transition period. They have provided good potential for the EC/EU in trade and economic terms and on account of their commitment to democratic ideals and environmental concerns. Whether the remaining EFTA states will become members depends to a great extent on the wishes of their peoples.

The 'Europe Agreement' states of Central and East Europe are certainly candidates for EU membership and have come a long way since 1989 when they were Communist-ruled states entrenched in a Soviet-dominated security organization. Their relationship with the EC and then the EU has developed rapidly and it has been accepted that the end-point will be membership of the EU. The degrees of change needed to meet the conditions of EU membership differ among these states, but it is possible that all will be members by 2010.

There are three other states that have lined up for membership: the two Mediterranean islands of Cyprus and Malta, and Turkey. These are associates of some years' standing, and although they have been subject to the rigours of the market economy for some time, each has its own particular mix of social, economic and political problems that have made their path to EU membership strewn with difficulties.

A different set of problems has been experienced by the states in the West Balkans region. These are the constituent republics of former Yugoslavia (with the exception of Slovenia) and Albania. Here the greatest problems are those associated with the various conflicts in the region and with the political nature and instability of the states and their consequent economic and social problems. Nevertheless, the EU has sought to bring the area into the mainstream of European political life and these states must hold the expectation of EU membership, if only in the longer run.

Finally, there are the states of the Commonwealth of Independent States (CIS), especially Russia, Ukraine, Moldova and Belarus. Though membership is not currently on the agenda for these states, they are nevertheless important European countries in security terms and are potentially large markets for the EU. Their relationship with the EU is of importance, especially for an extended Union that may have members bordering these four states.

The EFTA states

As outlined in the Introduction, once the Six ECSC countries had signed the Treaty of Rome in March 1957 to establish the European Economic Community, some of the other Western European states started to consider an agreement among themselves based on creating their own industrial free trade zone. By May 1960 seven states – Austria, Denmark, Norway, Portugal, Sweden, Switzerland and the United Kingdom – formed for themselves the European Free Trade Association (EFTA), formalizing the trade divide of Western Europe. The relations between the two groups since then can be divided into three periods: the EFTA period, the European Economic Area (EEA) and the EU's northern enlargement and beyond.

The *first period* lasted from the establishment of EFTA in 1960 until the opening of negotiations for the EEA in 1990. Almost within a year of EFTA's implementation as a free trade association, one of the main founding members – the United Kingdom – was considering membership of the EEC. In order not to give its partners the feeling that they might be ditched, the British agreed, at the London EFTA Ministerial Council of June 1961, that the EFTA states would 'remain united throughout the negotiations' with the EEC. EFTA would be maintained until agreements had been reached with the EEC in order to meet 'the various legitimate interests of all members of EFTA, and thus enable them to participate from the same date in an integrated European market' (*EFTA Bulletin*, 1961: 1). This allowed each EFTA state to decide on its own form of relationship with the EEC but also gave the hint of a 'convoy approach' to ensure that all seven members would be accommodated by the Community and not necessarily by full membership. Indeed, only Denmark, Norway and the United Kingdom took that option at the time, with Austria, Sweden and Switzerland requesting talks for associate membership, mainly because of concerns about their neutrality.

After the French veto of the British application (see Introduction, p. 13), EFTA returned to creating an industrial free trade area among its members, which it achieved in December 1966, three years earlier than planned. A second attempt by the United Kingdom and some of its EFTA colleagues to apply for EC membership in 1967 was also vetoed by the French government. By 1969 a new French government had accepted the idea of extending EC membership; in 1970 negotiations opened with the British government, later joined by those of Denmark, Norway and Ireland (the last not being an EFTA member). From 1 January 1973, the United Kingdom, Denmark and Ireland became full members of the EC, the Norwegian electorate having rejected membership in a referendum in September 1972.

From 1973 until the mid-1980s, the remaining EFTA states entered into a period of 'pragmatic bilateralism' (Pedersen, 1991: 13) in their relations with the expanded EC. During 1972 and 1973 the EFTA states, which by then included Finland and Iceland, signed individual industrial free trade agreements with the EC that allowed for the mutual dismantling of tariffs by 1977 between each EFTA state and the EU on industrial goods and processed agricultural goods. These agreements were overseen by a number of joint committees of representatives of each of the EFTA states and the EC. All the treaties, except that with Finland (which was still concerned about its relations with the Soviet Union), had an 'evolutionary clause', which allowed matters not covered by the free trade agreement to be discussed.

In 1984 the remaining few tariffs between the EFTA states and the EC were swept away and a whole range of issues – non-tariff barriers, agriculture and fisheries, transport and energy – were discussed at the first joint meeting of EFTA and EC governments, held in Luxembourg in April 1984. Within the next few years modest progress was made in common action on matters such as technology and with meetings of joint commissions held twice a year.

A turning point came in the EFTA–EC relationship in January 1989 when Jacques Delors, the President of the Commission, alluded to the EFTA states in his address to the European Parliament. He saw two options for future EFTA–EC relations:

> ... we can stick to our present relations, essentially bilateral, with the ultimate aim of creating a free trade area encompassing the Community and EFTA; or ... we can look for a new, more structured partnership with common decision-

making and administrative institutions . . . to highlight the political dimension of our cooperation in the economic, social, financial and cultural spheres. (European Parliament, 1989)

The stark option that Delors presented to the EFTA states was to stand still or advance. The latter option, he suggested, would need EFTA to strengthen its own structures with co-operation resting on 'the two pillars of our organizations'. Otherwise any advance would be on the basis of EC rules being extended to the EFTA countries. Delors – with some foresight – expressed misgivings about the EFTA states 'being allowed to pick and choose' from elements of EC co-operation which involved a Common Commercial Policy, harmonization, supervision by the European Court and social conditions of fair competition, not to mention closer co-operation on foreign policy (European Parliament, 1989). The most likely reason for Delors's initiative was to prevent the EFTA states, with their 'excess of devotion to free-trade zones and insufficient zeal for integration, from applying for EC membership' (Ross, 1995: 48).

Two events affected the EFTA states' calculation at this stage. The first was the southern expansion of the EC that brought Greece, Spain and Portugal in as new members by 1986, thus enlarging – and making more attractive – the EC market. The second was the plan for the Single European Market, accepted at the Milan EC Council in 1985, and the consequent 1986 Single European Act, meaning that the Communities were deepening as well as widening. This increased the economic costs for those outsider states (Krugman, 1988: 1–4).

The EFTA states' response to Delors *démarche* was twofold. First, they increased their contact with the EC. After the joint EFTA–EC ministerial meeting in February 1988, the European Council had declared the EC's wish for stronger and expanded relations with EFTA. A High Level Steering Group of EC and EFTA officials, meeting in Brussels in March 1989, agreed to examine the possibilities of a more structured partnership between the two sides. This would be based on the four freedoms of movement – of goods, services, capital and persons – and on other areas of co-operation, the so-called 'flanking policies'. The second response by the EFTA states was to work more closely together, as recommended by Delors. This was given political impetus at the March 1989 summit of heads of EFTA governments, where it was decided that, to be effective, EFTA had to ' "speak with one voice", thus following a wish expressed by the Community to deal with one partner only' (*EFTA Bulletin*, 3/89: 1).

The *second period* began in 1990. In December 1989 the EC and EFTA ministers met in Brussels and agreed to start formal negotiations between the two sides in 1990 with a view to creating the European Economic Area (EEA) as from 1 January 1993. The aim was to extend the four freedoms of movement achieved from that date by the EC to the EFTA countries on a mutual basis and to strengthen and broaden co-operation between the two sides on matters such as education, social welfare and consumer protection. This would mean the EFTA states accepting the *acquis communautaire* – the existing stock of EC legislation – and in recognition of the differences between the rich members of EFTA and the poorer southern members of the EC, economic and social disparities between regions should be reduced (*EFTA Bulletin*, 4/89–1/90: 5–6). To this end a Cohesion Fund was proposed, whereby EFTA states would assist Greece, Ireland, Portugal and Spain. Negotiations started in June 1990 and, after a number of delays, were completed by October 1991.

The agreement of association created a homogeneous European Economic Area with free movement of goods, persons, services and capital; by ensuring that competition was not distorted and rules were equally respected; and by providing for closer co-operation in other areas such as research and development, the environment, education and social policy. There was to be no discrimination on the grounds of nationality for the citizens of the 19 countries party to the agreement.[2] Common institutions were to be established. However, the EEA was not meant to become a customs union like the EC: the EFTA states could still maintain their tariffs with the rest of the non-EEA world. Also the EFTA states could keep their agricultural and fisheries policies, with only limited freer trade in these products between EFTA and the EC. Freer trade in fish and fish products was exchanged for greater access to Norwegian waters for EC vessels. EFTA was to enforce state aid and competition law to comply with EEA rules, and public procurement was to be opened up on the basis of EC directives. The EFTA states were allowed some concessions: Norway could maintain its national legislation for fishing boats, Iceland could limit foreign investment in its fisheries, and the Swiss had a five-year transition period for the elimination of the law that prevented the acquisition of their land by non-Swiss. Separate transit agreements were made between Austria and the EC and between Switzerland and the EC about transport across those countries.

A number of common rules were established to ensure that competition in the EEA territory would not be distorted by monopolies, cartels or restrictive practices or by impermissible state aids. Further rules covered public procurement and the laws on intellectual property. Should serious economic, societal or environmental difficulties of a sectoral or regional nature arise, then a signatory could take certain unilateral measures to remedy the situation. However, other EEA states could then take their own counter-measures.

The EEA agreement included a section on 'the horizontal policies relevant to the four freedoms', which aimed to support the functioning of these freedoms. Under social policy, the parties agreed to promote improved work conditions and health and safety of workers; provisions were made for consumer protection and for the environment.

Co-operation between EFTA and the EC was strengthened by a number of 'flanking policies' which included research and development; information services; education, training and youth; social policy; consumer protection; Small and Medium-Sized Enterprises; tourism and the audio-visual sector. The EFTA states' Cohesion Fund, to help Greece, Ireland, Portugal and Spain, was established.

The EEA institutions mirror some of those of the EC, as detailed in Table 10.1:

Table 10.1 *EEA structure*

- **The EEA Council** lays down guidelines and gives a political impetus to the agreement; it consists of members of each EFTA government, of the EC's Council of Ministers and of the EC Commission. Decisions are to be taken by agreement between the EC on the one hand and the EFTA states on the other.
- **An EEA Joint Committee** was set up to ensure the effective operation and implementation of the agreement, and matters causing difficulties could be raised by either side. It consists of official representatives of EFTA states, the EC states and of the Commission, and meets monthly.
- **The EFTA Surveillance Authority** ensures the fulfilment of the EEA obligations. Acting with the EC Commission, the Surveillance Authority ensures a uniform surveillance throughout the EEA and receives complaints about the application of the agreement (http://www.efta.inst/structure/SURV/efta-surv.cfm).
- **An EFTA Court** has jurisdiction over actions concerning the surveillance procedure regarding the EFTA states, appeals about competition initiated by the EFTA Surveillance Authority and over disputes between two or more EFTA states. There is a system of exchange of information on the judgments from EFTA and EC courts. In the original agreement of October 1991, an independent EEA Court was created, but the European Court of Justice (ECJ) ruled that this would interfere with the internal order of the EC and the autonomy of the EC legal order. The new arrangement with an EFTA Court and a division of labour between the EFTA Surveillance Authority and the EC was agreed in February 1992 (http://www.efta.inst/structure/COURT/efta-crt.cfm).
- **An EEA Joint Parliamentary Committee** consists of equal numbers from members of the EFTA parliaments and of the European Parliament.
- **An EEA Consultative Committee** is made up of equal numbers of the 'social partners' in the EC and EFTA – the workers and the employers – drawn from the EC's Economic and Social Council and EFTA's Consultative Council.

The decision-making procedure laid down for the EEA allows the EC Commission to seek expert advice informally from within EFTA when preparing new legislation in a field covered by the EEA agreement, and requires a copy of any proposal to be transmitted to EFTA governments. A continual process of consultation should follow, with every effort made to reach mutually acceptable solutions.

Another setback to the EEA agreement was its rejection in December 1992 by the Swiss electorate in a ratification referendum. The remaining 17 EEA states made some adjustments and the agreement came into force on 1 January 1994.[3]

The long negotiations leading to the EEA and the upset about a court reminded the EFTA states of the unsatisfactory nature of the arrangement. The former EC Commissioner Franz Andriessen commented that 'it will be the Community which sets the EEA agenda. The common rules of the EEA will be those of the Community's *acquis*' (cited in Gstöhl, 1994: 350). What had started as an easy exercise between familiar partners ended up as a loss of operational sovereignty by the EFTA states without any great gain in the freedom to participate in joint decision-making (*ibid.*: 335). After the three EFTA states of Austria, Finland and Sweden joined the EU on 1 January 1995, the three remaining EFTA members of the EEA – Iceland, Liechtenstein and Norway – faced an EU of 15 members. Despite this, the three decided to continue the agreement, though its importance in the eyes of the EU had been substantially diminished.

The *third period* has been that since the start of 1995 when the three EFTA states joined the EU. In a sense, the start to this phase can be traced back to early 1989 when Austria filed its application for full EC membership. It was followed by Sweden in June 1991, Finland in early 1992 and Norway in November 1992. The end of the Cold War meant an end to the security policy considerations that had previously restrained the neutral states – Austria, Finland and Sweden – from applying for full membership. Economic factors were also a consideration, with the EEA soon showing itself to be a disappointing alternative to full membership.

The Commission gave positive opinions of the four applicants, and a few issues were flagged up for negotiation. Generally these were agriculture, regional policy and competition policy; more specifically they were the foreign and security policies of the neutral states, the state monopolies of the Nordic countries and Norwegian fisheries (Commission of the European Communities, 1993a: 2–3).

Negotiations began with the four states in early 1993 and were substantially complete by March 1994. The next major problem was that of ratification of the agreements. (The results can be seen in Table 10.2.) The electorates of Austria, Finland and Sweden voted to accept membership from 1 January 1995; that of Norway rejected it for the second time. Broadly, those in the north of the Nordic states were most against membership, whereas city-dwellers tended to be more in favour.

From 1 January 1995 the division of Western Europe that had started back in the 1950s was substantially ended. Still excluded from EU member-

Table 10.2 *Referendum results for membership of EU by EFTA states, 1994 (per cent)*

	Yes (%)	No (%)	Turnout (%)
Austria (June)	67	33	81
Finland (October)	57	43	74
Sweden* (November)	52	47	83
Norway (November)	48	52	89

* In the Swedish vote 1% of ballots were spoiled.

ship were the mini-state of Liechtenstein; Iceland, with its North Atlantic fisheries dominating any consideration; and Switzerland and Norway; both with sizeable parts of their population demonstrating a wish to remain outside the EU and which are rich enough to survive. Switzerland had its own individual arrangement with the EC, but by the late 1990s Norway was finding that the EEA agreement was very one-sided and its governments had to accept a whole range of legislation from the EU without having had any input into its formulation. The issue of membership will return to the Norwegian political agenda after their September 2001 general election, and a further Norwegian application is a distinct possibility.

Europe Agreements

The European members of the former Council for Mutual Economic Assistance (CMEA or Comecon) were the Soviet Union, Bulgaria, Czechoslovakia (now the Czech Republic and Slovakia), the German Democratic Republic, Hungary, Poland and Romania. Taking their lead from the Soviet Union, the governments of these countries regarded the EC as a capitalist enterprise and refused to recognize its competence in trade matters. Even when the EC took over the right to conclude commercial agreements from its member states in 1973, EC members and the Comecon countries found ways round this seeming monopoly. When the EC Commission tried to open negotiations with Comecon states on a wide range of trade matters in 1974, they were rebuffed (Pinder, 1991: 11). A direct EC–Comecon relationship failed to emerge as the EC refused to accept Comecon as being on its own level. In particular, the EC did not want to provide the opportunity for greater central control within Comecon, as this would have meant more Soviet influence to the detriment of the East European presence (Pinder, 1991: 193).

With the liberalization of the Soviet leadership from the mid–1980s, relations quickly improved. Contact was made between the Commission and Comecon, and, after relations between the EC and individual Comecon states were 'normalized', a joint declaration between the two sides was signed on 25 June 1988. By October 1990 agreements had been signed between the EC and all the Comecon European members (Pinder, 1991: 25).

The revolutions in Central and East Europe during the winter of 1989 changed matters dramatically. The fall of Communist regimes there meant curtailment to the state-trading economies, their tight links with the Soviet Union and to Comecon and its military equivalent, the Warsaw Treaty Organization. The EC responded quickly to these events, sponsoring a meeting of the G24, the industrialized countries, which in May 1990 established the European Bank for Reconstruction and Development (EBRD); this could provide aid for the ex-Communist states and establish its own assistance programme. Since then, the relationship between the EC/EU and these Central and East European Countries (CEECs) has developed through a number of stages and its intensity has often differed with the proximity of the state involved.

One former Comecon member – East Germany – received special treatment. Less than a year after the collapse of the Communist regime there in November 1989, Germany was unified, on 3 October 1990. East Germany, formally known as the German Democratic Republic (GDR), had been created as a state by the Soviet Union in 1949 from its post-war occupation zone in Germany. When negotiating the EEC's Treaty of Rome, the Federal Republic of Germany (FRG) – formed from the three Western occupation zones and whose government insisted it was the only legal government of Germany – required that trade between the GDR and FRG should be treated as internal German trade and so remain free of tariffs.

Once the GDR ceased to exist in 1990, its territory became five Länder (regional governments) in the FRG and by July 1990 there was already economic and monetary union with the FRG. The EC acted quickly to make sure that East Germany could become part of the EC as well as of the FRG. No treaty revisions were necessary as they had all been signed by the FRG, which was merely increasing its size. With the unification of Germany, EC legislation automatically applied to the ex-GDR, except where decided otherwise by the Council, acting on a Commission proposal. One result was that tariffs were introduced on goods coming from other CEECs, although they were given a year's grace (to December 1991) to adjust (Commission of the European Communities, 1990: 5–27).

The CEECs

The governments of the Central and East European Countries that emerged from the collapse of Communism in 1989 looked west for their trade, and economic and political links. The response of the EC/EU has differed over the years, depending on the stage of economic and political development of the states involved, which were Poland, Hungary, the Czech Republic, Slovakia, Slovenia, Bulgaria, Romania, Estonia, Latvia and Lithuania.[4]

Until the 1988 EC–Comecon accord, these states were not even considered for inclusion in the EC's Generalized System of Preferences or for bilateral agreements, not so much because of their state-trading or undemocratic practices, but more because their exports were in direct competition with EC products (Tovias, 1991: 291). The 1988 accord led to bilateral agreements with Hungary in September 1988, Czechoslovakia in December 1988 and with Poland in December 1989.

After the CEECs' move to democratic government at the end of 1989 and start of 1990, the EC helped them with the structural changes needed in changing to market economies. With the help of the G24 industrial countries, the EC initiated the Phare (Poland–Hungary Aid for the Reconstruction of the Economy) programme in July 1989; Czechoslovakia and other former Comecon states plus Yugoslavia were added in September 1990. The priority areas for reconstruction were agriculture, industry, investment, engineering, training, environmental protection, and trades and services, especially in the private sector. From 1989 to 1999 Phare provided some ECU11bn in assistance for the CEECs, 'making it the largest technical assistance programme in history' (Avery and Cameron, 1998: 18). In 1990 the EC Commission proposed the Trans-European Mobility Programme for University Students (Tempus) for the CEECs, followed by programmes in economics (Ace), infrastructure (Cosine) and government and management (Sigma). From 1990 the EIB was able to assist the CEECs and further aid came from the European Bank for Reconstruction and Development (EBRD). All this activity aimed to transform the formerly state-run economies into more open markets.

The next stage in EC–CEEC relations was that of the 'second generation agreements' (the first generation being those resulting from the EC–Comecon accord). These were treaties of association known as Europe Agreements. The idea was advanced by the United Kingdom in 1990 and the agreements were only concluded by December 1991 for Czechoslovakia, Hungary and Poland, after resistance by France and Portugal to giving concessions to the three on their agricultural and textile exports (Kramer, 1992: 15). These agreements did not come into force until 1994 (or 1995 in the case of the Czech Republic and Slovakia after the break-up of Czechoslovakia), with interim agreements filling the void before ratification (Phinnemore, 1999: 73–5).

The Europe Agreements' limitations reflect not just the problems of the CEEC states but also the concerns of EC members. Their aim was the phased achievement of industrial free trade between the associate and the EU, with tariffs and quotas being abolished, apart from some exceptions such as on textiles. Only limited access has been allowed to EU markets for the agricultural produce of the associates, and their workforce has not been allowed free movement of labour into the EU. The fear has been that, until the associates' markets are stronger, such freedom could result in a mass movement of economic migrants into Germany and other EU countries.

Both Bulgaria and Romania signed Europe Agreements with the EU in 1993, with interim arrangements sufficing in the period before ratification in 1995. Both countries benefited from Phare aid from 1990 but are regarded as less well developed than the Czech Republic, Hungary and Poland.

The Baltic states of Estonia, Latvia and Lithuania were independent in the inter-war period but were forcibly integrated into the Soviet Union in 1940. National revivals took place in these states in the 1980s and each declared its independence in 1990. After the failed military coup in the Soviet Union in August 1991, the three were able to put their declarations into practice and their return to sovereignty was recognized by other European states, the USA and, finally, the Soviet Union and its successor state, Russia.

The three republics have a range of outstanding problems. They are small countries – Estonia has 1.6m inhabitants, Latvia 2.7m and Lithuania 3.7m – with limited natural resources whose economies had been fully integrated into that of the Soviet Union. Latvia and Estonia, in particular, have sizeable non-native minorities.

After regaining their independence, they signed 'first generation' trade and co-operation agreements in May 1992, which came into force in February 1993. In June 1995 the three countries signed Europe Agreements; these came into force in February 1998.

When Yugoslavia fragmented into its component republics at the end of 1991 and the beginning of 1992 (see pp. 203–4), Slovenia, to the north-west of the country and bordering Italy and Austria, was the one republic that managed to avoid the subsequent conflicts. It was also the most economically advanced part of Yugoslavia, conducting 60 per cent of its trade with the EU (Commission of the European Communities, 1993b: 3). It received Phare aid and signed a 'first generation' agreement with the EU in 1993 and a Europe Agreement in June 1996 after a dispute with Italy about the status of former Italian property in Slovenia had been solved. This agreement came into force in February 1999.

The road to membership

It soon became apparent that the Europe Agreements were not ends in themselves but steps towards full membership by the aspiring CEECs. Not least, the rather restrictive nature of the agreements offered the CEECs by the EC/EU persuaded some of them that they would not taste the full fruits of modern western economies until they were full members of the emerging European Union. Furthermore, many politicians in Central and East Europe – and their voters – regarded EU membership (often together with NATO membership) as the final proof that their country had 'returned to Europe' after some 45 years of Soviet domination (longer in the case of the Baltic states). The Europe Agreements had indicated that accession to the EC/EU had become the aim of the associates, but did not show this to be an EC/EU aim.

It was the EC Copenhagen Summit of June 1993 that accepted that the CEECs could become full members, but it set no deadline. In 1995 Hungary and Poland formally applied for EU membership, followed by Romania, Slovakia, Latvia, Estonia, Lithuania and Bulgaria in 1995 and the Czech Republic and Slovenia in 1996. The Copenhagen Council talked about the associates being 'able to assume the obligations of membership by satisfying the economic and political conditions' (Commission of the European Communities, 1993c). The 'Copenhagen criteria' to be fulfilled by the applicants before they could don the robes of membership are:

- they should have stable institutions that guarantee 'democracy, the rule of law, human rights and the respect for and protection of minorities' (the political criterion);
- they should have a 'functioning market economy' and a capacity to cope with competition and market forces within the EU (the economic criterion);
- they should be able 'to take on the obligations of membership, including adherence to the aims of political, economic and monetary union' (the administrative criterion);

Added to this was a criterion to be fulfilled by the EU itself:

- the Union had to have the capacity to absorb new members while maintaining integration (institutional reform criterion) (*ibid.*).

A further implicit condition is that new members should not import into the EU any dispute with neighbouring states over, for example, borders or minorities.

As with the membership of previous applicants, the starting point for any new member was that it had to accept the *acquis communautaire* of the EU, which was defined by the Danish President of Council in 1993 as including:

- the content, principles and political objectives of the Treaties [of the EC], including those of the Maastricht Treaty;
- legislation adopted pursuant to the Treaties, and the case law of the Court of Justice;
- statements and resolutions adopted within the Community framework;

- international agreements and agreements concluded among themselves by the Member States relating to Community activities.

The inclusion of the Maastricht Treaty and now the Amsterdam Treaty has created a wider '*acquis* of the Union' to be accepted by potential EU members.

However, the EU recognized that these requirements could not be made in a vacuum – their achievement had to be aided by assistance and guidance, and a process created that would plot the path to full membership for the aspirants. In March 1994 the EU Council set out plans for an increased dialogue with the Europe Agreement states. These included meetings between the President of the European Council and the heads of state or government of the CEECs, briefings of their ambassadors after each European Council, common discussions of CFSP, human rights and JHA matters, and the possibility of common action (Commission of the European Communities, 1994: 68). The leaders of the then six Europe Agreement states were invited to the Essen European Council in December 1994, and changes were made to the Agreements in order to improve access to the EU markets for the agricultural, steel and textile exports of the six states.

The Madrid European Council in December 1995 asked the Commission to prepare a report on the effects of enlargement, including the financial aspects, and Opinions on the ability of the candidates to fulfil the criteria for membership. This was to be ready by the completion of the IGC that led to the Amsterdam Treaty in 1997 (Commission of the European Communities, 1996). The Commission decided to send questionnaires in April 1996 to the ten CEEC applicants (Bulgaria, Czech Republic, Estonia, Hungary, Latvia, Lithuania, Poland, Romania, Slovakia and Slovenia) to elucidate their progress on the administrative Copenhagen criterion. Statistics from other organizations provided information on the progress in the economic criterion and a variety of sources helped in deciding advances in the political area (Avery and Cameron, 1998: 37–40).

The Commission's Opinions were ready in July 1997, just after the signing of the Treaty of Amsterdam. The Commission had asked itself whether the applicants would be ready for membership in the medium term, that is, within five years, thereby taking 2002 as a 'hypothetical date for accession' (Avery and Cameron, 1998: 41). On the basis of these Opinions, the Council decided – also on the Commission's recommendation – to open negotiations with five CEECs – Hungary, Poland, the Czech Republic, Estonia and Slovenia – as well as with Cyprus. This represented a political compromise. The three central states that had just been admitted to NATO – Hungary, Poland and the Czech Republic – were obvious candidates. The inclusion of Estonia was a response to the Nordic EU states that wanted all

three Baltic states included but had to be satisfied with the most economically advanced. Slovenia was the candidate of France and Italy, and Cyprus
of Greece. The disappointment felt by the states not included was assuaged
by the promise that their cases would be kept under review. Indeed, the
other candidates – Bulgaria, Latvia, Lithuania, Romania and Slovakia, –
together with Malta and Turkey – were given the green light for their
accession negotiations at the Helsinki European Council in December 1999
(http://presidency.finland.fi/netcomm/news/).

If the candidates seemed ready for membership, what of the EU? After all,
the final Copenhagen criterion referred to reform of the Union's institutions. There were two related matters that needed attention. The first was
the size of the Commission. There are 20 Commissioners of the 15-state EU.
It was felt that a larger Commission would be both unwieldy and inefficient,
with some Commissioners scarcely having any real tasks to perform. Should
the five largest present members forgo their second Commissioner, then the
size of the College of Commissioners could be kept to 20 if only five more
states were allowed membership, each having their own Commissioner.
Clearly the long list of applicants meant that even this solution would not
suffice. The second issue was that of Qualified Majority Voting (QMV) in
the Council. As the number of member states with relatively small popula-
tions grows, so does the possibility of a couple of large members having
legislation imposed on them by a QMV vote of countries that represent even
a minority of the total EU population. Solutions to this quandary would be
either to increase the weighted vote of the larger countries or to change the
weighting formula, for example by having a formula that reflects population size. These two issues are related as a number of the larger members are
unwilling to give up their second Commissioner unless they have a reassur-
ance about a more balanced – from their perspective – QMV. Furthermore,
other members want the extension of QMV, but again this is unlikely to be
accepted as long as the QMV formula remains unchanged.

At the December 1999 Helsinki European Council, the EU made a
commitment to holding an IGC on institutional reform by December
2000, so that – after ratification of the reforms – it would be ready 'to
welcome new Member States from the end of 2002 as soon as they have
demonstrated their ability to assume the obligations of membership and
once the negotiating process has been successfully completed' (http:/
/presidency.finland.fi/netcomm/news/).

Cyprus and Malta

In 1989 the President of the Commission, Jacques Delors, referred to these
two Mediterranean countries (together with Yugoslavia) as 'the orphans of
Europe', presumably because they did not belong to any trade or defence

group. Both Cyprus and Malta became independent from the United Kingdom in the 1960s and have precarious economies based on tourism.

In 1974 Cyprus was invaded by Turkey, one of the island's guarantor states, after a coup brought to power a group that wanted to join the country to Greece, always a Turkish fear. The Turkish government claimed that it was defending the Turkish minority in North Cyprus and established a republic there led by the local Turkish politicians. This administration has not received any international recognition and a solution to both the international and internal aspects of the Cyprus question has eluded the UN, NATO, the OSCE and the EC/EU (Kramer, 1997: 18).

Cyprus signed an association agreement with the EC in December 1972, in preparation for entry into the EC of the United Kingdom, one of the island's major trading partners. The original plan was a two-stage move to a customs union between Cyprus and the EC, with the first stage to be completed in 1977 and the second in 1982. The Turkish invasion of 1974 introduced an element of turmoil into the working of the agreement. The second stage of a transition to a customs union was postponed from 1977. Generous access to the EC markets was prevented by the Mediterranean member states, with whose produce Cypriot imports might have competed. Also there was the practical problem of how to implement the customs union for the northern Turkish-occupied part of the island.

A unilateral declaration of independence by the northern occupied part of the island in 1983 was condemned by the foreign ministers of the EC and the European Parliament and gave some impetus to EC–Cypriot relations (Tsardanidis, 1984: 352–76).

A Customs Union Agreement (to complete the second stage of the Association Agreement) was signed between Cyprus and the EC in October 1987, with completion of the union planned for 2002. In July 1990 the Cypriot government announced that it wanted full membership of the EC. The Commission accepted Cyprus's eligibility but pointed out that membership would be difficult as long as the island remained politically divided and the fundamental freedoms for all the islanders were denied (Commission of the European Communities, 1993d: 17; Nugent, 1997). In 1994 the European Council decided that Cyprus would be included in the next round of enlargement. The question of a free trade treaty between the EU and Turkey allowed Greece – the main supporter of Cyprus within the EU – some leverage on its fellow EU member states in 1995. In July 1997 Cyprus was on the Commission's list of applicants with whom negotiations should be initiated, and talks were begun between Cyprus and the EU on 31 March 1998. Negotiations about the division of the island started in New York under the aegis of the UN Secretary-General in December 1999, and this gave some hope that a political settlement might be reached on Cyprus's internal and international problems. The 1999 Helsinki

European Council noted that a settlement 'will facilitate the accession of Cyprus to the European Union' without 'being a precondition' (http://presidency.finland.fi/netcomm/news/).

The Maltese government signed a treaty of association under Article 238 of the EEC Treaty in 1970, in time for British entry into the EC in 1973. This was negotiated by the pro-EC National Party government, but then became a source of disagreement between the later Labour government and the EC. This government tried to play off the EC against Libya to the south but a change back to National Party government in 1987 brought the country closer to the EC again. In 1990 Malta applied for full membership of the EC and the Commission's Opinion in 1993 was positive about negotiations, although issues about the economy and Malta's non-alignment were raised (Commission of the European Communities, 1993e: 14). When the Labour party won the 1996 election, it declared that it would not pursue membership but by 1999 the return of a National party government meant that Malta's application was again active and the country was included on the list of states with which the EU would open negotiations.

Turkey

Turkey's relations with the EC/EU have been difficult for a number of reasons. After the First World War the reformist government in Turkey decided on the adoption of Western ways. Now, with a foothold on the European continent and membership of NATO and the Council of Europe, Turkey regards itself as a European state as well as one situated in Asia Minor. The population is Islamic although the state is secular. Its level of development is high compared with its neighbours although below that of the EU members where many Turks are resident as 'guest workers'. It has developed democratic institutions but the army seized power on a number of occasions (in 1960, 1971 and 1980) and has seen itself as the guardian of the secular state. Turkey has been constantly in dispute with Greece, especially about the seas between the two countries and over the island of Cyprus (see above). Turkey can be seen either as a bastion for Europe against the unrest and Muslim fundamentalism of the Middle East or as an area of possible instability that could impinge on Europe.

Turkish relations with the EC until Greek membership in 1981 demonstrate an anxiety not to be treated any less favourably than their Greek rivals. After several false starts in negotiations, Turkey obtained associate membership of the EC in 1963, partly as a response to a similar Greek move. The idea was for a 22-year transitional phase from December 1964. The Turkish invasion of Cyprus in 1974 lowered the country's estimation in the eyes of EC leaders, especially as an EPC/EC *démarche* was upset by further Turkish action. Greek application for EC membership in 1975 led Turkey to seek – and obtain – assurances that Turkey would be kept informed of the progress of the Greek negotiations. The period from 1975 until 1981 saw EC–Turkish relations take on an erratic nature, especially as the prospect of Greek membership drew closer (Tsakaloyannis, 1980: 46–54). The issue also arose of Turkish treatment of the Kurds, a mountain people who live in Turkey, Iran and Iraq.

The military takeover in Turkey in January 1980 froze relations with the EC until civilian government returned. With a partial restoration of democracy in 1983 and in the expectation of full parliamentary elections, the Turkish government applied for EC membership in April 1987.

Turkey had to wait over two and a half years for a Commission Opinion on membership and when it came, it was unfavourable. A number of factors counted against membership:

- the Commission said it could not start negotiations with any candidate before 1993 because of the Single Market programme;
- it was stated that, because of its economic and social situation, Turkey 'would find it hard to cope with the adjustment constraints with which it would be confronted in the medium term if it acceded to the Community' (Commission of the European Communities, 1989: 88);
- political pluralism and human rights were still a problem;
- 'the persistence of a dispute with a member state' (Greece) was a negative factor;
- as was 'the lack of solution of the Cyprus problem' (*ibid.*).

The Commission set out measures to help Turkey modernize itself politically and economically in line with the 1963 association treaty. This involved the completion of the customs union with the EC, greater financial, industrial and economic co-operation and the strengthening of political and cultural links. In June 1990 the Council of Ministers adopted the Commission Opinion on Turkish membership and called for specific measures such as the completion of the customs union by 1995, greater co-operation in reducing the development gap between the EC and Turkey and the re-establishment of financial co-operation suspended in 1981.

Turkey's role in the Gulf conflict with Iraq from August 1990 to February 1991 and in the subsequent operation among the Kurds reminded the EC of the importance of the country in Middle Eastern affairs but also of its vulnerability to outside factors and internal rifts (Aybet, 1994). The Commission recommended that further 'appropriate steps' be taken in the relations between the EC and Turkey (Commission of the European Communities, 1992: 17). The intention was to work towards creating the delayed customs union between Turkey and the EU by 1996. However, this met Greek opposition and only entered into force at the last moment – 31

December 1995 – with its full implementation being delayed by further Greek–Turkish disagreements.

The presence of a government in Athens that wished to improve its relations with Turkey, and the mutual suffering of the two countries when they were both hit by earthquakes in 1999, led to the Greek government lifting its veto on Turkish EC membership in time for the December 1999 Helsinki European Council. This meeting welcomed positive developments in Turkey as seen in the Commission's report and stated that Turkey was 'destined to join the Union on the basis of the same criteria as applied to the other candidate States' (http://presidency.finland.fi/netcomm/news/). However, progress still had to be made on the following points:

- the settlement of disputes with Greece
- the Cyprus question
- human rights

Although Turkey still has some way to go on these issues and on the question of economic development, it is now closer to EU membership than ever before. What is given little public consideration is the effect on the EU of membership of a large state, the frontiers of which stretch to Syria, Iran and Iraq, and whose traditions and political system is quite different from those of both the existing EU members and the other candidate states.

The West Balkans

Yugoslavia, although a Communist country after the Second World War, was not controlled by Moscow as were other East European states. Under President Tito, it took a more open approach to the West and in the 1960s and 1970s became a leading member of the non-aligned movement. Because of its precarious position between East and West and its ability to keep out of the Soviet bloc, individual EC states had granted a Most Favoured Nation status to Yugoslav exports before the formulation of the EC's common commercial policy. The EC concluded a trade agreement with Yugoslavia in 1970, confirming this privileged position, and established a joint EC–Yugoslav committee to deal with mutual problems. A second trade agreement in 1973 led to the reduction of tariffs and import duties on Yugoslav exports to the EC (Pinder, 1991: 18).

Just before Tito died in 1980, the EC tried to develop its trade agreement to include co-operation, with the aim of helping to stabilize the country in the post-Tito period. This confirmed Yugoslavia's position in the EC's Generalized System of Preferences (granted in 1971) and also encouraged mutual co-operation over finance, labour, science and technology. Loans from the EIB helped to ease transport between Italy and Greece (Pinder, 1991: 18).

Yugoslavia's favoured position with the EC was soon eroded after the events in Eastern Europe of 1989–90. The country only received a small share of the Phare programme and the EC's interest in Yugoslavia was no longer determined only by its strategic position in the East–West struggle, but was also influenced by the move to multi-party democracy and a market economy. Yugoslavia's journey down that road proved hazardous in 1990 and Poland, Hungary and Czechoslovakia soon overtook it. The disintegration of Yugoslavia in 1991 changed the country from being – in the EC's eyes – an object of its commercial policy, albeit for political reasons, to being the subject of political debate, but with economic consequences.

By the end of 1991 Slovenia and Croatia, then constituent republics of Yugoslavia, were attempting to break away from what they regarded as the increasingly Serbian-dominated and nationalistic Yugoslavia. The EC tried to keep Yugoslavia together, even signing a loan agreement with the federal republic the day before the two breakaway republics declared their independence (Cviic, 1992: 88). This was a crisis on the doorstep of the EC and there were expectations of EPC/EC action in what the Luxembourg Foreign Minister, Jacques Poos, called 'the hour of Europe'. However, the recognition of the Yugoslav republics as sovereign states was followed by a war between the Serb-dominated rump Yugoslavia and, at first, Croatia and Slovenia, and then Bosnia-Herzegovina. Once conflict broke out, the EC–EPC was involved in four ways.

First, the EPC was delegated by the CSCE to resolve the conflict and it convened a number of conferences to that end, chaired originally by Lord Carrington, the former Secretary-General of NATO. In September 1991 the Commission was asked to chair the three working groups of the conference. The EC/EU later provided co-chairmen for peace conferences held with a UN-appointed co-chair.

Second, the EPC attempted to broker ceasefires between the warring factions and sent unarmed monitors to observe them (Nuttall, 1994: 21–4). The most successful of these was the Brioni Agreement of July 1991 when the EPC–EC troika arranged for a peaceful solution of the crisis in Slovenia.

Third, the EC ministers in November 1991 invoked sanctions against those elements it considered responsible for the continued fighting – mainly the Serbian government and the Yugoslav federal army (Cviic, 1992: 88–90). These sanctions, which had UN blessing, were monitored by the Western European Union (WEU) with NATO help. The WEU, with NATO assistance, carried out search operations against ships in the Adriatic in Operation Sharp Guard and a WEU police and customs unit helped Bulgaria, Hungary and Romania implement sanctions inland.

Finally, the EPC meeting in December 1991 decided to recognize in January 1992 those separate Yugoslav republics that wished international recognition. This line had resulted from a German declaration that it intended unilaterally to recognize Slovenia and Croatia on 23 December 1991. In order to keep a united front, the other EC members agreed on recognition provided it was postponed until 15 January 1992. In April 1992 recognition was extended to Bosnia-Herzegovina. Greece prevented the EC recognition of another constituent republic, Macedonia.

The conflict was mainly between the Serb-backed federal forces – together with local Serb militia – and Croatia and then Bosnia-Herzegovina, where Serb forces occupied over half the territory. During 1992 and 1993 efforts were made to produce a peace plan for the area which would be acceptable to all sides. This was the work of the co-chairmen of the peace conference: Cyrus Vance, nominated by the UN Secretary-General (later replaced by Thorvald Stoltenberg); and David Owen, Lord Carrington's successor, nominated by the EC states working through the EPC. Meanwhile the Serb forces removed Muslim Bosnians from the east of Bosnia-Herzegovina in what became known as ethnic cleansing, and surrounded the Bosnian capital of Sarajevo. The Croat forces within Bosnia-Herzegovina clashed with the mainly Muslim government forces over the town of Mostar which was placed under EC/EU administration in July 1994 with Hans Koschnik, the former mayor of Bremen, acting as administrator (Allen and Smith, 1995: 70).

During 1994 the Serbian-Croat war ended and the Croats in Bosnia formed a loose federation with the mainly Muslim Bosnian government. NATO bombing of Serb forces and their reverses on the ground against Croat and Bosnian forces led to the US-brokered Dayton Peace Accord in November 1995. David Owen's successor as EU special envoy in former Yugoslavia, Carl Bildt (replaced in 1997 by Carlos Westendorp, who was himself replaced in 1999 by Wolfgang Peritisch), was overshadowed by the diplomacy of the US special envoy, Richard Holbrooke (Allen and Smith, 1996: 64). The implementation forces for this agreement – the Implementation Force (IFOR) and then the Stabilization Force (SFOR) – were based on NATO forces and planning. However, the EU took on the task of implementing the civilian side of the agreement. In short, the EC/EPC/EU contribution to solving the Yugoslav imbroglio was one that was long on resolutions and missions, but short on action and determination. It was hobbled by differences among member states, a lack of willingness to send troops to an area where they might be in danger, the ability of the parties in the dispute – the Serbs in particular – to call the bluff of any threat, and by a basic disagreement about the mix needed between armed action and diplomacy.

When Serb forces took action in 1998 against ethnic Albanians in the Serb province of Kosovo (which is populated overwhelmingly by ethnic Albanians), it seemed that the Serb-dominated Milosovic government of the rump of Yugoslavia was again going to 'ethnically cleanse' an area. This time the international community, led by the USA and NATO, was quicker to respond and in March 1999 an operation was launched under NATO leadership to evict Serb military forces from Kosovo. The subsequent peace agreement in June 1999 – partly brokered by President Ahtisaari of Finland acting for the EU – involved an EU-led reconstruction plan for the whole of what is called the West Balkans (former Yugoslavia and Albania). A wider EU Stability Pact for South East Europe offered the states in the region Stabilization and Association Agreements, which would prepare them for eventual EU membership (Cameron, 1999: 88).

The work of the European Community Humanitarian Office (ECHO) was augmented under the Obnova Assistance Programme (of aid to the former Yugoslav region); an Agency for Reconstruction established responsibility for implementing the continuation of the Obnova aid with the inclusion of Kosovo (http://europa.eu.int/comm/dg1a/see/intro/index.htm). At the time of the Helsinki European Council in December 1999, the EU was anticipating urgent reports on the economic and political situation in the region and to improving its relations with those particular states. As part of this process it hoped for the democratization of the Federal Republic of Yugoslavia,[5] supporting democratic forces in Serbia and the government of Montenegro. The Council also pledged €500m for the Reconstruction and Recovery Programme for Kosovo from 2000, additional to contributions from member states (http://presidency.finland.fi/netcomm/news/).

Albania is one of the most problematic of the Central and East European states as it only returned to international relations in the early 1990s after having been isolated under an inward-looking Communist dictatorship since 1945. EU initial involvement was in the form of Phare and humanitarian aid to what is one of the poorest parts of Europe, and the signing in May 1992 of a 'first generation' treaty. Economic collapse in 1997 led to civil war in the country and an exodus of people to Italy and other neighbouring states. The idea of a WEU-led force to keep order was overruled by the United Kingdom and Germany and instead an ad hoc force under Italian leadership helped to restore a form of order to the country.

The country is now included in the EU's Stability Pact for South East Europe and the Common Strategy for the West Balkans, both of which aim to bring the states in the area closer to the EU norm in terms of democracy, human rights, social peace and economic development. This is clearly a long-term development but the EU has decided that if it is to enlarge its membership to Central and East Europe and possibly to Turkey, then there is no reason in principle why the countries of the West Balkans should be excluded.

Russia

Before the late 1980s, the Soviet Union[6] did not recognize the EC and its trade relations were based on individual arrangements made by the Soviet Union and the EC member states. Once the USSR recognized the EC in 1988, the situation changed and by the end of 1990 the European Council offered the Soviets an agreement covering economic, political and cultural co-operation, expanding on that signed in Brussels in December 1989. However, the use of force by the Soviet Union in the Baltic republics in January 1991 led to a suspension of EC aid.

A failed coup against Mr Gorbachev, the reformist leader of the USSR, in August 1991 eventually led to the collapse of the Soviet Union, which was formally disbanded on 25 December 1991, leaving the component parts of Russia and 14 republics. Concerned lest the economic and social conditions in these republics caused security problems for the area to the east of the Communities, EC ministers took action at two levels.

The first was economic. The attempt to deal with the long-term economic problems was the task for the European Bank for Reconstruction and Development (EBRD) – set up after an EC initiative by the G24, the group of industrialized countries (Pinder, 1991: 86–103). The EC supplied the Soviet successor states with food and medical help in order to survive the 1991–92 winter. The EC also had its own effort to support reform in the new states: the Technical Assistance to the Commonwealth of Independent States (Tacis) was established in 1990 first to provide technical help to the Soviet Union and then to the CIS. It faced a much greater task than Phare, its Central and East European equivalent, insofar as it covered 12 republics – some Asian – spread over a vast area. In June 1994 the EU signed a Partnership and Co-operation Agreement (PCA) with Russia, but its implementation was immediately endangered by Russian military action against the rebellious province of Chechnya (Commission of the European Communities, 1994: 3) and it only came into force in December 1997.

The other response was by the EPC (the political facade of the EC – see Chapter 9) and it was a diplomatic recognition of the successor republics, including Russia, and support of their membership of the CSCE (later OSCE) and the United Nations. The political link between the EC/EU and Russia is important for both sides. From the Russian perspective, it is a recognition of the country's status and of the need for it to be brought into decisions about the future of the continent. From the EU's viewpoint, it is part of the process of trying to modernize and stabilize Russia so that it may no longer be a source of great uncertainty in Europe. In March 1998 President Chirac of France and Chancellor Kohl of Germany met President Yeltsin of Russia in Moscow in order to reassure him that EU expansion would not isolate his country. Although previous Russian prime ministers have broached the question of eventual Russian membership of the EU, this has not been officially taken up.

It was with this in mind that the EU accepted the Northern Dimension initiative of the Finnish government in 1997 with the aim of engaging Russia in a co-operative relationship in the Barents-Baltic region (Jopp and Warjovaara, 1998). Furthermore, the first Common Strategy agreed at the Cologne European Council was that for Russia. The areas of co-operation were to be political – with strengthened dialogue on foreign and security issues – and economic reform, and concerning challenges such as the environment and international crime. Again, relations were somewhat overshadowed by Russian action against Chechnya at the end of 1999, and the Helsinki European Council condemned the severity of this action and the effects on civilians, although 'did not question the right of Russia to preserve its territorial integrity nor its right to fight against terrorism' while this should not warrant wholesale action against a people. It called for a political solution, and an end to the 'indiscriminate use of force' and the safe delivery of humanitarian aid. The Council promised to re-examine the PCA, Tacis aid and the implementation of the Common Strategy on Russia in this light (Annex II of the Presidency Conclusions, http://presidency.finland.fi/netcomm/news/). After Vladimir Putin's election as Russian President, the EU resumed a dialogue with Russia, withdrawing even the modest sanctions imposed in early 2000 because of the situation in Chechnya.

The others

On the break-up of the Soviet Union at the end of 1991, the EPC recognized the successor states that – apart from Russia – ranged from Ukraine in Eastern Europe to Tajikistan in Central Asia. In doing this, the EPC ministers also set out guidelines of expected behaviour by the new states and postponed recognition of Georgia, where there was a civil war.

The EU signed Partnership and Co-operation Agreements (PCAs) with Moldova and Ukraine in 1994; Kyrgyzstan, Belarus and Kazakhstan in 1995; and Armenia, Azerbaijan, Georgia and Uzbekistan in 1996. These Agreements allow for a degree of market access for the exports of these countries, with the eventual prospect of free trade with the EU.

A Partnership and Co-operation Agreement was concluded with Ukraine in 1994. In October 1995 the EU provided ECU200m in balance of payments aid, linking this to the closing of the Chernobyl nuclear power station (Allen and Smith, 1996: 75), a move that had not been achieved by 2000. Nevertheless, the Helsinki European Council adopted a Common Strategy on Ukraine, recognizing the importance of the country in between the CEECs and Russia. This strategy took account of 'Ukraine's European aspirations and pro-European choice', suggesting that membership could be a question for consideration in the future (Annex V to Presidency Conclusions, http://presidency.finland.fi/netcomm/news/).

Belarus is a former Soviet republic that has little history as a separate state or national identity. The anti-democratic nature of the Belarus government and its poor human rights record has led to the PCA not being implemented and all aid, except humanitarian and that for democratization, being suspended in 1997 (Allen and Smith, 1998: 80). In 1998 EU states withdrew their ambassadors from Belarus after eviction from their residences by the Belarus government.

Conclusions

As the EU embarks on its next enlargement, so its relations within non-EU Europe will change. States presently external to the EU will become part of the Union, meaning new links with new neighbours and changing trade patterns. Two countries will remain important in their relationship with the EU – Russia and Turkey. Both these have sizeable territory outside Europe and have their own identity and traditions that are not in the mainstream of those of the EU countries. Yet both have their own, quite different, European aspirations. Turkey wants to be a member of the EU and Russia does not want the option ruled out. Membership of the EU by either would change its nature more than in the case of membership by the CEECs, Malta and Cyprus. There would be no 'other' in Europe that could be regarded as an outsider, especially if the authoritarian governments in Serbia and Belarus were to disappear. The methods used to work the Community of the Six in the 1950s and 1960s have been adapted for the Union of the 15 and, at a pinch, will survive in a reformed mode for the Union of 20 or 27. However, the very nature of the EU will be severely challenged by Turkish membership and could not survive membership of Russia.

Notes

1 The EFTA states were originally Austria, Denmark, Norway, Portugal, Sweden, Switzerland and the United Kingdom. Iceland joined in 1970 and at the end of 1972, Denmark and the United Kingdom left to join the EU. Portugal did the same at the end of 1985, but Finland joined EFTA as a full member in 1986 as did Liechtenstein in 1991. Austria, Finland and Sweden left to join the EU at the end of 1994, leaving Iceland, Liechtenstein, Norway and Switzerland as EFTA members.
2 The 19 states were the 12 members of the EC plus Austria, Finland, Iceland, Liechtenstein, Norway, Sweden and Switzerland. Austria, Finland and Sweden later joined the EU and Switzerland rejected EEA membership.
3 The figure became 18 when Liechtenstein ratified the agreement on 1 May 1995. The Swiss rejection had meant that Liechtenstein – tied to Switzerland by a customs union – took extra time to join the EEA.

4   From 1990 until 1993 the Czech Republic and Slovakia formed the Czech-Slovak Federal Republic. The old name of Czechoslovakia will be used here. Until 1991 Estonia, Latvia and Lithuania were incorporated into the Soviet Union. Slovenia was a constituent republic of Yugoslavia until its collapse at the end of 1991.

5   At that time Serbia and a smaller republic, Montenegro, made up what was still called the Federal Republic of Yugoslavia, although in reality it was dominated by Serbia and its political leader, Slobodan Milosovic. His seeming defeat in the September 2000 Yugoslav presidential election gave the opportunity for political change in the country.

6   The Soviet Union came into existence in the years following the 1917 Russian Revolution in which the Communist Party came to power. Although the Soviet Union – or Union of Soviet Socialist Republics (USSR) – had a federal structure on paper, it was, until the late 1980s, ruled by the Communist Party of the Soviet Union (CPSU), which brooked little opposition. Mr Gorbachev, the last head of the USSR, attempted to reform the system but failed. When the USSR dissolved, it fragmented into the following 15 republics: the Russian Federation, Ukraine, Belarus, Moldova, Estonia, Latvia, Lithuania, Kazakhstan, Uzbekistan, Turkmenistan, Kyrgyzstan, Tajikistan, Armenia, Azerbaijan and Georgia. These states – minus the three Baltic states of Estonia, Latvia and Lithuania – formed the loose association of the Commonwealth of Independent States (CIS).

References and further reading

Allen, D. and Smith, M. (1995) 'External policy developments', in N. Nugent (ed.), *The European Union 1994: Annual Review of Activities*. Blackwell, Oxford, pp. 69–86.

Allen, D. and Smith, M. (1996) 'External policy developments', in N. Nugent (ed.), *The European Union 1995: Annual Review of Activities*. Blackwell, Oxford, pp. 63–84.

Allen, D. and Smith, M. (1998) 'External policy developments', in N. Nugent (ed.), *The European Union 1997: Annual Review of Activities*. Blackwell, Oxford, pp. 69–92.

Avery, G. and Cameron, F. (1998) *The Enlargement of the European Union*, Contemporary European Studies 1. Sheffield Academic Press, Sheffield.

Aybet, G. (1994) *Turkey's Foreign Policy and Its Implications for the West: A Turkish Perspective*, Whitehall Papers 27. Royal United Services Institute, London.

Buzan, B. and Dietz, T. (1999) 'The European Union and Turkey', *Survival*, 41 (1): 41–57.

Cameron, F. (1999) *The Foreign and Security Policy of the European Union: Past Present and Future*, Contemporary European Studies 7. Sheffield Academic Press, Sheffield.

Commission of the European Communities (1989) *Bulletin of the European Communities* 10/89. European Communities' Commission, Brussels.

Commission of the European Communities (1990) *Bulletin of the European Communities*, 4/90. European Communities' Commission, Brussels.

Commission of the European Communities (1992) *Bulletin of the European Communities*, 3/92. European Communities' Commission, Brussels.

Commission of the European Communities (1993a) *Background Report: The Enlargement of the Community*. Office of the Commission, London.

Commission of the European Communities (1993b) *Target 92, No. 5*. Office for Official Publications, Luxembourg.

Commission of the European Communities (1993c) *Bulletin of the European Communities*, 6/93. European Communities' Commission, Brussels.

Commission of the European Communities (1993d) *Bulletin of the European Communities*, 5/93. European Communities' Commission, Brussels.

Commission of the European Communities (1993e) *Bulletin of the European Communities*, 4/93. European Communities' Commission, Brussels.

Commission of the European Communities (1994) *Target 92, No. 7*. Office for Official Publications, Luxembourg.

Commission of the European Communities (1996) *Bulletin of the European Communities*, 1/96. European Communities' Commission, Brussels.

Cviic, C. (1992) 'Implications of the crisis in south-eastern Europe', *Adelphi Papers*, 265, International Institute for Strategic Studies, London.

Cyprus Press and Information Office (1991) *The Development of EC–Cyprus Relations*. Press and Information Office, Nicosia.

EFTA Bulletin. August/September 1961; 2/84; 3/89; 4/89–1/90.

European Parliament (1989) *Debate of the European Parliament No. 2–373, 1988–89*, report of Proceedings from 16 to 20 January 1989, *Official Journal EC*, 2/373.

Grabbe, H. and Hughes, K. (1998) *Enlarging the EU Eastwards*. Cassell, London.

Gstöhl, S. (1994) 'EFTA and the European Economic Area or the politics of frustration', *Cooperation and Conflict*, 29 (4): 333–66.

Jopp, M. and Warjovaara, R. (eds) (1998) *Approaching the Northern Dimension of the CFSP: Challenges and Opportunities for the EU in the Emerging European Security Order*. UPI and IEP, Helsinki.

Kramer, H. (1992) 'The EC and the stabilisation of eastern Europe', *Aussenpolitik*, 43 (1): 12–21.

Kramer, H. (1997) 'The Cyprus problem and European security', *Survival*, 39 (3): 16–32.

Krugman, P. (1988) *EFTA and 1992*, Occasional Paper No. 23. EFTA, Geneva.

Mayhew, A. (1998) *Recreating Europe: The European Union's Policy Towards Central and Eastern Europe*. Cambridge University Press, Cambridge.

Müftüler-Bec, M. (1999) *Turkey's Relations with a Changing Europe*. Manchester University Press, Manchester.

Nikolaidis, K. (1998) 'Exploring second-best solutions for Cyprus', *Survival*, 40 (3): 30–4.

Nugent, N. (1997) 'Cyprus and the European Union: a particularly difficult membership application', *Journal of Mediterranean Politics*, 2 (3): 53–75.

Nuttall, S. (1994) 'The EC and Yugoslavia: *deus ex machina sine deo*', in N. Nugent (ed.), *The European Union 1993: Annual Review of Activities*. Blackwell, Oxford, pp. 11–25.

Pedersen, T. (1991) 'EC–EFTA relations: an historical outline', in H. Wallace (ed.), *The Wider Western Europe*. Pinter, London, pp. 13–27.

Phinnemore, D. (1999) *Association: Stepping-stone or Alternative to EU Membership*, Contemporary European Studies 6. Sheffield Academic Press, Sheffield.

Pinder, J. (1991) *The European Community and Eastern Europe*. Pinter, London.

Rhodes, C. (ed.) (1998) *The European Union in the World Community*. Lynne Rienner, London and Boulder, CO.

Ross, G. (1995) *Jacques Delors and European Integration*. Polity Press, Cambridge.

Tovias, A. (1991) 'EC–Eastern Europe: a case study of Hungary', *Journal of Common Market Studies*, **29** (3): 291–315.

Tsakaloyannis, P. (1980) 'The European Community and the Greek–Turkish dispute', *Journal of Common Market Studies*, **19** (1): 35–54.

Tsardanidis, C. (1984) 'The EC–Cyprus association agreement: 1973–1983', *Journal of Common Market Studies*, **22** (4): 351–76.

Web sites

europa.eu.int/comm/enlargement/ intro/ag2000_opinions.htm	Agenda 2000
europa.eu.int/comm/enlargement/ pas/turkey.htm	EU and Turkey
europa.eu.int/comm/external_relations/ see/intro/index.htm	EU and South East Europe
europa.eu.int/pol/enlarg/	EU: enlargement process
presidency.finland.fi/netcomm/news/	Finnish Presidency of EU
www.europarl.eu.int/dg7/summits/en/ lux1.htm	Luxembourg Summit, 1997
www.europarl.eu.int/enlargement	European Parliament briefings on enlargement
www.efta.inst/structure/COURT/efta-crt. cfm	EFTA Court
www.efta.inst/structure/SURV/efta-surv. cfm	EFTA Surveillance authority

11 The EU and the world

Introduction

The EU has a layered relationship with the world outside Europe, both in terms of trade and in political relations. The links with former colonies have been some of the most intense with their basis in the Treaty of Rome, while the United States is a key player in the world economic and political system to which the EU must react over a wide range of issues. The Asian states of China, India and Japan and those within the ASEAN group are a large and vibrant market for the EU, while the Middle East, North Africa and Latin America are all areas to which the EU has given increased attention in recent years.

It should be noted that for much of the post-war period, most of the world's trade relations were conducted in the wider context of the General Agreement on Tariffs and Trade (GATT), which tried to liberalize trade by breaking down barriers to trade and by preventing new ones arising. This was the aim of a succession of rounds of GATT negotiations including the Kennedy Round (1962–67), the Tokyo Round (1974–79) and the Uruguay Round from 1986 to 1992, which also led to the creation of the World Trade Organization (WTO) on 1 January 1995. While GATT had been a loose arrangement with weak enforcement instruments and concentrated predominantly on the trade in goods, the WTO is more organized, has an enforcement structure and deals with a much wider definition of trade, including issues such as intellectual property and the trade in services.

The EU's relations with other states should also be seen in the context of the Common Commercial Policy whereby the EC/EU have taken over existing commercial arrangements that the member states have with other countries. The EU will increasingly place these commercial arrangements in the framework of the Union's external policy aims such as the encouragement of peace and stability in regions of conflict, the furtherance of human rights and economic reforms, and the underwriting of regional economic co-operation. The structures created in the Common Foreign and Security Policy in the Maastricht and Amsterdam treaties will now have to interact with the Common Commercial Policy of the EU so that the Union is seen to act in a co-ordinated fashion on the world stage. The Prodi Commission has set such cohesion in external policy as its aim; the coming years will determine their success.

ACP agreements

The EU's relationship with a number of African, Caribbean and Pacific (ACP) states dates back to the EEC's links with the colonial and former colonial territories of the signatories of the 1957 Treaty of Rome.

The ACP countries form a large proportion of the total number of less-developed and developing states and their special relationship with the EU is derived largely, but not completely, from their former colonial status. The members of the group are non-Asian former colonies of the EU member states, with two states (Ethiopia and Liberia) having no prior colonial status.

Association and Yaoundé

Part Four of the Treaty of Rome was devoted to the structure of the EEC's relations with colonies and ex-colonies. This had been included at the insistence of the French government, which saw the opportunity of trade and aid gains for its colonies and overseas territories from the other members of the EEC.

Part Four of the Treaty created the Association of the Overseas Countries and Territories with the purpose of promoting 'the economic and social development of the countries and territories and to establish close economic relations between them and the Community as a whole' (Article 131). In Article 132 the Associates were given a 'most favoured nation' status for trading access, and non-discrimination in the rights of establishment and commercial ventures. While Article 133 abolished customs duties for EEC and Associate countries' products on a mutual basis, the Associates were permitted to 'levy customs duties which meet the needs of their development and industrialisation', although it was expected that these would be of a temporary nature. Article 136 required an Implementing Convention in order to detail the specific procedures governing Association, with commitment lasting for an initial period of five years.

The EEC also recognized the need for investment with the European Development Fund (EDF), which was subsequently set up and disbursed $581m over the first five-year period of Association (Lister, 1988). During this initial period many of the Associates benefited from the EDF with improved administrative structures, although, because of the slow implementation of the provisions of Association, the expected 'payoffs' of trade creation did not materialize (Lister, 1988: 20–9).

Nevertheless, both sides agreed that the formal basis of Association should be developed. During the 1960s a revised set of agreements between the Community and the Associates were drawn up. The first, the *Yaoundé Convention*, was signed in 1963 when many of the Associates had already gained their independence. Eighteen newly independent African states took the title of the Association of African and Malagasy States (AAMS). The Yaoundé Conventions (1963–68; 1969–74) maintained the system of Association, although between the EC and a group of sovereign states. AAMS goods received preferential and duty-free access to the EC market.

The first Yaoundé Convention also introduced a set of joint AAMS–EC institutions directly to manage decisions and issues arising from the relationship. These consisted of a Council, supplemented by a Committee, Parliamentary Conference and a Court. The EDF was enlarged in volume by 20 per cent and money was made available in the form of grants and loans in order to encourage economic diversification and the stabilization of commodity prices.

With the second Yaoundé Convention the AAMS members stressed their own problems of transition and the inability of the Convention to redress major weaknesses of manufacturing and industrial capability. Despite the EC's full agenda at home and some intransigence on behalf of the AAMS, Yaoundé II was concluded. The Group of 77 (mainly African, Latin American and Asian states) and other members of the United Nations Conference on Trade and Development (UNCTAD) were relatively successful in pursuing the extension of the Generalized System of Preferences. The assertiveness of the developing states during the 1970s allowed the AAMS to maintain and reform their economic relations with the EC. On the United Kingdom joining the EC in 1973, the African and Caribbean members of the Commonwealth acceded to Yaoundé II, while Asian Commonwealth states were linked to the EC in bilateral trade agreements.

The Lomé Conventions

The first Lomé Convention, named after the capital of Togo in which it was signed in 1975, seemed to usher in a new era of co-operation between the EC and developing states. The Convention referred to the African–Caribbean–Pacific group (ACP) as 'equal partners' of the EC. The 46 states that then made up the ACP group were varied in levels of development, geography and historical background.

While Lomé reproduced some of the content of Yaoundé, there were some novel features, largely as a result of pressure from the ACP members. Unlike the earlier reciprocal trade preference scheme, Lomé introduced a non-reciprocal regime whereby ACP members were not obliged to offer special access to EC imports but could still enjoy preferential trade access to

Community markets. Under Lomé equal trade access applied to all members. There was also a separate Sugar Protocol, of importance for the sugar-producing Caribbean ACP members, that guaranteed the purchase of a quantity of their sugar at a fixed price linked to that received by EC sugar-beet farmers.

Lomé I also introduced an export revenue stabilization scheme, known as Stabex. This innovative feature developed practices begun under Yaoundé to provide aid in special circumstances. Export revenues of the ACP states could be stabilized by the EDF, through which Stabex operated according to certain criteria:

- primary products covered were those such as coffee, tea, cotton, bananas, iron ore and animal hides;
- ACP states whose export revenue depended heavily on these products could apply for reimbursement if export earnings fell by more than 7.5 per cent. The poorest ACP states could be reimbursed if their earnings dropped by more than 2.5 per cent.

This scheme and the Sugar Protocol helped to bring a greater sense of economic security to many ACP producers, and it was hoped that this would lead to a greater diversification of ACP economies. This was also to be assisted by the European Investment Bank (EIB) with the EDF funding industrial co-operation between the EC and ACP and by the creation of the Centre for Industrial Development to act as a forum for identifying projects.

The aid provisions in Lomé I had to address the doubling in the number of Associates since Yaoundé and their disparate economic and social needs. EC aid was set at EUA3.4bn (European Units of Account), a doubling in real terms of the aid allocated under Yaoundé II. However, it was still the EC that very much determined the direction of aid.

The institutional framework was reformed by Lomé I. The ACP–EC Council of Ministers had the power to take decisions. The Council of Ambassadors complemented and supported the infrequent Council meetings by providing an element of continuity. A Consultative Assembly provided a forum for debate and consultation but had no real powers.

After Lomé I expired in 1980, it was followed by Lomé II 1980–85, Lomé III 1985–90, and Lomé IV 1990–2000. A number of issues and developments can be seen in these agreements.

First, there was the effort to diversify the economic bases of the ACP states and to stabilize their export earnings. Lomé II widened Stabex's product coverage and introduced Sysmin to support mineral exports. Lomé III tried to encourage regional economic self-reliance and also relaxed the requirement to repay Stabex funds.

Second, development aid has always been an issue. It has been shared between the EC and its member states and the Union has stressed the match between EU and bilateral official development assistance. The nature of aid has changed from being project-based under Lomé I and was aimed more at structural adjustments, debt relief and economic recovery programmes in Lomé II and Lomé III. During the 1990s, about half the EDF funds went on national indicative programmes and about a quarter on structural adjustments. Regional and intra-state co-operation was also a feature of this period. During the reference period of 1996–2000 EU aid to the ACP states was ECU14.6bn, compared with ECU6.7bn aid given to Central and East European states in the 1995–2000 period (http://europa.eu.int/comm/development/faq/en-faq07.htm).

Third, issues such as integrating the environment and human rights issues have increasingly been elements in programmes. This has brought to the fore the question of the ACP's involvement in Lomé. The EU has tried to respond to the ACP states' request to decide where aid should best go, but has been under increased pressure from its own politicians and peoples to attach environmental and human rights' requirements to any assistance. Economic Impact Assessments for projects were introduced in 1992 and became mandatory in 1996, providing an important input from the EU side into any Lomé programmes.

A *new relationship?*

When the time came in 1999 to negotiate the successor to Lomé IV, a number of factors had to be taken into account.

First, Lomé IV had been revised mid-term and this took into account the return of South Africa to the international community after the end of white minority rule there. Also commodity prices were falling and the debt burden was increasing. Already in 1994 the ACP states were asking the EU 'to write off all public debt with ACP states' (ACP–EC Joint Assembly resolution, OJC 167, 20 June 1994: 23). Aid had also been suspended to states that had not honoured pledges to hold democratic elections, such as Liberia and Togo. As political conflict spread in Africa the European Community Humanitarian Office (ECHO) became increasingly active in Liberia, Somalia, Rwanda and Burundi in providing humanitarian assistance (European Commission, 1994a).

Second, the collapse of the Soviet bloc in Eastern Europe has changed the geostrategic position of the 'Third World', especially as there is no longer a 'Second World', meaning a Communist bloc. This shift has weakened the developing states' bargaining power. Furthermore, the existence of candidate states in Central and East Europe has meant a reordering of EU aid and trade priorities in favour of those states.

Third, the globalization of trade and finance seems to be leading to an international system in which the poorest countries are increasingly excluded (http://europa.eu.int/comm/development/publicat/rep97/chal_en.htm).

Negotiations between the ACP states and the EU lasted from September 1998 until February 2000. In June 2000 a 20-year partnership agreement was signed between the EU and 77 ACP countries at Cotonou, Benin. The Cotonou Agreement is to replace the Lomé Convention and has provisions on the political dimension, participation, development strategies, trade and financial cooperation. The key elements are:

- The agreement lasts for *20 years*, will be open for revision every five years, with some components up for annual review, and key elements (such as the economic partnership agreements) will be negotiated by 2002.
- There is an emphasis on *political dialogue* between the EU and ACP states with important elements being peace-building policies and conflict prevention; respect for human rights, democratic principles and the rule of law; and a commitment to good governance.
- Provisions promote *participation* by civil society and social and economic participants.
- *Development strategies* aim at poverty reduction with a multi-dimensional and integrated approach. Three themes are gender equality, environmental sustainability and institutional development and capacity building.
- The new *trade framework* aims at integrating the ACP economies into the world economy and at introducing a new trading arrangement after a preparatory period, with the existing one in place until then. The EU will liberalize almost all imports from least developed countries (LDCs) on the basis of the Generalized System of Preferences (GSP). Negotiations for a new economic partnership agreement would start by September 2002 at the latest, with new trading arrangements in force by the start of 2008 at the latest. The aim is to produce a regime that will be compatible with the World Trade Organization.
- *Financial cooperation* – in effect, the 9th European Development Fund (EDF) and EIB assistance to the ACP states – is to be rationalized. There will be a 'grant envelope' for long-term development, with each state allocated a lump sum, managed by the Commission and the ACP state concerned. Part of the EDF will be reserved for regional programmes under this heading. The Investment Facility will deploy a slice of EDF money and be managed by the EIB. A single Country Support Strategy (CSS) for each state will analyse economic, political and social factors and will contain a review mechanism.
- *The financial resources* for the next seven-year period are €13.5bn for the EDF, of which €10bn is for long-term allowances, €1.3bn

for regional allowances and €2.2bn for the Investment Facility; €9.9bn from remaining balances from previous EDFs; and €1.7bn from the EIB's own resources (http://europa.eu.int/comm/development/cotonou/overview_en.htm).

This agreement is likely to be tested in the new trade environment dominated by the World Trade Organization, even after the failure of the Seattle negotiations to widen its remit. Some of the preferential systems created between the EU and ACP may fall foul of WTO rules. This has already happened to the banana regime. Lomé created a system whereby ACP banana exports – coming mainly from the Caribbean islands – were given preferential trade access to the EC/EU that included a system of tariffs and quotas (Thagesen and Matthews, 1997: 615–27). By the mid-1990s US-based banana producers, whose trade came mainly from the non-ACP states of Central America, complained to the WTO about this preferential treatment. In 1997 the Dispute Settlement Body of WTO ruled that certain aspects of the EU banana regime were not in conformity with WTO rules and that these had to be amended by the end of 1998. The EU Council adopted a modified regime to come into force on 1 January 1999. The WTO Dispute Settlement Body ruled that this was still not compatible with WTO rules and allowed the USA – the complainant – to 'suspend concessions' to the value of $191.4m, which meant punishing EU trade to the USA with tariffs to that extent. The WTO Dispute Settlement Body in particular ruled against a separate quota for ACP bananas and also against import licences being distributed on the basis of a 1994–96 reference period which 'perpetuated the distortions of the previous regime' (IP/99/828, http://europa.eu.int/rapid/start/cgi/guesten.ksh). The Commission proposed a new system at the end of 1999 based on an interim arrangement that would give preference to the ACP states but that would lead to a flat tariff after 1 January 2006. However, this proposal could still be challenged and also depends on a new arrangement being negotiated before 2006 and on assistance for the ACP states that will suffer from the freer trade (*ibid.*).

The example of the banana regime could be ominous for the ACP states. It shows that their arrangements with the EU can no longer be made to suit the needs of the two sides, but must now take into account WTO rules. Furthermore, the advocates of freer trade in the USA may be willing to press the US government to attack other aspects of the EU–ACP agreement. ACP negotiators will increasingly have to keep an eye on Washington, DC, as well as on Brussels.

North America

The United States' presence in Europe had a long pedigree in the twentieth century. It was a liberator and occupier in both the First and Second World

Wars and a founder member and *the* guarantor of NATO after 1949. US troops stayed in Europe after 1945. With the Marshall Plan in 1947, the United States encouraged the Europeans to make the most of the reconstruction process financed by this scheme by intensifying their own economic co-operation. The USA became a supporter of the integration process in Western Europe, not least to build up European countries as bastions against the Soviet Union. An economically viable Western Europe would not only be a market for American goods but would also be able to take on its share of the defence burden. Indeed, the USA also became a market for the EC/EU: by 1998 it took 22 per cent of EU exports. It also provided over 40 per cent of Foreign Direct Investment (FDI) in the EU, with EU members accounting for over a half of FDI in the USA. Underpinning these economic and political links between the USA and EU members is a common belief in democracy and the market economy; this has been demonstrated in the support for NATO by the USA and most EU states and in the foundation and membership of the OECD.

However, the relationship between the USA and the Western Europeans has not always been easy. US administrations clashed with President de Gaulle in the 1960s on defence and foreign affairs issues – but then so did the United Kingdom. The formation of the EEC as a customs union may have been encouraged by US governments, but that did not prevent a number of disputes arising as the EEC created its Common External Tariff. Although the Kennedy Round of GATT tried to blunt the effects of EEC policies by wider global agreements, the EEC's negotiator stoutly defended the Common Agricultural Policy (CAP) to the extent that no deal was done in that area. From the early 1960s through to the start of the 21st century, there have been a number of trade disputes between the USA and the EC/EU that have arisen mainly from the creation of the Single European Market. There have also been a number of disagreements arising from political differences. For example, USA diplomatic sanctions on Islamic fundamentalist Iran (from 1979 to 1980), sanctions against the Soviet Union in 1980 because of its invasion of Afghanistan in December 1979, and then against Poland in 1982 after the imposition of martial law there in December 1981, were seen as strong-arm tactics by most EC members. The USA considered European action through the EPC as too circumspect (Bowker and Williams, 1988: 253).

Many of these disagreements over the response to Soviet action disappeared after Mr Gorbachev came to power in the Soviet Union in 1985 and later signed a number of arms control agreements with the West. At the end of the 1980s and the start of the 1990s, the USA sought EC assistance to manage the end of the Cold War, the freeing of Central and East Europe and the collapse of the Soviet Union. However, even with the election of President Clinton in 1992, a person sympathetic to the aims of the EU, policy differences between the Union and the USA – for example over the management of the disintegration of Yugoslavia – could not be disguised (Smith and Woolcock, 1994; 470–4). In another dispute – that between Greece and Turkey in the Aegean Sea – the US negotiator, Richard Holbrooke, accused the EU of 'sleeping through the night' while the USA toiled to end the dispute (Jakobsen, 1998: 257). Furthermore, the election of a Republican Congress in 1994 and 1998 helped the move to an 'America First' policy and led to tiffs with the EU over sanctions on Libya and Iran and the US punishment of EU firms investing in Cuba under the Communist – and anti-US – leadership of Fidel Castro. In the latter case a head-on collision was only prevented by President Clinton's intervention. Disputes between the EU and the USA over the trade in bananas and the EU's banning of hormone-enhanced beef from the USA have both been sent to WTO arbitration with the USA winning their cases (Guay, 1999). The inability of the USA and the EU to agree on a new round of trade talks at the Seattle meeting of the World Trade Organization in 1999 can be seen as another stand-off in the succession of trade disagreements between the two sides.

Does this mean that the EU is facing a trade war with the USA? It would be of little advantage to either side to see such an economic conflict between interdependent blocs. Furthermore, the EU–US relationship has been institutionalized. In November 1990 the two sides signed the Transatlantic Declaration, which expressed the common goals of assuming responsibility for the worldwide mediation of conflict, contributing to a healthy world economy, backing political and economic reform in developing countries, and providing the necessary assistance to Central and East Europe. They also agreed to liberalize multilateral world trade through GATT. The US President and the Presidents of the European Council and Commission were to meet twice yearly, and there were to be ministerial meetings, as well as regular consultation on crisis matters. The Gymnich Arrangement, whereby the EU kept the USA informed of its activities, was to be continued, as were regular meetings of members of the European Parliament and of the US Congress. In 1995 the signing of a New Transatlantic Agenda enhanced the EU–US relationship on each side by providing a more specific list of policy areas for co-operation, including the creation of a Transatlantic Business Dialogue.

It might be concluded that the EU and the USA are in a competitive rather than in a conflictual relationship and this involves disputes within a framework of co-operation. The EU and USA have dealt with their trade disputes in a way that has not endangered their basic relationship (Featherstone and Ginsberg, 1996). The Second EU–US summit, held in December 1999 in Washington, was attended by the Commission President, the EU Presidency and President Clinton of the USA. It dealt with a wide range of political and trade subjects but did not mend the rift between the two sides over the progress of the WTO talks (EU–US relations, http://europa.eu.int/comm/dgs/external_relations/us/intro/index.htm).

Relations between the EC/EU and Canada have been somewhat overshadowed by the EU–US relationship. A framework agreement on trade and co-operation was agreed with Canada in 1976, although this did not include any preferential trade regime. In 1990 Canada and the EC signed a Transatlantic Declaration, similar to that agreed between the USA and the EC. As with the USA, a number of bilateral disputes have arisen between the two sides, especially over EU fisheries rights in the Grand Bank off Newfoundland which in 1995 led to a 'Turbot War' between the two. A 1996 Joint Political Declaration on EU–Canada relations included an Action Plan that intensified the links between the two sides. A Europe–Canada Trade Initiative in 1999 aimed to reduce and eliminate trade irritants between the two sides (IP/99/998 at http://europa.eu.int/comm/dgs/external_relations/index_en.htm).

North Africa and the Middle East

The EC/EU has had an abiding political and economic interest in both these regions. They border the common sea of the Mediterranean and over the centuries the peoples of these areas have interacted with Europeans both in the form of trade and in warfare. In the nineteenth and early twentieth centuries, some European powers established colonies in North Africa and political control over much of the Middle East; European states, along with the USA, fought both world wars in the regions. Since 1945, the countries there have become independent and their relations with their former European overlords have sometimes been difficult. The rise in the importance of nationalism mixed with pan-Arabism and Islam in both areas has often tested the co-operative links with Europe. Petroleum has been a much-sought-after product of the Middle East and North Africa, and the presence of an independent Israel as a home for the Jewish people in an area claimed by the Palestinians has been a constant source of conflict in the region.

In North Africa the EC signed first-generation association agreements with Tunisia and Morocco in 1969 and a trade agreement with Egypt in 1972. In 1972 the EC decided to take 'a global approach in all the Community's relations with the Mediterranean countries' (Commission of the European Communities, 1972: 119). In 1973, British entry into the EC meant a renegotiation of previous individual agreements with North African states. The Arab oil embargo of October 1973 to March 1974 made the EC conscious of its dependence on raw materials – especially oil and gas – from the southern Mediterranean states such as Algeria and Libya. From 1972 to 1973 onwards, EC/EU policy towards North Africa has to be seen in the context of its evolving Mediterranean strategy and the Euro-Arab Dialogue (see p. 225).

Co-operation agreements were signed with the three Maghreb states of Algeria, Morocco and Tunisia in 1976 and with the four Mashreq countries of Egypt, Jordan, Lebanon and Syria in 1977–78. These were based on reciprocal trade preferences, financial and technical aid, and an improved status for Maghreb migrant workers residing in the EU.

However, relations with the North African states cooled during the 1980s. By the middle of that decade the fear of the Arab states withholding oil from the West had declined with the price of oil. Greece, Spain and Portugal redirected their trade towards the other EC states once they became EC members, weakening their solidarity with North African states especially as these often wanted access to the EC market for produce that would compete with exports from the three new EC Mediterranean countries. In 1989 the European Council did, however, ask the Commission to flesh out a policy of 'neighbourly relations' with the Maghreb Union (Commission of the European Communities, 1990: 9), possibly in response to a Moroccan hint that it wished to apply for EC membership. After the Gulf conflict of 1990–91, the EC increased its aid and loans available to the Maghreb and Mashreq states.

In 1990 Jacques Delors described the EC's interest in North Africa in terms that defined the EC/EU concerns about the region for the following decade:

> We must make it our concern, firstly because of traditional trade flows and cultural and historic links, and secondly because we cannot ignore ... the urgent development needs of countries faced with a steep rise in population, the environmental pressures on the sea we share, and the flashpoints of social and religious tension which are a major source of instability. (Commission of the European Communities, 1990: 9)

The EC's New Mediterranean Policy, adopted in December 1990, reinforced trade links and supported economic reform and social adjustment in the southern Mediterranean partners of the EC. The hope was to stabilize these countries and to co-operate with them, especially over energy, drug smuggling and migration. It was realized that adverse conditions in this area provided 'sources of instability leading to mass migration, fundamentalist extremism, terrorism, drugs and organized crime'. The response was to be an increase in funds for the Mediterranean countries and a move towards free trade with the Maghreb countries (European Commission, 1994b: 3–4).

The next major move was by the European Union: this was an attempt to deal with the all of the Mediterranean region in a holistic fashion that included political, social and economic policies. With Israel and the Palestinian authorities moving towards peace (see p. 225), the Commission felt ready in 1994 to publish a communication on 'Strengthening the Mediterranean Policy of the European Union' (European Commission, 1994c). This led to the signing of the Barcelona Declaration of November 1995 between the EU and Algeria, Cyprus, Egypt, Israel, Jordan, Lebanon, Malta, Morocco, Syria, Tunisia, Turkey and the Palestinian territories. This is the basis for the 'Euro-Med Partnership'.

The Barcelona Declaration has three chapters. The first deals with the political and security aspects and includes the acceptance by all parties of human rights and fundamental freedoms, the rule of law and democracy, co-operation in combating terrorism, organized crime and the drugs problem. This chapter also sees the Mediterranean as a common area of peace and stability. The second chapter covers economic and financial matters and is built on the progressive establishment of a free trade zone, economic cooperation and an increase in EU aid to the partners. It is hoped that a free trade area will be established in the region by 2010. The EU budget for the Euro-Med Partnership from 1995 to 1999 was ECU4.6bn with an extra ECU4bn of loans from the EIB. The third chapter covers social, cultural and human issues and aims to bring together the peoples of the area by exchanges and conferences, while strengthening co-operation over crime, illegal immigration, terrorism, corruption and the fight against racism and xenophobia. As a result of this agreement there have been a number of Conferences of Foreign Ministers of the Euro-Med states, including those in Malta 1997, Palermo 1997 and Stuttgart 1999 (http://www.euromed.net).

Whether the EU states can maintain their interest in the North African states, once the process on enlargement into Central and East Europe starts, remains to be seen. Membership of the EU by Cyprus and Malta – and certainly by Turkey – would strengthen the southern perspective of the Union. The ability of the North African states to deal with the EU in a united and comprehensive fashion is also open to question. There are high stakes – the social, economic and political stability of the Mediterranean world – at risk.

The Middle East reflects on a larger scale many of the problems of the North African states. Added to these have been wars between Israel and its neighbours (1948, 1956, 1967, 1973 and 1982), between Iran and Iraq (1980–88) and between Iraq and its neighbours plus an alliance of Western states (1990–91).

Apart from states included in Mashreq (see p. 223), the EC/EU has found other partners in the Middle East region. In 1989 the EC signed a cooperation agreement with the Gulf Co-operation Council (GCC) – Bahrain, Kuwait, Qatar, Oman, Saudi Arabia and the United Arab Emirates – and the first Joint Co-operation Council was held in March 1990. It was agreed to focus on industry, energy, agriculture, trade, services and science and technology. By October 1991 a free trade agreement had been drawn up between the EC and the GCC but implementation has been difficult because of the issue of unhindered access to European markets of refined oil.

EU relations with Iraq and Iran are difficult. In the case of Iraq, this is because of sanctions on the regime of Saddam Hussein after his invasion of Kuwait in 1990 and continued human rights abuses and manufacture of weapons of mass destruction. For Iran, the causes have been its support for terrorist movements and its refusal to lift the *fatwa* or religious ruling that condemned the British author, Salman Rushdie, to death. By the close of the 1990s, a more reforming regime in Iran meant that the EU started to open up relations with that country, although with much caution.

The start of a wider EC interest in the Arab world came in 1974 with the opening of the Euro-Arab dialogue on a wide front and using such forums as the UN. This was a response to the oil embargo of 1973–74 and the rise in oil prices; the EC members wanted to secure their oil supplies.

In 1980 the EPC took its first initiative on the Arab–Israeli dispute with its Venice Declaration. This was seen as a balanced approach, advocating international guarantees for mutually recognized borders and the creation of a Palestinian homeland. It was ignored by the Arab states and rejected by Israel. However, it was followed by visits to the region by the EPC Council President in subsequent years. The initiative on the Middle East Peace Process (MEPP) was taken away from the EU in 1993 by the United States and Norway, although that emphasized a deal between Israel and the Palestinians rather than the wider settlement sought by the EU. Nevertheless, as a result of the 1993 Israeli-Palestinian accord, the EU updated its association agreement with Israel and gave ECU87.4m in aid to the fledgling Palestinian authority in Gaza and Jericho in 1994. Between 1994 and 1998 the EU provided €600m in grants and loans for the Palestinian authority, with another €800m coming from member states (Chris Patten, 'The Middle East Peace Process, http://europa.eu.int/external_relations/ speeches/ patten/speech_00_12.htm). The progression of the MEPP means that the EU could have the opportunity to deal with the Middle East region as a whole and to encourage regional organizations and peace-building projects in the area.

Japan

The EC/EU has had an often uneasy relationship with Japan. It was only in the 1970s, after the country had experienced an annual 10 per cent real growth in its GNP in the previous 20 years, that the EC attempted trade negotiations with Japan. However, Japan restricted imports and gave financial assistance to exports, and the EC's insistence on a 'safeguard clause' against a sudden expansion of Japanese imports led to a breakdown of trade treaty negotiations in 1971. However, a mutual exchange of permanent delegations was agreed in 1975 and by 1980 the EC had turned its attention from criticizing Japan to opening up the Japanese market for EC products. Japan responded by liberalizing some of its markets, restraining its export growth and agreeing a number of Voluntary Restraint Agreements with EC states, as well as stimulating its home demand.

Attempts by the Japanese to establish car assembly plants within the EU received a varied response. The French opposed such moves on the grounds that they undermined the indigenous European car industry, whereas the British welcomed them for their employment potential. In 1991 an agreement was made between Japan and the EC on the export of motor vehicles from Japan, with national measures removed by the end of 1992 and provisions being made to monitor the situation.

The 1991 Joint Declaration between Japan and the EC led to regular meetings between the two sides and a dialogue in three areas. The first has been the political dialogue that culminates each year in a summit between the President of the Council, the President of the Commission and the prime minister of Japan. There are other meetings at ministerial and official levels, although by the time the Commission prepared a communication on the EU–Japan relationship in 1995, these had still not produced much more than 'exchanges of views and information' (European Commission, 1995: 7). The second area is that of economic and trade co-operation, where the emphasis has been on enhancing industrial co-operation and increasing deregulation and competition. There has also been an effort to increase EU investment in Japan, helped by the economic downturn and banking crisis in Japan in 1998. Finally, there has been an effort to co-operate on common and global challenges, especially on the environment and nuclear safety issues. This is recognition by the EU that Japan has become more of a political force in the UN and in regional and functional agencies during the 1990s (http://europa.eu.int/comm/trade/bilateral/japan/japan.htm).

ASEAN

The Association of South East Asian Nations (ASEAN) is an international organization devoted to economic, social and cultural development and was set up in August 1967 by Indonesia, Malaysia, the Philippines, Singapore and Thailand. Brunei Darussalam joined in 1984, Vietnam in 1995, Laos and Myanmar (Burma) in 1997 and Cambodia in 1999. These states, with a population of some 500 million, represent a resource rich area that has been developing fast. Between 1994 and 1997 their GDPs grew by an annual average of 7.1 per cent, although a decrease of 6 per cent was registered in the recession year of 1998 and a modest increase of 2.5 per cent was seen in 1999.

ASEAN has attempted to liberalize trade among its members and has a Preferential Trading Agreement, established in 1977 and enhanced in 1987, aimed to expand intra-regional trade. In January 1992 the members decided to form the ASEAN Free Trade Area (AFTA). The 1995 Agenda for Greater Economic Integration included an acceleration of the AFTA timetable in order to achieve free trade in ten rather than 15 years. In 1997 an ASEAN economic region was planned that would see freer movement of services and capital as well as goods, and in which some of the socio-economic disparities would be addressed. ASEAN has established the ASEAN Regional Forum (ARF), which includes not just the ASEAN states but also Australia, New Zealand, Canada, the USA, Russia, Mongolia, Papua New Guinea, China, India, Japan, the Republic of Korea and the EU (http://www.aseansec.org/). This discusses political and security issues, whereas the Asia–Pacific Economic Co-operation (APEC) meetings deal with trade and other economic matters.

In 1974 an ASEAN–EC Study Group was established to examine mutual problems, but little happened until the first ASEAN–EC Ministerial Meeting (AEMM) in Brussels in 1978. Further meetings were held every 18 months and, although the EC became more involved in ASEAN development projects, results were limited. An ASEAN–EC Co-operation agreement was signed in 1980, committing the two sides to closer co-operation in trade, industry, investment and technology transfer. A Business Council was set up in 1983. A Joint Co-operation Committee was established in 1980 to oversee collaborative activities and a first meeting of the two sides' economics ministers was held in Bangkok in 1985. Meetings of ASEAN and EU ministers have stressed the development of trade links but there has been some tension over the increased EU's wish to include human rights issues. The 1980 agreement expired in 1997 and was replaced by a new joint action plan (Allen and Smith, 1998: 83–4).

Market access is still an important issue. This was originally centred around the textile exports of ASEAN states to the EC/EU but has expanded to include a number of industrial goods. The EU fear is that these might be dumped on the European market, while the ASEAN concern is to obtain entry into the lucrative European market. The sharp economic downturn in the 'Asian Tiger' economies in 1998 and the political problems experienced in Indonesia – not least those concerning the occupied territory of East Timor – undermined the bargaining potential of ASEAN. However, the area is clearly still one of great potential as a trade partner for the EU.

After 1995 the ASEAN–EU relationship became part of a wider EU strategy on Asia that involved EU participation in such multilateral forums as APEC; the EU held an Asia–Europe Meeting (ASEM) in Bangkok in

1996, in London in 1998, with a follow-up in Seoul in 2000. These meetings have covered more than economic matters and have had to deal with differing views on political issues, not least those of human rights in Myanmar and Indonesia, as well as Indonesia's relations with East Timor.

China and India

Neither of these countries had strong links with the EC until the late 1990s. This was partly a result of their economic systems: China was a state-trading nation with a comparatively small external trade sector and the Indian government regulated aspects of its foreign trade. Also many Chinese and Indian exports are of the type that the EU wishes to restrict, such as clothing and textiles; their low per capita incomes have made them unattractive markets for EU exporters until the mid-1990s.

A general trade and economic agreement was signed with China by the EC in 1978 and renewed in 1985, and a textile settlement was reached in 1978 with renewal in 1984 (Redmond and Zou Lan, 1986: 133–55). However, the events in Beijing in June 1989, when student demonstrators were killed, led the EC to hold back the development of economic links with China to show their displeasure of the government's repressive action. In October 1991 members of the EC Commission visited China and had their first joint meeting since 1987, and in 1992 the Chinese Foreign Minister, Qian Qichen, met Jacques Delors, then President of the Commission. A memorandum on technical arrangements for co-operation in information technology and in telecommunications was signed and a meeting of trade experts in order to examine trade barriers was arranged. In 1994 a political dialogue was started between the EU and China but interrupted on human rights grounds until 1997.

In 1995 the Commission, as part of its effort to reconsider EU relations with Asia generally, issued a communication called 'A Long-Term Policy on China-Europe Relations', which was supplemented in 1998 with 'Building a Comprehensive Partnership with China' (European Commission, 1998). A second summit was held between Chinese and EU leaders in April 1998. In December 1999 the President of the European Council, Erkki Lipponen, met the Prime Minister of China, Zhu Rongji, on an EU–China summit on the occasion of the handover to China of the Portuguese enclave on the coast of South China, Macao. During this meeting co-operation was reviewed and each side brought up issues of interest: China put its case for joining the WTO, the EU expressed concern about China's evolution to a more open and transparent society.

The EU cannot ignore China, with its vast population, natural resources and political importance, and is now giving serious consideration to its relations with the country. There is a delicate balance that has to be struck between encouraging economic co-operation and protecting EU economic interest, and also between having a dialogue with China over issues such as human rights and being seen to be too neo-imperialist.

Early EU contact with India was about the textile question and that of intellectual property, with the Commission trying to prevent the pirating of books and patented material (Commission of the European Communities, 1991: 73–4). A partnership and co-operation agreement was signed in 1993, replacing two earlier agreements from 1973 and 1982. A joint statement on political dialogue was agreed with India in 1994, although India's testing of nuclear weapons has been a sore issue. The first EU–India summit was held in Lisbon in June 2000 and set out plans for a future EU–India dialogue.

Contact has been maintained between the EC/EU and the South Asian Association for Regional Co-operation, which includes India, Bangladesh, Bhutan, the Maldives, Nepal, Pakistan and Sri Lanka, but which has not been able to form as cohesive a grouping as ASEAN.

Australasia

Both Australia and New Zealand had close trade ties with the United Kingdom under the Commonwealth preference scheme, which existed before the United Kingdom joined the EC. However, since British membership in 1973, Australia has re-oriented its trade away from its former European market and towards the Pacific Basin. It has looked more to Japan for its markets and to the United States for investment. In trade matters it had been an active member of the Cairns Group in the GATT Uruguay Round, demanding the elimination of agricultural subsidies. This Group – which included Argentina, Brazil, Canada, New Zealand and Uruguay, among others – was often supported by the United States, especially in its attacks on the CAP (Woolcock, 1991: 19). In 1997 the EU concluded a Joint Declaration with Australia which covered economic issues, multilateral trade and human rights.

New Zealand was granted special continued access to its traditional British market after the United Kingdom joined the EC. The Luxembourg agreement of 1971 set the pricing arrangement for New Zealand butter exports to the UK for the 1973–77 period. They managed to maintain a 25 per cent share of the British butter market in 1977 but had a constant battle to keep their market share for both butter and lamb, a vital element in the 70 per cent of New Zealand's exports that are agricultural. In 1999 the EU concluded framework agreements for trade and co-operation with both Australia and New Zealand.

Latin America

Latin America was another area in which EC co-operation was traditionally weak. It was seen as an area of US interest and, until Spain and Portugal became members of the EC in 1986, Latin America only had Italy as an interlocutor in EC councils to advance its case (Muniz, 1980: 55–7).

The main aim of EC/EU relations with Latin America has been trade co-operation and the encouragement of regional groups. Under the first heading, early agreements were signed with Argentina (1971), Uruguay (1973) and Brazil (1974), and new economic co-operation agreements were signed with Chile, Mexico, Uruguay and Paraguay in 1990. A framework co-operation agreement was made with Brazil in 1992.

Contact with regional groups included that with the Andean Community – Bolivia, Colombia, Ecuador, Peru and Venezuela – which resulted in a Joint Declaration in 1980. A 'third generation' agreement followed in 1993, with members being granted duty-free access for their exports to the EC/EU in order to help undermine the economic grip of illegal drugs in those states by encouraging the growing of other cash crops. The EU established a dialogue in 1990 with the diverse Rio Group – Argentina, Brazil, Colombia, Mexico, Panama, Peru, Uruguay and Venezuela – with the major issues being debt, drug trafficking and trade (Piening, 1997: 130). The EU has also had a 'third generation' agreement with all the members of the Mercosur customs union (or Southern Cone Common Market, with Argentina, Brazil, Paraguay and Uruguay as full members and Bolivia and Chile as associates). An agreement was reached in 1995 of an EU–Mercosur accord leading to trade liberalization and a political dialogue between the two blocs. This could be the basis for a strong economic presence in South America when Mercosur becomes a fully fledged customs union in 2006. After all, the Mercosur states showed a trade growth of 400 per cent between 1990 and 1997 (http://www.mercosurinvestment.com/).

EC/EU involvement in Central America has shown a more political slant. During the 1980s El Salvador, Guatemala, Honduras and Nicaragua all had internal political disputes – some in the form of civil wars – which were interpreted in US administrations in Cold War, Communists versus the West, terms. The EC saw a more complicated situation, and, after some preparation, in 1984 the ten EC foreign ministers and those of Spain and Portugal (then candidate members) visited San José, Costa Rica to help the peace process in Central America. This began the San José process of ministerial and other meetings which helped to differentiate the EC strategy in the region from that of the more interventionist and militarist United States (Smith, 1995). A trade and co-operation agreement was signed with the Central American states in 1985 (implemented in 1987) with a 'third generation' agreement, that made benefits conditional on human rights and democracy, signed in 1993. Between 1990 and 1996 many of the internal conflicts in Central America came to an end, and 'the diplomatic support and encouragement of the EC ... provided essential moral and political backing to the efforts of the Central Americans ...' (Piening, 1997: 127). In January 2000 the Commission formally approved the results of free trade negotiations with Mexico. This aims to create free trade between the two sides by 2007 but with Mexican exports to the EU entering duty-free by 2003 (see IP/OO/54, 18 January 2000, http://europa.eu.int/comm/external_relations/news/).

Latin America is a potentially rich and expanding market to which the EU is paying increased attention. The emergence of Mercosur as a customs union and its link with the EU could be the basis of flourishing co-operation. The EU and its member states provided over 60 per cent of development funding for Latin America during the 1990s and the EU managed 20 per cent of this (the EU and Latin America at http://europa.eu.int/int/comm/dg1b/). This economic interest, and the political distance of the EU compared with the United States, makes the European Union an attractive partner for Latin American states.

Conclusions

The regions and countries mentioned above show, in their diversity, the task of any Commission in trying to bring cohesion to the external policies of the EU. First there is the task of unifying the response of the member states with all their historical and geographic differences. Spain and Portugal have close links with Latin America; the United Kingdom with North America. France keeps a proprietary eye on its former colonies in Africa. There is often commercial rivalry over markets in East Asia and in the Middle East. Second, there is the need to bring together external trade policy, development policy and the EU's Common Foreign and Security Policy. What may make sense in security terms in the Middle East may transgress the trade interests of a majority of EU states. Finally, there is the need to balance and often to choose between partners. Not all regions can have priority in EU policy. The rotating Presidency of the EU allows the different members to advance differing priorities, but choices still have to be made. Increasingly, the EU is making those choices not merely on economic and trade grounds but also on wider considerations. This reflects the power that the EU may exercise in the wider world as the CFSP develops and as its membership widens.

References and further reading

ACP–EC (1994) Joint Assembly Resolution, OJC 167: 23.

Allen, D. and Smith, M. (1998) 'External Policy developments', in G. Edwards and D. Wiessala (eds), *The European Union 1997: Annual Review of Activities*. Blackwell, Oxford, pp. 69–91.

Bowker, M. and Williams, P. (1988) *Superpower Detente: A Reappraisal*. Sage, London.

Commission of the European Communities (1972) *Bulletin of the European Communities*, 5 (10). European Communities' Commission, Brussels.

Commission of the European Communities (1990) *Bulletin of the European Communities*, 1/90. European Communities' Commission, Brussels.

Commission of the European Communities (1991) *Bulletin of the European Communities*, 24 (10). European Communities' Commission, Brussels.

European Commission (1994a) *Humanitarian Aid: Annual Report 1993*. COM (94) 40 final, Brussels.

European Commission (1994b) *Background Report: Europe and the Mediterranean*. European Commission, London.

European Commission (1994c) *Strengthening the Mediterranean Policy of the European Union: Establishing a European–Mediterranean Partnership*. COM (94) 427 final, Brussels.

European Commission (1995) *Europe and Japan: The Next Steps*. COM (95) 73 final, Brussels.

European Commission (1998) *Building a Comprehensive Partnership with China*. COM (98) 181 final, Brussels.

Featherstone, K. and Ginsberg, R.H. (1996) *The United States and the European Union in the 1990s: Partnership in Transition*. New York, St Martin's Press.

Guay, T. (1999) *The United States and the European Union: The Political Economy of a Relationship*, Contemporary European Studies 8. Sheffield Academic Press, Sheffield.

Jakobsen, P.V. (1998) 'Sleeping through the night? EU member involvement in military conflict management in the 1990s', in A. Wivel (ed.), *Explaining European Integration*, Copenhagen Political Studies Press, Copenhagen, pp. 256–69.

Krenzler, H.G. and Schomaker, A. (1996) 'A new transatlantic agenda', *European Foreign Affairs Review*, 1 (1): 9–28.

Lister, M. (1988) *The EC and the Developing World: The Role of Lomé Convention*. Avebury Press, Aldershot.

Lundestad, G. (1998) *Empire by Integration: The United States and European Integration, 1945–97*. Oxford University Press, Oxford.

Muniz, B. (1980) 'EEC–Latin America: a relationship to be defined', *Journal of Common Market Studies*, 19 (1): 55–64.

Petersen, J. (1996) *Europe and America: The Prospects for Partnership*, 2nd edn. Routledge, London.

Piening, C. (1997) *Global Europe: The European Union in World Affairs*, Lynne Rienner, London and Boulder, CO.

Redmond, J. and Zou Lan (1986) 'The European Community and China: new horizons', *Journal of Common Market Studies*, 25 (2): 133–55.

Rhein, E. (1996) 'Europe and the Mediterranean: a newly emerging geopolitical area?', *European Foreign Affairs Review*, 1 (1): 79–86.

Roberson, B.A. (ed.) (1998) *The Middle East and Europe: The Power Deficit*. Routledge, London.

Smith, H. (1995) *European Union Policy and Central America*. Macmillan and St Martin's Press, Basingstoke and New York.

Smith, M. and Woolcock, S. (1994) 'Learning to cooperate: the Clinton administration and the European Union', *International Affairs*, 70 (3): 459–76.

Thagesen, R. and Matthews, A. (1997) 'The EU's common banana regime: an initial evaluation', *Journal of Common Market Studies*, 35 (4): 615–27.

Woolcock, S. (1991) *Market Access Issues in EC–US Relations*. Pinter, London.

Web sites

europa.eu.int/comm/development/cotonou/overview_en.htm	Cotonou Agreement
europa.eu.int/comm/development/faq/en-faq07.htm	EU Commission aid to ACP countries
europa.eu.int/comm/development/publicat/rep97/chal_en.htm	EU Commission post-Lomé negotiations
europa.eu.int/comm/dgs/development/	EU Development Directorate General
europa.eu.int/comm/dgs/external_relations/	EU Commission External Relations
europa.eu.int/comm/dgs/external_relations/speeches/patten/speech_00_12.htm	The Middle East Peace Process
europa.eu.int/comm/trade/bilateral/japan/japan.htm	EU–Japan relations
europa.eu.int/comm/dgs/external_relations/us/intro/index.htm	EU–US relations
europa.eu.int/int/comm/dg1b/	EU–Latin America relations
europa.eu.int/rapid/start/cgi/guesten.ksh	EU's banana regime (IP/99/828)
www.aseansec.org/	ASEAN
www.euromed.net	Euro-Med partnership
www.mercosurinvestment.com/	Mercosur trade and investment report
www.oneworld.org/	Oneworld (development policy coalition)
www.wto.org	World Trade Organization

Index